The Nye County Brothel Wars

A TALE OF THE NEW WEST

by Jeanie Kasindorf

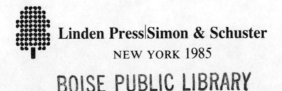

Linden Press|Simon & Schuster

NEW YORK 1985

Published by Linden Press/Simon & Schuster
A Division of Simon & Schuster, Inc.
Simon & Schuster Building
Rockefeller Center
1230 Avenue of the Americas
New York, New York 10020
LINDEN PRESS/SIMON & SCHUSTER and colophon are trademarks
of Simon & Schuster, Inc.
Designed by Irving Perkins Associates
Manufactured in the United States of America
1   3   5   7   9   10   8   6   4   2
Library of Congress Cataloging in Publication Data
Kasindorf, Jeanie.
The Nye County brothel wars.
1. Prostitution—Nevada—Nye County.   2. Nevada—
Social conditions.   3. Judicial corruption—Nevada—Nye
County.   4. Mafia—Nevada—Nye County.   I. Title.
HQ145.N3K37   1985   979.3'34   85-10399
ISBN: 0-671-41591-3

*This book is dedicated to
the memory of my grandparents,
Jeanie and William Russell.*

CHAPTER

One

Nevada is a state that seems to exist in defiance of itself. Although Nevada means snowy—the Donner party perished in the snow in the Sierra Nevada, from which Nevada takes its name—the climate over much of the state is dominated by a killing heat that makes the land inhospitable to all living things. It looks as if the winds that come out of the west, those hot, dry winds that come in over the Sierra Nevada and across Death Valley, have stripped the land of all life. As far as the eye can see there are no trees, nothing to provide any shade from the unrelenting sun, nothing to break up the endless miles of desert but the dark volcanic hills that, in the early mornings and late afternoons, cast thin shadows across the hot sand.

All that will grow in the low deserts of Nevada are sagebrush, mesquite, cactus and creosote bush, and a collection of desert shrubs that have learned to kill their own offspring in competition for the little water in the land. Even the few rivers that flow through Nevada flow not to the sea but to alkali sinkholes in the earth; they are rivers to nowhere.

Nevada has always been one of the least populous states. President Lincoln, in need of votes to pass the Thirteenth

Amendment against slavery, signed Nevada into statehood in 1864 even though the western territory had only seven thousand people and did not meet the population requirement.

It is therefore fitting—almost biblical—that gold and silver have come out of this tortured earth. Lead, zinc, antimony, arsenic, tungsten, copper, iron, mercury. To those few dreamers willing to endure the hardship of the land, the rewards were immense. In the nineteenth century the mining camps of Nevada, at places such as Tonopah and Goldfield, grew into the raw and raucous boom towns of those dreamers, made infamous in literature and film for their hard gambling and whoring. Nevada quickly became known as the ideal location for doing what in the rest of America would be considered outside the realm of civilized activity.

In the twentieth century, when the precious metals gave out, there was nothing left for the dreamers to do but gamble and whore. And so the gambling and the whoring became the state's new industries. And if one cared to see the hand of God or the Devil in its history, one could envision the Nevada mining boom as merely a catalyst to get the serious business of Sodom and Gomorrah under way.

Today the state is still occupied by men who, like the miners before them, have come to Nevada to follow their own particular dream. Some men dream of going there and making that one big score at blackjack or craps or poker. Some dream of going there to become a casino pit boss or a tuxedo-clad dealer. And others dream of setting up a cozy little brothel in the desert and whiling away their later years in the pleasant pursuit of counting profits.

In the winter of 1976 Walter Plankinton was such a man. A large man, who looked as if he had just come in off the range and gotten duded up for the day with hand-tooled boots, a polyester shirt, and two diamond pinkie rings, Plankinton had begun life as a poor Kansas farm boy. The year he turned sixteen he did the two things poor boys often do: he married his hometown sweetheart and joined the Marines. When he left the Marines, he became a cross-country trucker. Then, in 1966, at the age of thirty-eight, he started his own trucking company, Cowboy Van Lines. Then he founded Cowboy Trash, which became the largest garbage collection service in Denver, Colorado, and started to make big money for the first time in his life.

He soon began to risk his newfound money in other ventures. He bought an International Harvester distributorship in British Honduras, and a shrimp-fishing operation in Brownsville, Texas. He invested in a Denver nightclub called the Gladiator, and got into a bitter fight with the former owner, which one man who was involved describes as "two hustlers hustling each other." Then in 1970 he invested in his own short-lived political career, unsuccessfully running for Governor on the American Independent Party ticket.

As he neared fifty, he suffered a major heart attack, and decided it was time to retire to the desert to open the one business he had always dreamed about running: a nice little whorehouse in Nevada, the only state in the Union that had legal whorehouses. During his years as a trucker, he had spent many long hours running up and down those Nevada highways, dreaming of owning a brothel. He had also spent enough hours as a customer inside those brothels to learn what the business was all about. He knew you could buy yourself a plot of desert land for $10,000, spend another $50,000 on a half-dozen old house trailers and some used furniture, and soon be spending your working days surrounded by pretty young "working girls" while you and the girls took in a cool one million dollars a year.

Whether or not Plankinton understood what he was getting into when he arrived in Nevada no one will ever know. Perhaps, as he wanted people to believe, he was truly naïve and thought that in a land that big and that empty there was room enough for any man to make his place in the sun doing whatever it by God pleased him to do. But it is more likely he knew that, by muscling in on the entrenched politics of the prostitution business there, he would end up in a nasty fight, and he was looking forward to it.

Whatever the case, it was not in Plankinton's character to philosophize, but to act. As soon as he had arrived in Nevada, he moved into one of the thousands of cheaply constructed town houses that dot Las Vegas, this one decorated with pale-blue carpeting, brown velvet sectionals, and mirrored walls. Then he got into his Thunderbird and drove across town to I-15, the interstate highway that runs through the city, parallel to the Las Vegas Strip. Instead of taking I-15 north, where most of the tourists go, he took it south. Then, just outside Las Vegas, he turned west at the Blue Diamond cutoff to Highway 160. He followed the old desert highway for sixty miles through the shimmering white sands until he reached the town of Pahrump, in the southeastern corner of Nye County, where he planned to open his whorehouse.

Nye County takes its name from the one-time Syracuse, New York, Police Commissioner, James W. Nye, whom President Lincoln appointed as governor of the Nevada Territory in 1861. In terms of square miles, it is the third largest county in America, yet it is so desolate that, in 1951, the United States Atomic Energy Commission chose Nye County as the place to put the nation's Nuclear Testing Site. It stretches across eighteen thousand square miles of land that the men who first mapped the continent called the "Great American Desert." Its boundary looks like a large cubist mushroom on the map, the stem of the mushroom lying west-northwest of Las Vegas, and the cap stretching up into northern Nevada and the Toiyabe and Shoshone mountains.

In many ways it is still a frontier county: in 1976 the men in Nye County outnumbered the women three to two. Although it is twice the size of the state of Vermont, its eigh-

teen thousand square miles of land held only five thousand
people, who lived in ten desert towns hundreds of miles
apart. There were only two doctors in the county, plus
fourteen churches, thirty-five bars, thirteen motels, two hotels, seven schools, one weekly newspaper, three swim-
ming pools, one hospital, and three legal whorehouses.

Its five thousand residents were not wealthy people: their
average household income was $11,000 a year. They had
weathered, windburned faces and the trace of a midwestern
twang in their voices, even if they hadn't come from the
Midwest. Their clothes were a curious mix of western jeans
and cowboy boots, and pastel blue and green leisure suits.
In the north they worked the cattle and sheep ranches, the
old gold and silver mines, a molybdenum mine, and the
motels and restaurants along the interstate that housed and
fed tourists traveling between Reno and Las Vegas. In the
south they commuted to work in Las Vegas, or in Death
Valley, where they worked the borate mine. Or they
worked on construction crews at the Nuclear Testing Site.

That sociopolitical history, however, was of little concern
to Walter Plankinton. His sole interest in Nye County was
that it provided him a place to open a whorehouse only
sixty miles from Las Vegas. In 1971, five years before Plankinton's arrival, legal whorehouses were outlawed in Las
Vegas' Clark County. Which meant that tourists staying at
the MGM Grand, the Stardust, and Caesar's Palace had to
travel anywhere from eighty to two hundred miles north on
I-95 to get to Nye County's three legal whorehouses: the
Shamrock, eighty miles north in the desert crossroads town
of Lathrop Wells; Fran's Star Ranch, 113 miles away in the
town of Beatty; or Bobby's Buckeye Bar, the oldest whorehouse in Nye County, a full two hundred miles away in the
county seat of Tonopah.

Plankinton's plan was to open his whorehouse in the
Pahrump Valley, in this little southeastern corner of Nye

County, and take the other brothels' Las Vegas business away. As he entered town, Plankinton wheeled his Thunderbird past the fancy new Calvada restaurant and real-estate complex where salesmen peddled plots of desert land to tourists they brought out from Las Vegas. He continued on past a half-dozen other desert real-estate offices operating out of house trailers, past Stanton's Union 76 and Mankin's Texaco gas stations, past the Starlite Motel and the Saddle West, a coffee shop–casino in a big, red, barnlike building. Then he drove past the Cotton Pickin' Saloon, The Drugstore, the post office, and a one-room cinderblock building that housed the sheriff's station, and he had seen about all there was to see of Pahrump.

Being a careful man, Plankinton started asking around about the prospect of opening a brothel there. And Plankinton discovered that, eleven years before, the township of Pahrump had outlawed prostitution within its boundaries. But there must be plenty of land in this desert that isn't in the township, Plankinton said to everyone he talked to. That don't matter, they all told him. The "men who run the county" don't want no whorehouse there.

A man like Walter Plankinton was not about to let that stop him. He talked to several real-estate agents. Then, with fine white sand collecting on his windshield, he drove around the gravel roads that crisscrossed the desert near the Clark County line, looking at land that was for sale. It didn't take long for Plankinton to find what he was looking for: a plot of land on Hafen Ranch Road, which intersects old Highway 160 only sixty miles from Las Vegas, just inside the Nye County line.

He knocked on the door of the trailer nearest that land and jokingly inquired of the couple who lived there whether they would have "any ill feelings about me raising chickens there." The couple, who had recently moved to Nevada from Pennsylvania and bought a 7-Eleven franchise in Las Vegas, had been in the state just long enough to understand what Plankinton meant. Not only did they not object, they agreed to invest in the embryonic chicken farm, which

Plankinton said he was going to call the Chicken Ranch, after the legendary Texas whorehouse where farmers once paid for working girls with chickens. The couple kicked in $10,000 of their life savings.

Plankinton looked up his plot of land in the County Recorder's Office, duly jotting down the file number: 482-3327. When he had assured himself that the land was outside the limits of the township of Pahrump, he bought ten acres at $1,000 per acre. He went back to Clark County and looked around the mobile-home lots in North Las Vegas. He paid $14,000 for two eleven-foot secondhand Hillcrest house trailers, had them hauled to Pahrump on a flatbed truck, and planted them on cement blocks on his new land.

Than Plankinton decided it might be a smart idea to get to know those "men who ran the county." When he had run for governor in Colorado in 1970 he had collected only 2,052 votes to the winning candidate's 350,690, but he had had a hell of a good time. As long as he was about to try his hand at running a business in Nye County, Plankinton decided, he might as well also try his hand at running the county.

He drove out to Interstate 95 and took it north around the Nuclear Testing Site. He drove for nearly two hundred miles, until he reached the county seat of Tonopah, a rocky desert landscape dotted with small wood-frame houses and rusting mobile homes and abandoned mining equipment from the turn-of-the-century silver-boom days.

Plankinton drove down Main Street in Tonopah until he saw the Nye County Courthouse, the center of power in this vast eighteen-thousand-square-mile county. It was a small, square two-story building made from white sedimentary rock and topped with an incongruous dome that someone had seen fit to paint a shimmering silver. Walter Plankinton wheeled his Thunderbird up to the courthouse, walked purposefully through the wide wooden doors, and set the stage for all that was to come.

CHAPTER

TWO

In that winter of 1976 when Walter Plankinton arrived in Nye County, the rest of the country was still recovering from the Watergate scandal. In New Hampshire, Florida, and Illinois, a little-known former Georgia governor named Jimmy Carter was winning Democratic primaries by telling people that what the nation needed was an "outsider" in government.

In Nevada there was none of that talk of bringing outsiders into government. Nevada had not changed very much in the one hundred or so years since it achieved its somewhat questionable statehood. Its boundaries held only 610,000 people—fewer than in what most states constitutes a good-sized city—and those people did not take well to outsiders coming in and shaking up the normal order of things.

In a rural "cow county" like Nye County, with only five thousand people, the same man had been running county government for twenty-one years. That man was Judge William P. Beko, the fifth District Judge of the state of Nevada. And almost anyone you asked in Nevada could tell you that Nye County was "Bill Beko's county."

A tall man with a long, narrow face and sharp features that have softened over the years, Bill Beko had been born and raised in Tonopah in a house that still stands across the street from the courthouse. His father, Pete Beko, was one of hundreds of men who came to Tonopah from southern Yugoslavia to work the silver mines. In Tonopah they called those men the Serbians and called Pete Beko the father of all the Serbian people; on Saturdays and Sundays he would sit in his house and the Yugoslav miners would come to ask him for help with their problems.

Bill followed right in his father's footsteps. "Bill Beko," says a member of one of Tonopah's oldest families, "is like a god to these people." For twenty years Beko had been the district attorney of Nye County and legal counsel to the Nye County Board of Commissioners, old miners and bar owners and desert ranchers who came to Tonopah two days a month to conduct county business and were happy to have Bill Beko around to run the county the rest of the time. Toward the end of those twenty years, he started grooming his successor, a small, shy Nye County boy named Peter Knight, whose father, the 1939 bronc champion at the Cheyenne Rodeo, had begun courting his mother, a little dark-haired cowgirl, when both had appeared at New York City's Madison Square Garden Rodeo. Beko took Knight straight out of law school in 1971 and made him deputy district attorney.

Then in 1975, when Beko was named to the Fifth District judgeship, Beko asked the Nye County Board of Commissioners to appoint Knight to succeed him as district attorney. And so Peter Knight moved into Bill Beko's office in the Nye County Courthouse, and Beko moved across the hall to the Fifth District Judge's office. And although he was now supposed to be removed from the rough-and-tumble of everyday politics, it was hard to find anyone in Nye County who didn't believe that Bill Beko was still running things.

• • •

So it was something of a rude surprise in that election year of 1976 when the forty-seven-year-old Walter Plankinton, with his big crooked grin and brash manner, arrived in the Nye County Courthouse and challenged the fifty-four-year-old Bill Beko's power by filing to run for Nye County commissioner and declaring his intention to open a whorehouse in Pahrump, all at the same time.

On a blistering August day that summer, while he was campaigning for that commissioner's seat, Plankinton stopped to visit Peter Knight at the Nye County Courthouse. Their versions of the meeting are as different as the two men. Knight, a small, shy man with a round, almost pretty face, whose eyes darted nervously around his office as he spoke, says Plankinton barged in "like a pimp" and laid out his plans: "I'm going to open a whorehouse whether you like it or not, whether Judge Beko likes it or not, and whether the people of Nye County like it or not. It's legal in Nevada, and I have my rights."

Or words to that effect.

Plankinton says he simply thought it would be polite to introduce himself to the District Attorney, who to Plankinton's surprise was more interested in his plans for a whorehouse than in his political campaign.

"Glad to see you, Plankinton," Knight said. "You're just the man I've been waiting to see. I hear you're planning to open a brothel in the area. If that's what you want to do, you've got to get permission from the people who count."

"What are you talking about?" Plankinton asked.

"Well," Knight persisted, "Pahrump's a lucrative spot. It's closer to Las Vegas than any brothel in the county, so it's a costly item. It'll cost you seventy-five thousand dollars and five percent of your take."

Or words to that effect.

There were no notes taken, no tape recordings. Their words were gone in the air, like dust devils on the sand.

Knight calls that version of history "a figment of Walter Plankinton's imagination." Plankinton swears by it, saying, "I told him to go screw himself. I told him that I never paid no crooked politicians in my life and I wasn't about to start now."

On September 15, 1976, the news in the rest of the nation was that President Gerald Ford had formally kicked off his Presidential campaign against the "outsider" candidate, former Georgia Governor Jimmy Carter. In Nye County the news—which came as no surprise to anyone in the county—was that an outsider named Walter Plankinton had lost the race for Nye County commissioner by a hopeless margin to an Amargosa Valley man named Don Barnett, who operated heavy construction equipment at the Atomic Energy Commission's Nuclear Testing Site.

The very next day after that election, Plankinton went back to the business that had brought him to the Nevada desert: he began to ready his ten acres and two Hillcrest trailers for the purpose of diverting the tourist-and-gambler trade from Las Vegas to his whorehouse, before it got anywhere near any other whorehouse in Nye County.

Plankinton had married and divorced three times and liked to brag that he had helped raise three children and four stepchildren. Now that some heavy work needed to be done, he brought in his stepson, Doug Harkalis, from Denver to help him turn the two Hillcrest trailers into the Chicken Ranch. They drilled a well to bring water into the bathrooms, carted in a propane tank to provide hot water in the bathrooms and the kitchen. They laid tile in the bathrooms, hung cheap curtains on the windows and drapes across the bedroom doorways, and brought in all the cheap sofas, chairs, lamps, and wooden Formica-top tables they could squeeze into the front room of one of the trailers, which would serve as the whorehouse parlor. They moved single beds and small dressers into the bedrooms. And on the floor outside each bedroom door they placed a white kitchen egg timer, so that their customers would always be sure to get only what they paid for, right down to the minute.

Then Plankinton started visiting the Shamrock and Fran's Star Ranch and Bobby's Buckeye Bar as a paying customer and getting the word out to the girls that he was looking for employees: the Chicken Ranch was ready to open for business.

One week before it did open, however, Jay Howard, the red-faced, potbellied Sheriff of Nye County, walked into Plankinton's trailers, sucking his teeth and adjusting his side arm.

"Well, I hear you're going to open this place," he bellowed.

"Yeah, Mr. Howard," Plankinton said. "I think I will."

Howard, a native Texan who had been a Tonopah bartender, a twenty-one dealer, and a stable manager before he decided to run for sheriff, told Plankinton that the Chicken Ranch happened to be located within the town boundaries of Pahrump.

"You're wrong," Plankinton said. "This is outside the town."

Plankinton was sure Howard was bluffing him or was honestly misinformed. In either case, there was nothing Plankinton could do about it now. If the Sheriff insisted on making trouble, Plankinton would have to straighten him out in court.

"You've let other people operate whorehouses in the county for thirty years," he told Jay Howard. "So I figure I'm just as good as the rest of 'em."

Jay Howard slapped his gun and sucked his teeth some more. "Well, Plankinton, I'm going to come and get you. And don't you resist me, 'cause you're mine."

• • •

The rules governing prostitutes in Nye County were more a matter of frontier tradition than of county law: you couldn't find them on file anywhere in the Tonopah courthouse. But every brothel owner knew that Nye County expected two things: that you have your girls examined once a week by old Doc Cecil, and submit to a blood test if Doc Cecil thought it was necessary; and that you have them fill out a working card with the Sheriff.

A week after Jay Howard's visit, Plankinton hired his first working girl, a cute little blonde named Kathy who had heard that the Chicken Ranch was opening and had come knocking on the trailer door. He drove her the 165 miles from Pahrump to Nye County Hospital in Tonopah for the doctor's exam and the blood test. Then he drove her over to the Sheriff's office in the silver-domed County Courthouse.

Kathy presented her new health certificate to the deputy behind the desk. The deputy stood her up and snapped her picture with a Polaroid camera he kept in a filing cabinet for such occasions. Then he fingerprinted her. He filled out a small blue-lined index card with her name and Social Security number, turned the card over, and wrote "Prostitute" on the back. Kathy was officially a whore.

Before Plankinton could leave the building, word got back to Jay Howard. He wandered out to take a look at his tall and lanky adversary.

"Well, Jay," Plankinton told the Sheriff, "I'm gonna be open tomorrow afternoon."

Jay Howard grinned widely. "Well," he said, "I'll be down knocking on your door."

Plankinton grinned back at him, took Kathy by the arm, and walked out into the desert sun. And as soon as Plankinton was out of sight, Howard turned, went back to his office, and began to plan a raid on the Chicken Ranch.

He called three deputies who worked in Pahrump, Larry Massoli, Frank Homstad, and Mike Upton, and told them to meet him at the one-room cinder-block station the following evening. Then he called Lieutenant Max Carnes in

Tonopah. He told Carnes he was sure Plankinton would recognize the Pahrump deputies, so he wanted to use Carnes as the deputy who would go into the Chicken Ranch to buy a girl. He told Carnes to meet him at the Pahrump station the following night wearing "truck driver's clothes."

"We want to make sure the red light is on," Howard told the four men when they had finally assembled. "That way we'll know Plankinton's in business. When we're sure it's on, Max is going to go inside the place. And Max is going to get himself solicited." Once Max had "got himself solicited," Howard said, he would arrest Plankinton for operating a house of prostitution inside the town boundaries of Pahrump.

The five men started out in four cars: Howard and Massoli drove two white sheriff's cars, Upton and Homstad took the department's new Chevy pickup, and Max Carnes drove his own Pinto. They took Highway 16, heading toward Las Vegas. Then just before they came to the county line they turned right on Hafen Ranch Road. They stopped a short distance from the two Hillcrest trailers.

Howard, using a walkie-talkie, told Massoli to drive past the trailers to make sure the red light was on. So Massoli turned off his patrol car's headlights and drove slowly toward the trailers until he could see a dim red light in the desert blackness. He turned his car around on the gravel road, drove back to the other three cars, and told Howard the red light was on. Howard told Carnes to go in.

Carnes walked up to the front door of the first trailer and rang the bell. The door was opened by Kathy, who stood in the doorway in a sheer negligee. She led Carnes into the whorehouse "parlor", from which he could see several cheaply curtained doorways leading to other rooms. There were two other girls in the parlor that night—Rita and Gina, a mother-and-daughter team who had arrived a few hours before to inquire about employment.

Max Carnes hired Kathy and followed her into a small

bedroom. Kathy had been given just one instruction by Walter Plankinton: Don't take less than twenty dollars a trick. Kathy told Max Carnes he could get a straight lay for twenty dollars, and Carnes handed Kathy a twenty-dollar bill. And before Kathy even had time to take off her negligee, Sheriff Jay Howard and the three deputies came through the front door.

As soon as he heard the front door open, Carnes stepped out through the curtain that covered Kathy's bedroom doorway and told Jay Howard he had placed Kathy under arrest. Howard looked at Carnes, then looked around the parlor. As his eyes passed over a double doorway covered by two curtains, the curtains were pushed aside and out walked Walter Plankinton.

"You're under arrest," Jay Howard said.

CHAPTER
Three

There would come a time when reporters from all over the country would be calling Walter Plankinton to talk about the raid on the Chicken Ranch. But in October 1976, the only reporter to call was Milt Bozanic, the publisher, editor, and sole reporter of the Pahrump Valley *Times*. Bozanic had started the paper as a monthly six years before and had expanded it into a weekly just a month before the arrest. For Bozanic—who covered five thousand people spread out over eighteen thousand square miles of barren desert—the arrest of Walter Plankinton was one of the biggest stories his fledgling paper had ever had.

The day after his arrest, Plankinton was quick to point out to Milt Bozanic that he had gone to the Nye County Recorder's Office and found the map of Pahrump there. It was in Nye County Recorder File 482-3327, Plankinton said, in case anyone doubted he had checked the map, and it clearly showed that the Chicken Ranch lay outside Pahrump Township. If Plankinton's research had not shown that to be the case, he would have bought his plot elsewhere. He was certain that he was in the right.

That same day, District Attorney Peter Knight told Milt Bozanic what only a handful of men in Nye County knew:

that Pahrump Ordinance Number Three, the ordinance that outlawed prostitution, applied to the town of Pahrump, not the township depicted on the map. In 1962 residents of Pahrump had filed a petition with Judge Beko's County Commissioners to establish the unincorporated town of Pahrump and to set new boundaries to allow for future growth. The Commissioners had simply rubber-stamped the petition to create the new town, which now circumscribed and contained Pahrump Township with plenty of room to spare. They had never bothered with the formality of filing a new map with the County Recorder's Office.

"We've checked the map," Knight said, "and the ordinance. And the brothel is in the town."

A month later Plankinton filed suit in Judge Beko's Fifth District Court challenging Pahrump Ordinance Number Three. When Beko, who had been district attorney when the town of Pahrump was created in 1962 as well as when Ordinance Number Three was written, heard that Plankinton's attorney was going to move to disqualify him for bias, he beat them to it by removing himself. District Judge Joseph O. McDaniel was brought in from Elko to hear the case.

Plankinton's lawsuit argued that Pahrump's Ordinance Number Three was invalid because there had "never been a validly created town of Pahrump." Plankinton based his argument on two counts: that the map of Pahrump had never been filed, which meant that the town had never been validly created as state law requires; and that only 12 percent of the property owners in the proposed town had signed the petition, while state law required that 60 percent sign.

When Knight filed his response, he didn't even try to argue that the town of Pahrump had been legally created. He argued instead that "a private person in private litigation cannot question the validity of a town's existence," especially when a town has "enjoyed the powers and privileges of a town" as long as Pahrump had.

Judge McDaniel dismissed Plankinton's case. When he

did, the way was legally cleared for the powers of Nye County to put Plankinton into jail, or at least give it a good try.

The court was in the same one-room cinder-block sheriff's station that Plankinton had passed so many times going out the north end of Pahrump toward the interstate. It sat by itself, about a mile north of the Texaco gas station and the Saddle West coffee shop–casino that marked the center of Pahrump. From the front door he could see Charleston Peak rising twelve thousand feet from the shimmering hot white desert floor. In every other direction, just a hot wind and emptiness. Even the scorpions went indoors at noon.

The cramped concrete hall of justice was furnished with an assortment of chairs and tables of different lineages, and a dispatcher's desk off to one side where the police scanner emitted occasional bursts of static and someone's dissonant drawl, as life went on in the desert against heat and drought and all other natural obstacles. At the rear of the single airless room were two jail cells. One was empty, used as an open latrine and smelling of it. The other contained evidence in a few pending cases, while at the same time housing extra tires for Jay Howard's sheriff's car.

The Justice of the Peace, Dow Chenoweth, came in and set up a folding table, motioning for Knight, Plankinton and his attorney, Jeffrey Shaner, to sit behind it. Then Chenoweth took his place behind another table and the trial was on. The prosecution's case, which is to say Peter Knight's case, was simple. He had Sheriff Howard and Lieutenant Carnes, who had paid Kathy twenty dollars for sexual acts yet to be performed, testify to the events that took place the night of the arrest.

Then Plankinton's attorney rose to cross-examine. A big, boisterously friendly Las Vegan, who talked faster than most of the people in the Justice Court could listen, Shaner reeled off a series of questions in a rat-a-tat, rapid-fire manner he was sure would overwhelm everyone in the room.

"How can you prove Mr. Plankinton operates the Chicken Ranch?" he insisted of Sheriff Howard. "Are you sure the deeds to the Chicken Ranch are in Mr. Plankinton's name? Have you seen the deeds in Mr. Plankinton's name? Did Mr. Plankinton do anything consistent with the ownership of a house of prostitution? Did Mr. Plankinton offer anyone a girl? Did Mr. Plankinton tell you he was offering Lieutenant Carnes a girl? Did Mr. Plankinton take any money from Lieutenant Carnes for a girl?"

His cross-examination of the witnesses was, indeed, overwhelming. So overwhelming, in fact, that Justice Chenoweth ignored it completely, banged on the table when Shaner was done, and said, "I find the defendant guilty of violating Pahrump Ordinance Number Three."

The trial lasted about thirty minutes. Plankinton was fined $500 and sentenced to sixty days in the Tonopah jail.

Walter Plankinton had never accomplished anything in his life by walking away from a fight. And he was not about to start now. He instructed Jeffrey Shaner to file an appeal to try to keep him out of the Tonopah jail. Then he drove straight up to Tonopah, walked into Bill Beko's courthouse, and began searching the property records until he found a chunk of land that the founding fathers of Pahrump had forgotten to take into their town. The land was a half mile past the end of Homestead Road, a gravel road which came off Highway 160 about a mile inside the Nye County line. As soon as he found it, he bought twenty acres for the same price he had paid for his Hafen Ranch Road land: $1,000 per acre.

This time he decided he was going to have the profits from the Chicken Ranch all to himself. He let the couple he had talked into investing in "raising chickens" know that they were no longer welcome at the Chicken Ranch—a bit of highhandedness for which he would eventually have to pay a $15,500 judgment in a lawsuit charging him with taking their money and services and then squeezing them out of the business.

He hired a ten-wheel rig and brought in truckload after truckload of gravel to extend Homestead Road the half mile to his land. He had a well drilled and a septic tank buried and a generator installed and moved his two silver Hillcrest trailers to his new twenty acres. He built a front porch out of rotting cedar and built a rotting-cedar roof over the porch and screwed a red light bulb into the socket on the front of the first trailer.

Then he started a new search for working girls. Kathy, his first official prostitute, had left the county after her arrest for whoring inside the Pahrump town boundaries. Rita and Gina, the mother-and-daughter team, had driven up the highway to Lathrop Wells and found work at the Shamrock. So Plankinton made his rounds of the desert whorehouses again and found a beautiful tall redhead named Sherri, who he hoped would be the first of a dozen working girls. Only one month after his conviction for operating the Chicken Ranch within the Pahrump town boundaries, Walter Plankinton was ready to reopen for business.

CHAPTER

Four

From the time the first Legislative Assembly of the Territory of Nevada met at Carson City in 1861, the men who made Nevada's laws have all but given their official blessing to the practice of prostitution. When that first Assembly established "offenses against public morality," it included selling the flesh of a diseased animal, selling an adulterated drink of liquor, obstructing or injuring any public road or highway, marrying someone else's spouse, and refusing to join a posse. It did not include prostitution.

When that early Assembly met, Nevada's towns, like those in the other western territories, were mostly silver- and gold-rush camps where prostitution flourished. As the heat of the gold and silver rush cooled down, miners began sending for their wives, as most wanderers sooner or later do. The population grew, and along with it the pressure for moderation. Churches and Women's Christian Temperance Societies were formed. And they soon began demanding an end to the whorehouses. In every other western territory where the women settled, their demands were met. But Nevada resisted settling, by the sheer insurmountable fact of its geography: it was a wide-open desert, and the few people brave enough to settle it thought there was space enough to allow any man to do what he damned well pleased.

It wasn't until 1881, twenty years after that First Legislative Assembly met, that the legislators of the new state of Nevada passed any law that even mentioned prostitution. That year they passed a bill to give any county commission that wished to control prostitution the power to "license, tax, regulate, prohibit, or suppress all houses of ill-fame." By 1887, when it became clear that no county commission was going to touch the red lights, the churches and the Women's Christian Temperance Societies started pressuring the legislature to act. But the best the women could do was pry out of the state fathers a bill making it unlawful "for any owner of a house of ill-fame to situate that house within 400 yards of any schoolhouse, or on the principal business street of any town."

Over the next sixty years, as more people started coming into the state, several rural counties took advantage of the 1881 law and passed bills prohibiting whorehouses from operating within certain sections of their towns. In 1965, Nye County District Attorney Bill Beko and the Board of Commissioners, at the behest of political allies who hoped to subdevelop plots of desert land in Pahrump Valley and encourage people to move there from Las Vegas, outlawed whorehouses within a certain section of Pahrump. It was that section where Walter Plankinton mistakenly bought his first ten acres.

In 1971 the state legislature took up the issue of prostitution one more time when the Las Vegas delegation to the legislature proposed emergency legislation to prohibit county commissioners in counties with more than 200,000 people from licensing a "house of ill-fame." The emergency bill was passed after the District Attorney of Las Vegas' Clark County proposed that Mustang Ranch brothel owner Joe Conforte be allowed to open a whorehouse on the southern edge of Las Vegas.

The state legislators—and the people of Nevada—were perfectly willing to allow whorehouses to continue to operate out in the desert counties, where there were few people in each town and the townspeople had grown up with the old-time whorehouses' owners, as the people of Tonopah had grown up with Bobby, of Bobby's Buckeye Bar. But they would be damned if they were going to allow the state to become the nation's laughingstock by letting Joe Conforte walk in and open a legal whorehouse in Las Vegas.

All of which meant that Nye County District Attorney Peter Knight would have had no legal way to close down Walter Plankinton, were it not for one other major law governing prostitution: one created by a 1949 Nevada Supreme Court decision. That year the District Attorney and County Commissioners of Washoe County decided to close down Mae Cunningham, a madam who ran a whorehouse in Reno. They could have used the 1881 law that allowed the county to outlaw prostitution. But for reasons that are seldom found in legal journals, they didn't want to get rid of all the whorehouses in the county, they only wanted to get rid of Mae. They decided to try something that hadn't been tried in Nevada before. They decided to declare Mae Cunningham's house a "public nuisance."

Mae Cunningham took the case all the way to the Nevada Supreme Court. There the District Attorney argued that since there was no state law to regulate houses of prostitution, the Supreme Court must follow the common law, which says a house of prostitution is a public nuisance. On March 7, 1949, the Nevada Supreme Court ruled for Washoe County. It was a controversial ruling; it meant that from then on a district attorney could use the public-nuisance law to arbitrarily decide who could run a whorehouse in his county and who couldn't.

One week after Walter Plankinton opened the second

Chicken Ranch, sheriff's deputies Larry Massoli, Frank Homstad, and Mike Upton—the three men who patrolled the Pahrump Valley and had been in on the raid at the first Chicken Ranch—began going door to door in their sheriff's uniforms, asking citizens to sign petitions and write letters asking the county to close down Walter Plankinton. Massoli claimed that Jay Howard and Peter Knight told them to get letters only from people who were against Plankinton, not from people who were for him. Howard said that Massoli's claim was "nonsense." Whatever the case, there was no denying that the deputies did start knocking on Pahrump Valley doors.

The Pahrump Valley had not been settled until the early 1950s, around the time that the Atomic Energy Commission chose Nye County as the spot for its Nuclear Testing Site. Now, in the spring of 1977, the valley still held only one thousand people, most of whom lived in double-wide house trailers scattered miles apart. They were largely blue-collar workers: waitresses, electricians and hotel security guards who commuted to Las Vegas; truckers, gas station attendants, mobile home salesmen; women who cleaned government houses at the Nuclear Testing Site; men who worked on construction crews at the test site.

They were people who had spent their lives moving west across America, out of the cities and the crowded suburbs, until they came to this lonesome desert, where you could buy five acres of land for $450 down and $50 a month and have plenty of space to call your own. And have no one around to tell you where to put the garbage, as one Pahrump man explained. Or tell you to quiet your dogs, as one retired couple said. Or tell you, as one test-site worker liked to say, "not to take a piss in the sand."

If they had one common bond, it was that they believed in the inalienable right to lead whatever life you damn well wished to lead. And they thought that that right should also apply to Walter Plankinton. If legal prostitution wasn't the cleanest business in the world, well, they were willing to look the other way. So when the three sheriff's deputies started knocking at the "double-wides," they were surprised to find how few people were willing to complain about the Chicken Ranch.

There were, of course, people who bitterly opposed Plankinton. There were Bill Beko's political allies, many of whom were real-estate salesmen trying to entice Las Vegas tourists to buy Pahrump Valley retirement land. There were a handful of dyed-in-the-wool Christian fundamentalists, and a few Mormon families. And there were the mothers of teenaged sons who had tried to sneak out at night to peek in the windows of the Chicken Ranch. But there were fewer of those people than the deputies expected.

The three men were able to collect only thirty to forty letters complaining about the Chicken Ranch. Still, that was all Bill Beko's men needed. As soon as the letters arrived at the Tonopah courthouse, the Nye County Board of Commissioners declared the Chicken Ranch a public nuisance.

Plankinton immediately filed another lawsuit, charging that Nye County had acted unconstitutionally. He petitioned Judge Beko to remove himself from hearing the case. When Beko agreed, District Judge Stanley Smart, from 76 miles away in Fallon, was assigned to sit in his place.

The hearing was held in Beko's courtroom, a large, high-ceilinged room decorated with a bust of George Washington, a bust of Abraham Lincoln, and a calendar from the Hawthorne Gun & Tackle Shop. The attorneys began by arguing whether the common law could be applied to houses of prostitution, as it had been in the Mae Cunningham case. Plankinton's attorney argued that when the state legislature passed emergency legislation in 1971 to keep the Mustang Ranch out of Las Vegas, that repealed the common law. Peter Knight argued, of course, that it did not.

Then the attorneys turned to the emotional issues of the day. Peter Knight told Judge Smart that the only reason the county was acting against Plankinton was that it had received citizens' complaints. "We have attempted only to act with respect to brothels where we have received requests to take some action from a citizen of the county," Knight solemnly declared. "No requests have been received with regard to any other house of prostitution in the county. Not since I have been the District Attorney of Nye County have any been received with regard to any other brothel."

Plankinton's attorney told Judge Smart that Knight, Nye County Sheriff Jay Howard, and the Nye County Board of Commissioners had violated the equal-protection clause of the Constitution of the United States by declaring the Chicken Ranch a public nuisance without also declaring Fran's Star Ranch, Bobby's Buckeye Bar, and the Shamrock Brothel public nuisances.

The attorneys argued for only thirty-five minutes. When they were finished, Judge Smart recessed the court to give himself time to reach a decision. One hour later, he returned to the courtroom, took his place at Bill Beko's judge's bench, and startled everyone by delivering a spontaneous lecture on the nature of legal prostitution in Nevada.

"I think that the legislature, as well as the courts, have been something less than totally forthright and clear in their handling of the issue of prostitution in the state of Nevada," he said. "The legislature seems to want to avoid the problem and stick in our statutes various provisions that do nothing more than confuse the issue, instead of simply taking the bit in their teeth and either saying that prostitution in Nevada is legal and subject to regulations, or that it is illegal.

"The situation that we have, as a result, is that total, absolute discretion has been vested in the board of county commissioners of the various counties to either permit or not permit the operation of houses of prostitution. That is an unfortunate situation, as it is in any case where any one person, or any group of people, is given absolute discretion over who may and may not engage in any particular type of business.

"The particularly unfortunate part is that people come to feel—and I'm not implying that there is any truth to this anywhere—that those who are in a position of authority, whether it is the county commissioners or the District Attorney, are making their decisions as to who should operate and who should not operate for improper reasons, including allegations of receiving payoffs and everything that goes with that. This is an unhealthy situation and it is one that should not be allowed to continue in this state. And I would certainly hope that the legislature would do something about it."

Judge Smart stopped for a moment to heighten the drama a bit before he announced his decision. Then he turned to the notes before him.

"I agree with the argument that the 1971 state law did, by implication, repeal the common law," he said. "On that basis, it is the order of this court that a permanent injunction be entered, perpetually enjoining the defendant, Nye County, from seeking to abate the operation of the plaintiff, Walter Plankinton, of a house of prostitution."

There was not a sound in Bill Beko's courtroom. Judge Smart had just declared that all whorehouses were equal in the eyes of the Constitution of Nevada and the Constitution of the United States. In other words, one whorehouse could not be more legal than another. He had just told Bill Beko's men to leave Walter Plankinton alone, and let him live out his truck driver's dream in peace.

CHAPTER

Five

With the taste of victory still sweet in his mouth, Plankinton set about expanding the Chicken Ranch into something worthy of the label "public nuisance"—the whorehouse he had dreamed of on those long drives across the desert in his trucking days.

Plankinton's cowboy wisdom had taught him that no man would ever starve overestimating the worldwide demand for services of the flesh. So he bought four more trailers, planted peach trees and watermelon vines around the trailers—irrigating them with water from his well—and started talking about the day he would turn his miserable little twenty acres of southern-Nevada desert into a glorious southern plantation.

He hung several huge paintings of copulating couples on the parlor walls. The paintings had been executed in black ink on red velvet and were hung in gold-and-white antique frames. Then he added a plaster-of-paris statue of a nude woman—whose body was covered in metallic gold paint—to give the customers something to look at before they got the real thing. He bought one of the hundreds of premolded Jacuzzi tubs that sit out in the sun on pool company lots all

34

over Las Vegas, and had it installed in one bedroom. Then he turned another bedroom into a VIP room by pasting gold-flecked, mirrored tiles to the ceiling and moving in a king-sized water bed, complete with a fake leopard-skin comforter. And if the sum total was hardly an opulent southern plantation, it was certainly a cross-country truck driver's dream.

The four extra trailers gave Plankinton fourteen bedrooms in which he could employ twelve to fourteen girls, depending on whether he and his stepson, Doug, were staying in their town houses in Las Vegas or in their bedrooms at the Chicken Ranch. It wasn't hard to find the girls. The phone calls came in almost every day from girls in every state—New York, California, Idaho, Michigan, Texas—who wanted to know if he had a bedroom for them. There was a "national whore's grapevine," Plankinton liked to call it, of girls who traded information. And word was out on their grapevine that that new whorehouse only sixty miles from Las Vegas was open again and doing business.

Plankinton soon started his own grapevine, not unlike that of his girls. He would call Joe Conforte at the Mustang Ranch and the brothel owners in other Nevada counties, and they would exchange information about certain girls, the way baseball managers might exchange information about certain players. Plankinton just loved to talk about his whorehouse business. "You never know what the hell a trick wants," he said. "So we give him a variety. We've got Chinese girls, black girls, Mexican girls, white girls, redheads, blondes, brunettes, big-titted ones, fat ones, skinny ones—we got 'em all." And, indeed, it wasn't long before he did. He made sure that at any one time he could supply any man's fantasy.

Just as he had once prided himself on knowing a little something about every trucker he had out on the road, he now prided himself on knowing a little something about every girl. They were restless, liked to wander, he would tell you. There was one girl, Annie, "all tits and ass," he said, who worked the streets of Houston, then San Francisco or Tucson, and then would come back to one of the Nevada whorehouses for a while. The girls would get off the streets because the streets were dangerous; in a whorehouse the owner checked for guns and knives and could be counted on to come running when a girl started screaming. But after a few weeks they'd get bored with the sameness of it all and be back out on the street.

There was an occasional girl who was "working as an independent," Plankinton would say. There was Susanna, "tall, and strong, but a little too lean," he said, who got into the business at age fifteen when her parents lost their horse ranch in northern California. She was saving the money to buy the horse ranch back. And there was Julie, "pert little tits and sassy as they come," he said, who was using the money to put herself through college.

But those girls were few and far between. A far more common story was the story of Denise, "the skinniest little black whore you've ever seen," he said, who'd been raised in the Cleveland ghetto. The first profession she was taught there was forging checks, the second profession was whoring. Denise had two little boys, seven and eight, who lived in Ohio with her mother. They thought she worked as a cocktail waitress at Caesar's Palace. There was Janice, whose mother had turned her over to her father when she was eight, applying vaseline to the child before placing her in bed with him. There was Carol, who had been raped by her stepfather and brothers when she was thirteen, then turned out as a prostitute by them.

Almost every one of the girls had a pimp, and in many cases a girl's pimp was also her husband. Although by now Nye County District Attorney Peter Knight was routinely referring to the owner of the Chicken Ranch as "Walter Pimpington," Plankinton was not considered a pimp by the state of Nevada. Nevada state law prohibited a man whom the law defined as a pimp from living off the earnings of a prostitute. But it did not prohibit a man like Plankinton, whom the law defined as "the owner of a house of ill-fame," from living off the earnings of fourteen prostitutes.

The pimps lived all over the United States, and would call the girls as often as they could to check on how much they were making. Plankinton allowed the girls only two phone calls a week, otherwise he'd find them spending all their time on the telephone fighting with their pimps. They called it "sick love," and when they weren't busy whoring, they consumed most of their waking hours in conversation about it.

Days went by unnoticed in a whorehouse like the Chicken Ranch, where the girls worked fifteen hours, then went to bed, then awoke to work another fifteen hours. They might as well have been hurtling through space in an enclosed capsule as sitting in a trailer out in the Nevada desert. The girls worked three weeks on and one week off, and during those three weeks they were allowed to leave the trailers for a nine-hour stretch only once a week.

Plankinton woke them all at noon and gave them until one to be dressed in their slinky polyester evening gowns and be ready for "the lineup," a whorehouse ritual in which the girls formed a line and introduced themselves to each newly arriving customer so that he could see which girl fit his fantasy. They were on call from 1 P.M. till 4 A.M., when the two girls who had done the least business that day were given the chance to be the "early-up" girls, who stayed up to wait for the new men who came in between 4 A.M. and 1 P.M. of a new day.

It was not long before Plankinton started a limousine service from Las Vegas, and started advertising the service in the tabloid newspapers that are handed out to tourists. So a man in town from New York or Miami for his industry's annual convention, or a man in from San Francisco for a weekend of gambling, could simply look up the Chicken Ranch in the Las Vegas white pages and dial a

number, and the next thing he knew he'd have a limousine
whisking him sixty miles across the desert to a room full of
fourteen young women, all eager to please. Most of the
customers were men. But if a woman came in and wanted
another woman, and one of the girls was willing, well, that
was fine with Plankinton. And if a couple came in for what
Plankinton called a "three-way party," well, that was fine,
too, as long as they were willing to pay for it.

For that, after all, was what the whorehouse business
was all about. Plankinton charged each girl $20 a day, for
which she got room and board, and clean sheets once a
week. After that, Plankinton and each girl split everything
she made fifty-fifty. While it was largely a cash business,
Plankinton also offered his customers the services of VISA
and MasterCard and an easy way to disguise what they had
paid for: the company listed on the credit-card receipts was
Princess Sea Industries, his old shrimp-fishing company
from Brownsville, Texas.

Plankinton raised his minimum to $30 for a fifteen-minute
straight lay, $40 if a girl could get it. A half hour of oral sex
and intercourse went for $150 minimum, although there
was invariably one cute little blonde working there each
month who never took less than $200 for a half hour or $500
for an hour with a trick. A Jacuzzi Party was $115, just for
the privilege of stepping into the water; the price of sex was
added on top of that. A VIP Lounge Party cost $200 just to
get through the door; you negotiated the rest. Still, on Friday and Saturday nights there were always men waiting in
line to use the Jacuzzi and the VIP lounge.

Then there were men who liked to take a girl out of the
Chicken Ranch for eight hours on a date. The price ranged
from $600 to $1,000, depending on the girl. One night a
middle-aged man in an expensive three-piece suit came out
and wanted to take two girls on an "out date." He turned
over $2,000 and took them to the Harvest Festival and the
rodeo in Pahrump, and when his $2,000 and his eight hours
were up he called the Chicken Ranch and said he wanted

another eight hours. When the girls finally returned—$4,000 richer—they told Plankinton that all the man had done was check them into a run-down cabin of the Starlite Hotel, hold them in his arms, and fall asleep. "Money and problems," Plankinton said, happily pocketing $2,000 of the man's $4,000, "that's what makes the world go round."

Soon the lowest-grossing girl was clearing $600 a week, the highest was clearing $2,000, and most of the girls in the middle were managing to clear $1,000. And when it was all added up, Walter Plankinton was taking in the kind of money he had dreamed of when he arrived in the Pahrump Valley a year before. Although he would admit only to grossing $150,000 to $200,000, he was actually grossing $500,000 a year.

And so it seemed that Walter Plankinton had, indeed, been left alone to live out his truck driver's dream in peace. Until one day in April of 1977, when Plankinton started to post signs along Highway 160, advertising THE CHICKEN RANCH; LAS VEGAS'S CLOSEST BROTHEL.

No sooner had he put up a sign than he would find that it had disappeared. So one day in April, when the spring high was a pleasant eighty degrees, Plankinton drove out to the corner of Homestead Road and Highway 160 and put out a new sign that said, CHICKEN RANCH—8 MILES. Then he parked down the highway a bit and sat on the hot vinyl seat of the Thunderbird to wait.

In a few hours an old white Chevy pickup truck with the Nye County Sheriff's Department star on the doors pulled to a stop nearby. The side of the driver's door was stained with what looked like tobacco juice. A huge, wild-looking, florid-faced man emerged from the truck. He had a mashed-up cowboy hat on his head and a large automatic pistol in the back pocket of his baggy, dirty khaki pants. The front of his khaki shirt, like the patrol car door, was stained brown with tobacco juice.

On the brim of his cowboy hat was pinned an official star, which should have been on his breast pocket, designating the man as a lieutenant in the Nye County Sheriff's Department. The lieutenant lurched over to the sign and in one quick movement uprooted it and tossed it into the back of the battered pickup.

Plankinton got out of his Thunderbird and walked along the rocky edge of the road toward the wild-looking man. As Plankinton got close to the pickup, the man turned and, seeing him approach, reached down and pulled a hidden revolver from his boot. He pointed it at Plankinton, who stopped. This florid-faced man looked as though he might be in the habit of shooting people routinely and without remorse. He also looked like he might be crazy. There was ballpoint-pen handwriting all over his cowboy hat.

"The county don't want no sign here," he bellowed.

"Who're you?" Plankinton asked.

"Henderson," the wild-looking man bellowed again.

CHAPTER

Six

Glen Henderson was sent to Lathrop Wells, Nevada, the home of the Shamrock Brothel, in 1967, to keep the peace for District Attorney William P. Beko. On a small patch of desert not ten miles from Death Valley, Henderson built a wooden shack to serve as his sheriff's station and named it Fort Henderson. Outside the shack he hung a sign that read NYE COUNTY SHERIFF'S OFFICE; inside he hung a portrait of Bill Beko. Long after Beko had relinquished his job as district attorney of Nye County and become Fifth District Judge, Henderson still called him for orders instead of calling Peter Knight. He said Knight was "a pipsqueak." He said Beko was "the Godfather."

Henderson's beat included the Amargosa Desert, a forty-by-twenty-mile stretch of blistering white sand bordered by California's Death Valley on the southwest and the nuclear test site on the east. Across that stretch of desert were scattered a hundred or so trailers belonging to the men who had come to work the borate mines in Death Valley or work on the Nuclear Testing Site

It also included the Lathrop Wells "corner," as everyone in Nye County called it, the desert crossroads with less than a dozen buildings scattered along the highway that runs southeast to Death Valley and the highway that runs southwest to Las Vegas. Lathrop Wells was the site of Bill Martin's Shamrock Brothel, which had been the closest brothel to Las Vegas before the Chicken Ranch came into existence amid so much fanfare and consternation. When deputies were assigned to Henderson he told them, "Forget everything you learned. I don't need a cop, I need a lawman. Here's a car, here's a piece. Don't call me 'less you're bloody." Then he told them one more rule of his territory: "Leave Bill Martin alone."

A powerfully built man with the enormous beer gut that is symbolic of manhood on the modern-day range, Glen Henderson was known in Nye County as "the last of the old-time town tamers." His uniform consisted of a tan workshirt and baggy brown pants, in the back pocket of which he carried a nine-millimeter automatic.

Henderson would not have lasted long on an urban police force, but in the Nye County Sheriff's Department, his approach to police work seemed to suit everyone just fine. He kept a "drop box" in his car, filled with unregistered guns, and advised his deputies to do the same. "If you have to shoot some sumbitch," he explained, "you can put a gun on them afterward." When he had to kick some butts and take some names, he scrawled his arrest reports all over the surface of his Stetson.

When Henderson applied for the job of Nye County sheriff's deputy, he gave his place of birth in degrees of latitude and longitude, somewhere around 44 and 70, which put the blessed event just off the coast of Maine. In fact, he claimed he was born on a fishing boat in that vicinity. In 1955 he came to Nevada to escape "woman trouble," as an old friend of his put it. He had hated women ever since and made a habit of telling people that they were good for only one thing, "putting their legs over their heads."

He patrolled the southern half of Nye County during the years that District Attorney Bill Beko would put a light on the top of his car at night and go out on patrol with the Sheriff's Department. When anyone asked, Henderson would say he was sent to Lathrop Welis "for political reasons." The political reasons, he would explain, were that he was working with Judge Beko's sister in the sheriff's station at the entrance to the nuclear test site, lost his temper one day, and threw a telephone at her.

Henderson is the source of plenty of lore, some of it funny, some of it not so funny. On Sunday morning, February 4, 1973, a young prostitute named Heidi ran away from the Shamrock. She was a chubby blond twenty-one-year-old, the daughter of conservative Old World parents who had come to this country from Germany. Like other teenagers, she had run away from home after a fight with her parents, and quickly discovered that prostitution was an easy way to make a living. While working in Portland she became pregnant and had a baby girl. She left the baby with her sister and went to Nevada to see if she could make better money and get that jump on life so many who come to Nevada dream of.

She had worked at the Shamrock only a few months when she started to fight with the owner, Bill Martin. Not many people in Nye County remember Heidi, but the one man who does suspects that she had slept with Martin once or twice and then stopped. Heidi wished to leave the Shamrock. Martin didn't want her to. Heidi told people she was afraid of Martin, afraid of what he might do.

Saturday night, February 3, Martin took Heidi to Beatty for the evening. Sunday morning there was some kind of fight. Heidi ran out of the Shamrock, got into her car, and started driving up toward the atomic test site. Don Miller, a runty little man who worked for Martin and claimed he used to run the rackets in San Francisco, went after her in his powder-blue Lincoln.

Heidi was doing ninety miles per hour when her car ran off the highway. Her tires caught in the sand, and the car began to flip end over end. The first time the car went up in the air, Heidi was thrown through the windshield. The car came down on her body and crushed her, then flipped over twice more before it came to rest.

Brian Thayer, the Nevada highway patrolman who responded to the accident, was convinced that her car had been forced off the road by Don Miller. But in that desert wasteland, where there were no witnesses and the only law was Glen Henderson, he knew there was no way to prove it. She could have been the daughter of any one of us, Thayer thought. But in Nye County Heidi was just another dead whore.

One night nine days later, Brian Thayer and Glen Henderson both happened to answer a minor accident call in Lathrop Wells. In the darkness, Henderson walked up to Thayer, put a twenty-dollar bill into his hand, and said, "Bill says thank you for taking care of the bimbo."

Thayer sent the twenty-dollar bill, along with a report of his run-in with Henderson, to his Nevada Highway Patrol Lieutenant. The Lieutenant sent it to his boss in Carson City, with a recommendation that the report be sent to the Nye County sheriff. But no one in the Highway Patrol or the Sheriff's Department ever called Thayer to ask about Heidi, or Martin, or Henderson.

Brian Thayer was in a rage. He was the only law enforcement officer in Nye County, it seemed, who cared what happened to the girls in the whorehouses. Legal prostitution was supposed to offer those girls the kind of protection they couldn't find in any other state. But in Nye County there was no protection at all. If there was any trouble, the girls were on their own, out in the middle of the desert. Bill Beko's men simply looked the other way.

Three months later the Nye County Sheriff's Department held its annual banquet at the Elks Lodge Hall in Tonopah. District Attorney William P. Beko presented the Distinguished Service Award to Sergeant Glen Henderson of the Lathrop Wells sheriff's station and the Certificate of Appreciation for Continuous Support of Law Enforcement to Lathrop Wells businessman Bill Martin.

• • •

Bill Martin is the alias of a pale, puffy-faced New Yorker named William Louis Apfel, Jr. Born in 1919 on West 142nd Street in New York City, he grew up in the Bay Ridge section of Brooklyn and, after serving as a U.S. Army pilot during World War II, came home to work as a truck driver, then a cop. In his Lathrop Wells bar one night when he had had too much to drink, he told the men there that his brother, John, who was killed in World War II, had always been the good son, and that's why he became the bad one.

In November 1952, Apfel was found guilty in a Police Department trial of shaking down a Brooklyn tavern owner and muscling in on his business. In May 1953, having been dishonorably dismissed from the New York City Police Department, he walked into the small cinder-block Police Department building in downtown Las Vegas and filled out an application to become a patrolman.

He was quickly accepted. In 1953 Las Vegas was still a dry, dusty frontier town of 35,000 that was just starting to roll as an entertainment boom town, Bugsy Siegel had just opened the new Flamingo Hotel with Dean Martin and Jerry Lewis in his showroom. The streets were filled with weathered old cowboys and men in bib overalls who shook their heads in wonder at the new men coming into town in white slacks and pastel sports jackets. There were only forty-three men on the city police force, and the chief often hired new men when they walked through the door, then checked their records later.

It was only a few months before Apfel resigned from the force. The other patrolmen couldn't figure out whether he resigned because his New York record caught up with him or because he figured out how to make more than a street cop could earn in a city of 35,000. He was hired by Roxie's, the last of the great Las Vegas brothels and began to learn the business of running girls. Roxie's was four miles from the center of town, a neat wooden motel surrounded by cottonwood trees and a sign that said ROXIE'S —INNER SPRING MATTRESSES. Bill Apfel went to work there as a bouncer. His job was to keep both the customers and the girls in line.

Apfel spent the next two years in Las Vegas. He married a girl named Sallie Foster and bought her a red brick ranch house in Vegas Heights, a nice neighborhood north of town. In 1957, the year Howard Hughes married Jean Peters in a secret ceremony in Tonopah, Apfel drove to Lathrop Wells, walked into the Water 'N Hole café, one of the then half-dozen buildings on "the corner," and told the old man who owned it that he would "like to rent some land and put a red light there." The old man, who happened to own half the town, also happened to be one of the few people in the county who had a dim view of prostitution.

"Never," he said. "Never."

So Apfel walked across the street to the Coach House Bar and told the woman who owned it that he would "like to rent some land and put a red light there." And she, like most Nevadans, shrugged her shoulders and allowed that if there was one up in Beatty and one in Tonopah, there was no harm having one in Lathrop Wells.

Apfel drove down Highway 373 from Lathrop Wells to Death Valley, and when he reached the town of Death Valley Junction, just over the California line, he bought an old building that had been a railroad station and later a schoolhouse. He paid $200 to have it jacked up and lifted onto a flatbed truck, and on St. Patrick's Day it was installed on the corner where the Coach House and the Water 'N Hole had quietly existed for years. Apfel put a jukebox and a bar and a dance floor in the old schoolhouse, and put a red light on the roof. Then, since the schoolhouse had been moved on St. Patrick's Day, he named his new place of business the Shamrock.

As soon as he opened his new schoolhouse, he began leading two lives, much like some of the girls who worked for him. In Las Vegas, where he spent part of the week with his young wife in their new brick ranch house, where she would eventually raise his two children, he called himself Bill Apfel. Eighty miles north in Lathrop Wells, where he spent the rest of the week sleeping in one of the bedrooms at the Shamrock, he called himself Bill Martin. By 1967 Bill Martin owned the entire east side of the Lathrop Wells corner, and the vicious loyalty of its only law, Glen Henderson.

CHAPTER

Seven

Out on the desert by midafternoon everything begins to look like an overexposed Kodachrome. Colors begin to lose their distinction, and features of the land begin to burn into a uniform yellow-white glare. The sand, stretching low and away toward the atomic-test site, shimmers and dances with reflection—it might be glass or molten metal—until a puff of wind comes up to coax little funnel clouds out of the land.

On one such afternoon, just a week after Lieutenant Glen Henderson pulled Plankinton's Chicken Ranch sign out of the ground and drew his .22 on him, Bill Martin and Henderson drove down to Pahrump in Glen's patrol car and presented themselves in the one-room cinder-block building where Plankinton had been sentenced to sixty days in jail.

On duty that day were Sheriff's Deputies Larry Massoli and Frank Homstad. Massoli was a former Las Vegas television executive who, at age thirty-six, had come to work as a Nye County deputy sheriff because all he had ever really wanted was to be a cop. With his crisply pressed uniforms, his carefully cut and blow-dried hair, and the

elegant gold cigarette case and slim gold Cross pen he always carried in his shirt pocket, he looked preposterously
out of place in Nye County. Homstad was a quiet country
boy who grew up working in the farm fields of central California. Although he had three years' seniority over Massoli, Homstad had quickly become Massoli's sidekick.
When they saw Bill Martin walk through the door with Glen
Henderson—who by then had been put in charge of police
protection for Pahrump as well as Lathrop Wells—they
wondered what was going on.

Henderson and Martin pulled two old chairs into the center of the crowded room and started to talk about the
Chicken Ranch and Walter Plankinton. Plankinton's truck
driver's dream was now making thousands of dollars for
him, much to the consternation of Bill Beko's men in Nye
County, who seemed to have exhausted every legal means
of stopping him. Plankinton kept adding girls at the Chicken
Ranch. He now had fourteen, and the Shamrock had only
five. Plankinton was taking in $20,000 a week compared to
Martin's $7,000. So there was a great deal of muttering in
the quiet darkness of the cinder-block outpost about
"strangers comin' in causing all kinds of problems here."

"We gotta close that son of a bitch down," Henderson
said.

"Yeah," Martin agreed. "I don't like him coming in here
and hurtin' my business."

Martin and Henderson had been in the station only a few
minutes when Henderson stood up, hitching up his baggy
pants by the belt. "Let's go over to Saddle West and get
somethin' cold to drink," he said to Massoli and Homstad.
He told them one of Bill's men was coming to pick up
Martin to take him back to Lathrop Wells.

Homstad, Massoli, and Henderson went out into the
white-hot parking lot and got into the Lathrop Wells patrol
car. Henderson started the car. The steering wheel was so
hot he could hardly touch it.

"Martin and a couple of boys are going to go over to the

Chicken Ranch and burn it down," he said, turning to look Massoli straight in the eye. "One of these nights soon you're going to get a call to go over to the opposite side of the valley. I want you to respond to that call and I don't want you to respond to the fire." A sweat broke out over Massoli's body in the heat of the patrol car.

Henderson put the patrol car into gear and backed it out of the parking lot. Grabbing the steering wheel with two powerful hands, he drove down the highway toward the big red barnlike casino–coffee shop, the Saddle West. The three men went inside and ordered iced tea. No one had said a word.

Finally Henderson demanded, "Do you understand what I said?"

Massoli glared at him. "If I get a call to respond to a fire at the Chicken Ranch," he said, "I'll respond to the fire."

Larry Massoli and Frank Homstad had been in on the Chicken Ranch fight from the beginning. They had been the deputies assigned to the first raid on the Chicken Ranch. They had gone door-to-door in sheriff's uniforms asking people to sign petitions and write letters of complaint about the Chicken Ranch. Now they decided they were not going to go any further. They did not want to become involved in arson. They did not want to become involved in murder.

As soon as they could get rid of Henderson without arousing his suspicion, Massoli and Homstad decided to stake out the Chicken Ranch. For the next two weeks, when they got off work every day, they put on civilian clothes and drove out in Massoli's black Trans Am and sat at the end of Homestead Road and watched the Chicken Ranch through binoculars. Some nights they were out there for ten or twelve hours until the sun came up on the cold desert sands and ignited the mountains with little yellow and red fires. They knew that, out in the desert, things happened very differently when someone was watching and when someone wasn't.

One night, while sitting out there waiting for the henchmen of Bill Martin to burn down the Chicken Ranch, Massoli and Homstad decided that Nye County had just gotten too crazy for them. They were afraid to go to Judge Beko or Peter Knight or Jay Howard with their story. They knew they didn't stand a chance taking on crazy old Glen Henderson. It would be Glen's word against theirs. They knew that Henderson—with his portrait of Judge Beko on his office wall—would come out the winner. They thought it was safer to simply leave Nye County. In another few days Massoli located a friend who said he could get them interviewed for jobs in Panama City, Florida.

Massoli and Homstad asked Jay Howard if they could take a few days off to go on a fishing trip. Instead they flew to Florida. The Panama City Police Chief quickly hired them and as soon as they got back to Pahrump, they sent Jay Howard their letters of resignation, giving two weeks' notice. The letters said that they had found a better opportunity, with better pay, and that they would miss their fellow officers.

Jay Howard blew his stack. As soon as he saw the letters, he called Massoli and Homstad and ordered them to get their badges, cars, radios, and firearms into the office. Massoli and Homstad quickly gathered their equipment and drove to the one-room cinder-block sheriff's station. When they got there, a very red-faced Sheriff was waiting for them.

"Seein' as you boys don't want to work for the county any more," Howard told them, "then I don't think the county can trust you with its equipment for two more weeks."

Massoli stood and stared at Howard. He was sure that Howard had talked to Glen Henderson, and that Howard and Henderson now knew exactly what was going on.

CHAPTER

Eight

In that July of 1977, when Larry Massoli drove his black Trans Am out of Pahrump's Comstock Trailer Park, the men who ran Nye County thought they had seen the last of any trouble regarding this whole damned business with the Chicken Ranch. They could never have known that, just one month later, when a fifty-one-year-old, white-haired woman moved into the Comstock Trailer Park, their trouble would just be beginning.

Her name was Marcia "Joni" Wines. She was a small, round, ruddy-cheeked woman with pale-blue eyes and a nickname that everyone pronounced "Johnnie." She had been born in Iowa and raised in Rochester, New York, and had come west with her family in 1945. She attended college in Colorado, then became one of the first stewardesses to fly for United Airlines, flying DC-3s and DC-6s across the country. In 1952 she married a man named Blaine Wines, whose great-grandfather had ridden Pony Express across Nevada. She spent the next twenty-five years raising their six children and running a day-care center out of their Lake Tahoe home, in addition to working for a private investigator in Lake Tahoe, then for Harrah's Lake Tahoe Recreation Center.

In 1975 her husband, Blaine, moved to Pahrump, because it was the only school district in Nevada where he
could find a teaching job. He taught school during the day
and, like many people in Pahrump, commuted sixty miles
to Las Vegas at night to earn extra money working as a
shift supervisor at the keno counter at the Sahara Hotel.
Joni stayed at Lake Tahoe with their children until August
1977, when she agreed to join him.

Pahrump was only 473 miles from her handsome stone-
and-wood-frame home in the thickly forested hills above
Lake Tahoe, but it might as well have been in another
country. There were few women in the sagebrush-strewn
southern-Nevada desert who were lucky enough to live in
wood-frame houses. Most lived in "double-wide" trailers
(it took Joni a while to get used to having friends talk about
their "double-wides"). The fancier trailers came equipped
with sleek new kitchens. Some had fake wooden beams on the
ceilings. But they never felt quite like a home. The harsh
winds that came off the Sierra Nevada rattled the cheaply
installed windows, and the walls shook convulsively
each time the air-conditioner on the roof cut on and off.

Some of the women lived a turn-of-the-century lifestyle.
They raised their own pigs, cows, and chickens. They made
their own bread, canned their own food. When the pigs and
the cows were full grown, they would take them to the local
butcher, who could soothingly stroke the animal right up
until the second he sliced its throat, thereby guaranteeing,
they said, that the meat would not be tough.

For the women who did not choose that life, there was
little to do after they dropped their kids off at school and
stopped at the one-room post office to pick up the mail.
They spent most of their days sitting in their trailers, watching soap operas, and trying to keep up the unending battle
against the fine white sand that blew in the doors and the
windows and stuck to the floors and the walls and the furniture.

• • •

It was not long after she moved to Pahrump that Joni Wines began looking for something more challenging to do with her time than watch daytime television. One morning she went to a meeting at the Calvada coffee shop with other high school mothers to plan a fund-raiser for the school's athletic department.

"We'll have so many people we'll have to have somebody directing traffic," one mother said.

"You don't expect any help outa the Sheriff's Department, do you?" another asked bitterly.

The conversation immediately turned to the Nye County Sheriff's Department and the potbellied, red-faced Sheriff, Jay Howard, who was, the women agreed, an embarrassment to Nye County. Soon Jay Howard became a stock item of conversation among Joni Wines and her new friends. He had a reputation for rolling drunks when he was a young Tonopah bartender and rustling cattle up in Smoky Valley when he was a young rancher. More recently he was unseemly and unsightly, presiding at the Harvest Festival with a silly grin on his face and a can of beer perpetually in one hand.

The talk went on through the fall of 1977, when the women started talking about finding somebody to run against Jay. But it wasn't until the end of the year that Joni Wines's new friend Lola Binum made the fateful suggestion.

"Joni," she said, "I dare you to run for sheriff."

Nine

Sheriff Jay Howard was hardly in a position to notice that his territory was being threatened by outside competition of the political sort when he was so busy fighting outside competition of the commercial sort. In that winter of 1977, he was deeply engrossed in the business of trying to put Walter Plankinton into jail.

Plankinton's first attorney had made that quintessential mistake of all mistakes a lawyer can make, forgetting a filing date. Jeffrey Shaner, the fancy Las Vegas attorney who had defended Plankinton after the original Chicken Ranch raid, had forgotten to file a notice requesting a court date for a hearing on his appeal to stay Plankinton's sixty-day jail term until an appeal had been filed with the State Supreme Court. Shaner admitted that he had missed the filing date, but insisted that he'd been tricked by Peter Knight, who, he said, had led him to believe that Judge Beko's court would automatically set a hearing date. When the filing date had passed, a gleeful District Attorney Knight and Sheriff Howard issued a warrant for Plankinton's arrest.

With that arrest warrant, they finally pushed Plankinton

too far. No sooner had his new attorney, Leonard Smith, filed the necessary papers to keep him out of jail, than Plankinton drove to the United States Courthouse in Las Vegas to tell the whole story of Bill Beko and Peter Knight and Jay Howard and the tobacco-stained, six-gun-wielding Glen Henderson to the Office of the United States Attorney.

Plankinton was pale and nervous and shaking so badly when he walked into the small reception room of the U.S. Attorney's Office that the receptionist was convinced he was "a nut." Instead of letting him come through the locked door into the attorneys' offices, she asked Assistant U.S. Attorney Bill Turner to come out to talk to him.

Sitting in the small waiting room, his lanky body crammed uncomfortably into one of the straight-backed green leather government chairs, Plankinton launched into a rambling, impassioned speech about his fight with Nye County. "Peter Knight is my mortal enemy," he told Bill Turner. "The county is totally divided between the people who want government by the Constitution of the United States and those who want government by the good old boys. They run the county to suit themselves, and no one has had the inclination or the audacity to fight them except me."

When Turner had listened to Plankinton long enough to realize he wasn't "a nut," he escorted him through the security door and into his office and began to ask Plankinton more questions about Bill Beko's county. To Turner it sounded like the classic case for the U.S. Attorney: an investigation of political corruption by a county district attorney who was obviously not going to investigate himself. Turner picked up his telephone and called the FBI office on the second floor of the courthouse. He told FBI agent Jim Perry he thought he had a case for him.

In many ways Jim Perry was the perfect agent for the

case. A thirty-three-year-old former Air Force fighter pilot with prematurely silver hair, clear blue eyes, and a perpetual look of agitation on his ruddy South Dakota farm-boy face, Perry had wanted to do nothing but investigate political corruption since he joined the FBI. He had just come from Philadelphia, where he had helped get the conviction of Pennsylvania State Senator Buddy Cianfrani for taking political payoffs.

As he was winding up that case, Perry asked the FBI to transfer him to Las Vegas. When he and his wife, Caroline, were growing up in South Dakota, their families had often taken them to Arizona for vacations. They both loved the desert. They thought it would be a great place to raise their son and daughter. And Perry thought Las Vegas—"the black hole," FBI agents called it—would be a great assignment for him.

Now here comes this character Walter Plankinton with a story that seems to confirm it. Plankinton told Perry that after he had refused to pay Peter Knight a piece of the Chicken Ranch take, Knight had conspired with the Justice of the Peace Dow Chenoweth at his Pahrump Justice Court trial to find him guilty. There were two former sheriff's deputies, Larry Massoli and Frank Homstad, Plankinton said, who could confirm it. Perry could find them in Panama City, Florida.

Boy, this isn't bad, Perry thought. He wasn't that interested in the Justice Court trial. But he was very interested in the story that this young District Attorney out in the middle of the desert was demanding political payoffs. He decided to wire Plankinton up with a microphone and send him back to the Nye County Courthouse to have another talk with Peter Knight about that 5 percent of the take.

At that point Walter Plankinton folded like a bad poker hand. He had had a major heart attack just before he moved to Nevada, he said. He simply couldn't pull it off. Wearing a body mike was out of the question; his heart couldn't take it. He may have been a cowboy, he may have been a risk taker, but he drew the line at taking the risk of walking into Bill Beko's courthouse with a microphone taped to his chest.

While Jim Perry sat in Las Vegas in that February of 1978, trying to figure out what to do about this Chicken Ranch case, a small, dark Indian woman who lived with Bill Martin in Lathrop Wells walked through the door that separated Martin's office from the Coach House Bar, which Martin had come to own in the years since he founded the Shamrock. The Indian woman walked over to a giant, frightening-looking man with a long handlebar mustache and long, thick hair that hung to his waist.

"Bill wants to see you," she said.

The big man unfolded himself from his barstool, walked slowly around behind the bar, and went through the door into Martin's dimly lit office. Martin sat behind an enormous wooden desk. To one side was a safe. Against one windowless wall were filing cabinets. The two men glared at each other with undisguised hostility.

"That son of a bitch in Pahrump has been going too far," Martin said. "He has to be taught a lesson."

"What kind of lesson?" the man asked.

"I want Plankinton's arm broke," Martin said. "And his leg broke, and that whorehouse of his burned down. I'll pay you fifteen hundred dollars to do it."

The man continued to glare at Martin. For a moment he did not respond. Then he said, "You guarantee me seven hundred fifty up front and promise me a lawyer. Then I'll do it."

Martin said nothing. The big man left the room.

At the same time, in Pahrump, Joni Wines and her husband, Blaine, were arguing about whether she should run for Nye County sheriff. Blaine told her she was out of her mind to want to get involved in politics. He had been involved in school board politics in Lake Tahoe, and he knew how nasty it could get. He told her she shouldn't do it. And she told him to get used to the idea. She was going to do it.

When she was only twenty-one and living in Colorado, she had left her family and moved to New York City, determined to become a Rockette. She never got to dance in the spotlights, on the stage of Radio City Music Hall. Now, at fifty-one, she was being offered the opportunity few people ever get: the chance to try for the spotlight again.

On March 27, 1978, Joni Wines, dressed for the occasion in a dark-brown polyester pantsuit, set off by bright-red lipstick and bright-red polish on her nails, drove the 165 miles to Tonopah and walked into the County Clerk's Office in the silver-domed white stone Nye County Courthouse.

"I want to file to run for office," she informed the woman behind the counter.

"Fine," the woman said. "What office are you filing for?"

"Sheriff," she said.

The woman was speechless. She just stood and stared at Joni Wines. "All right," she said when she had finally gotten her voice back. She turned back to her desk to get the proper form.

As soon as Joni Wines finished filing to become a candidate for Nye County sheriff, she drove down Main Street to the Tonopah *Times-Bonanza,* a sixteen-page weekly that had been founded at the turn of the century, at the height of the silver boom. She handed the editor an envelope with her photograph and resumé.

"I've just filed to run for sheriff," she informed him. "I thought perhaps you'd be interested in the story."

"Thank you," the man said, without batting an eye.

On March 31, the Tonopah *Times-Bonanza* appeared throughout Nye County with a picture of Joni Wines on the front page, above the headline "Pahrump Woman Files for

Nye Sheriff Post.'' That afternoon a copy was delivered to the mailbox at Lieutenant Glen Henderson's trailer down the road from the Lathrop Wells corner.

When his deputy Tony Falcone walked into the wooden outpost called Fort Henderson later that afternoon, Henderson grabbed the newspaper.

"You've got to see this," he bellowed at Falcone, waving the *Times-Bonanza* in the air.

"What is it?" the deputy asked.

"There's some fat fucking woman running for sheriff."

Back in Las Vegas, FBI agent Jim Perry had not been able to get Walter Plankinton out of his mind. It was such an incredible story: a fight over a desert whorehouse. The agents back in Philadelphia would never believe it. Perry decided he had to make one stab at Plankinton's case. He sent a request to the FBI field office in Jacksonville, Florida. It asked them to send an agent to Panama City to find those two former Nye County sheriff's deputies, Massoli and Homstad, and ask them if they knew anything about the Justice Court trial Plankinton claimed had been staged to cheat him.

At the end of April, an FBI agent flew from Jacksonville to Panama City and found Massoli and Homstad. The two former Nye County deputies told him they did remember standing outside the Pahrump Justice Court the day Plankinton went on trial, and laughing about what a sure bet it was that he would be found guilty. But they had no evidence to back up Plankinton's story that Peter Knight had conspired with the Justice of the Peace to deprive him of a fair trial.

They did, however, have another story to tell the FBI agent. To the agent's surprise, they laid out the story of the day in April of 1977 that a crazy old Nye County sheriff's lieutenant named Glen Henderson walked into the Pahrump sheriff's station and warned them that a whorehouse owner named Bill Martin was going to have his boys burn down the Chicken Ranch.

On April 24, 1978, the FBI agent flew back to the field office in Jacksonville and dictated the report of his interview with Massoli and Homstad. The report was typed on the FBI's standard 302 form and was mistakenly set aside on a secretary's desk. It was never sent to Jim Perry.

CHAPTER

Ten

In the early-morning hours in the desert, just before the sun begins to rise, the sky is a fury of constellations, white and sapphire, while the land below is as black and impenetrable as the floor of the sea. In those early hours of June 10, 1978, in the southern-Nevada desert, a light-colored car turned off Highway 160, which runs out of Pahrump toward Las Vegas. It was a large four-door American car, the kind of car a man buys when he can't afford a Cadillac. The blackness made it seem as if the car had driven off the edge of the earth.

The car turned onto the gravel road that led to the Chicken Ranch. In the dead and chill night air the sound of vulcanized rubber churning stones carried across the desert. Crushing stone on stone, the car moved along the gravel road a short while and then came to a stop. The front doors opened and three men got out. The men did not look at all alike. One was a big man who might have been a bouncer. Another was short and narrow, nervous and jittery, like a ferret. The third was tall and thin, a sharp-featured Ichabod Crane.

Moving cautiously, they opened the back doors. The

three peculiar moonlit figures brought out a five-gallon Army fuel can, a small tin can, a bucket, and a round pot about a foot in diameter. Like three medieval warlocks about to begin some unfathomable ceremony, they placed the vessels on the edge of the desert.

The tall, lean man took over. Calmly and deliberately, like a man who knows his work, he lifted the small tin can and poured thick black kerosene into the round pot. Then he picked up the large Army fuel can and tipped the nozzle into the pot. The raw odor of gasoline filled the dry desert air.

The tall man poured the gasoline-kerosene mixture into a pool on the ground. Then he lit a match. Suddenly the three faces were illuminated in a warm yellow light. He touched the match to the ground and set off a little blue blaze that danced on the sand in the darkness.

After studying the color of the flame as it burned, danced, died, and went out, he picked up the Army can again and added more gasoline to the mixture. Once more he poured a sample into the sand and struck a match. This time the blue flame that danced across the sand was darker. The tall man was satisfied.

He nodded to the big man, who took the pot, opened the back door of the car, and got in. The tall man put the Army can into the trunk while the short man threw the tin can away at the side of the road and got into the driver's seat. Leaving the lights off and driving slowly to keep from spilling the gasoline-kerosene mixture, they made their way down the gravel road to the Chicken Ranch.

The Chicken Ranch had grown to six sixty-foot trailers in the twenty months since Plankinton first made a run at the entrenched politics of prostitution in Nye County. With twelve girls working in twelve bedrooms of those trailers, Plankinton was now taking in $20,000. a week. Or $1 million a year.

Inside the Chicken Ranch everything had quieted down for the night. The local cowboys and truckers who dreamed of one day owning their own whorehouses, the high-rollers with their credit cards and their limousines, had all come and gone, leaving $2,800 in the safe for the night's take. An exhausted group of working girls were getting ready to go to sleep on the same sheets on which they'd been working all day. The last customers, two high-school boys in baseball uniforms who had bought one girl each and had then come out into the parlor, counted their money, and bought one more apiece, had just left.

In the front parlor, with its chrome-and-plastic jukebox and cheap sofas and Formica-coated end tables, Rita, a buxom forty-three-year-old redhead, was manicuring another girl's nails. Rita was the mother in the mother-and-daughter team that had come to find work at the Chicken Ranch the night of Jay Howard's raid. She had gone to work at Bill Martin's Shamrock for a while, then returned to the Chicken Ranch after Plankinton opened it again.

Just off the parlor were two front bedrooms, furnished with single beds, flowered bedspreads, and small dressers. In one of the bedrooms, Suzi, a Taiwanese woman who was one of the house's leading girls, was about to go to sleep. Years ago Suzi had married an American GI and moved to Milwaukee and had a daughter. Sometime after that she had left her husband, moved to Nevada with her daughter, and gotten her first job in a whorehouse, where she could earn $2,000 a week, to support her gambling habit and her daughter. Although she was almost forty, she wore her long dark hair down to her waist and carried off the effect of a teenage Suzie Wong.

In the room to the right of the front parlor, Maria was awake and dressed because she was one of the two "early-up" girls. She would be on call for any customers who rang the bell between 4 A.M. and 1 P.M., when the rest of the girls started the day's work. Maria was the daughter of a military officer and had spent much of her childhood on military bases around the country. She was a beautiful six-foot-tall redhead with a slinky walk and soft henna curls that fell over her shoulders. She divided her time between the Las Vegas hotels and the desert brothels.

Farther down the slim corridor of the trailer, no wider than the aisle of the smallest airliner, were other, less elegant bedrooms, more like the compartments in a railroad Pullman car than rooms in a home. In one of them Lily was packing her bags for a trip to Las Vegas while she talked to April and Candy. Lily was the prettiest and youngest girl at the Chicken Ranch, only twenty years old, a tall brunette from back east. To see her you'd have thought she was a local college girl. Except that there were no local colleges near Pahrump, Nevada.

Beneath every whore's story lies another, the way arsenic and antimony lie beneath the desert sand. Lily's was hideous, and unfortunately not that unusual. She had been raped by her father and was walking the streets of Los Angeles by the age of thirteen. She moved to Las Vegas at eighteen. She had been working at the Chicken Ranch one month.

Farther back from Lily's bedroom was the Cat Room, a lounge where the girls watched television or played backgammon and talked while they waited for customers. Martha sat in the Cat Room talking to Barbara Perri, the new night maid, a sixty-two-year-old grandmotherly woman with a pretty, pale face and a gentle manner, who cleaned up and answered the door if the bell rang during the quiet shift.

The rest of the dozen girls, as well as Plankinton's stepson, Doug Harkalis, a handsome, friendly curly-haired young man in his early thirties, who served as the manager of the Chicken Ranch, were asleep in their rooms.

Maria was the first to hear the car. At about 4:15 A.M. she heard a car motor idling somewhere near the trailers. She pulled back the curtain on the small, high window, but could see nothing; she could only hear the motor in the quiet night. She went back to the magazine she was reading and waited, expecting to have to service a customer, whoever he might be, as soon as Barbara Perri let him in. For fifteen minutes she heard the motor idling outside. Then she heard the crushing of stones as the car moved slowly into the gravel parking lot outside her window.

Maria pulled the curtain back again. This time she saw one of the men get out on the passenger's side. She went to the bathroom to check her makeup and comb her long red hair, then walked back to the Cat Room.

"It looks like we have company," she said.

Barbara got up from the couch in the Cat Room. She maneuvered down the narrow aisle between the bedroom doors to the parlor. Without looking through the peephole cut into the wallpaper on the sliding glass door, she reached for the lock on the handle. As soon as the lock clicked, the door began to slide open on its own. When it had been opened several inches, two gloved hands reached in at her.

For a terrified instant, while the hands hung there in the still, dark desert air, Barbara Perri saw a man's head, the mouth covered in dark material, the eyes shaded by a floppy brown hat brim. The only clear feature was a sharp, narrow, pointed nose.

Then the hands closed on her throat and she was thrown onto her back. The hands disappeared for a moment, then reappeared holding a round pot. The hands splashed a thick black liquid on the shag carpeting, the end tables, the sofa. The yellow flame of a match appeared in one of the heavy gloves. The flame caught and began its dizzying course around the parlor of the Chicken Ranch.

The flame went up Barbara Perri's arm.

"Oh, my God, there's a fire! Oh, my God, there's a fire!"

She got back onto her feet and stumbled along the tiny aisle between the bedrooms. It was as if an airliner had caught fire in midflight. There seemed to be no way for the thirteen women and one man to get out. Barbara could hear the chorus of panicked screams begin as the girls realized what she was trying to tell them. Candy was the first to jump. The minute she heard the word "fire," she smashed the window of her tiny room and jumped out into the cold desert night.

Now Rita, who had leaped off the parlor sofa where she had been manicuring the other girl's nails, pushed past Barbara to get to the back door. She pounded on it in a panic to get out. It was latched on the outside. Candy made her way around the trailer, smoke and high-pitched cries pouring out of it, and unlatched the back door.

Doug awoke and ran in the direction of Barbara's screams. He immediately saw that they couldn't get out through the front door: flame and smoke had overcome the parlor. He began herding those girls he could find toward the back. As he moved down the narrow corridor one girl tried to push past him to get out the front. He spun her around and steered her back down the aisle.

Suzi jumped out of bed when she heard Barbara scream. She opened her bedroom door and was met by a wall of flame. She slammed the door again, and now she too began screaming. The lights went out and her tiny room was filled with smoke. She kept screaming. But no one came.

CHAPTER

Eleven

The emergency call came in to the Nye County sheriff's station at Pahrump at 4:49 A.M. Martha, who had been sitting with Barbara Perri before Barbara went to answer the door, had managed to report the fire to a telephone operator before running out of the trailers. The operator called Las Vegas by mistake, and the Las Vegas Fire Department dispatcher called Nye County. At 4:51 A.M. Sheriff's Deputy Steve Blackwell, sitting in the small cinder-block room ten miles across the desert from the Chicken Ranch, called the Pahrump Fire Department. He woke the duty man, who said he'd respond as quickly as he could. At 4:54 A.M. Blackwell called the Pahrump ambulance crew. He woke the woman on duty and she said she'd respond as quickly as she could.

At about 5 A.M., Blackwell called Sergeant Ray Shamblin and told him there was a fire at the Chicken Ranch. Shamblin told Blackwell to call him back at 6 A.M. with his regular wake-up call. Then Sergeant Ray Shamblin, a good old country boy from Alabama who had been appointed by Sheriff Jay Howard to run the Pahrump sheriff's station just eight months before, hung up the phone and went back to sleep while the Chicken Ranch burned to the ground.

It was one of the hottest fires anyone in that county had ever seen. Most people do not think of metal as flammable, but it is, aluminum especially, and the type of sheet aluminum that house trailers are made of even more especially. It is burning aluminum that gives fireworks their characteristic white-hot brightness.

The temperature inside the Chicken Ranch reached 2,400 degrees as the white heat—like an all-consuming ghost— possessed first one trailer, then another. The steel skeletons of the trailers began to twist in the agony of the heat. Inside, whiskey bottles, light bulbs, hair-spray cans exploded, as everything else—couches, clothing, cash, cloth and paper, jukebox—vaporized.

Standing in the sagebrush, half naked, the girls watched a vast mushroom cloud of blue-and-white ashes, punctuated by red and orange embers, rise into the sky. They saw something of what it must have looked like in the early fifties when the government still used the barren land just a few miles north for open-air nuclear tests.

As the bright-red glow spread across the desert, its heat reaching out farther and farther from the circle of light, Doug Harkalis steered the girls back into the creosote bush and sagebrush, fearing that the propane tank might go up with a horrible explosion and take them with it into the sky. They stood there, crying and screaming and talking all at the same time. Their nightgowns and thick makeup were caked with black smoke and blowing sand, and the smoke and the sand were smeared over their faces by their tears.

As the girls quieted down, bringing their hysterical sobbing under control, Doug counted heads to make sure everyone had gotten out. The exodus from the trailers had been so sudden, the fire had overtaken them with such devastating speed, that it did not surprise him to discover that one girl was missing. Suzi was trapped inside the Chicken Ranch in her place of honor in the front bedroom, which had already collapsed from the heat and ascended in glittering embers.

Even as Doug was trying to compose his words to tell

the others the obvious, that Suzi must be dead, a nude and bloody apparition lurched from the edge of the desert toward them. It was Suzi. Her huge breasts and cinder-black hair streaked with sand and soot, she was too stunned to make a sound. She was in shock. But she was—they all were—miraculously alive.

At 6:02 A.M. Nye County Sheriff's Dispatcher Steve Blackwell placed the routine six-o'clock wake-up call to Sergeant Ray Shamblin. At 6:06 A.M. Blackwell took a call from a woman who lived in a trailer out on the Tecopa Highway that runs from Pahrump to Death Valley. The woman told Blackwell that a man had stopped by her trailer to tell her there had been a wreck on the highway. Blackwell called the Nevada Highway Patrol.

Blackwell then called Sergeant Shamblin back and told him about the accident. And Shamblin, who now had the choice of going to the accident or the fire, responded to the auto accident.

One hour and four minutes later, another telephone rang in the bedroom of a spacious suburban ranch house on the west side of Las Vegas, more than seventy miles from the Chicken Ranch. The telephone was in the bedroom of FBI agent Jim Perry. The call that awakened him and his wife and two children on that lazy Saturday morning in June was from an FBI agent on the duty desk at FBI headquarters in Washington, D.C.

The agent told Perry he had just taken a call from an attorney named Leonard Smith, who said he represented a man named Walter Plankinton, who was the owner of a whorehouse somewhere out in the desert. Smith had told the agent that at four-thirty that morning a man had forced his way into the Chicken Ranch, knocked down a maid, thrown gasoline around, lit a match, and set the place on fire. It was now three hours later, Smith said, and no one from the local Sheriff's Department had done anything to investigate, even as the fire and the trail of the criminal were growing cold.

Perry shook himself awake and called Leonard Smith. Smith was agitated, upset. He told Perry he knew that the Sheriff, Jay Howard wasn't going to do anything. He begged Perry to go out there.

"OK," Perry said, "I'll go."

Even as he hung up the telephone, he couldn't believe that he had just agreed to go out to some whorehouse fire in the middle of the desert. But there was something about this case that had gotten under his skin. He somehow felt he had to. He dragged himself out of bed and dressed in a conservative gray business suit because he prided himself on the fact that when he went anywhere on bureau business he always wore a suit. By seven-thirty he was driving out of Las Vegas on the Blue Diamond Highway. By eight-thirty he had arrived in Pahrump.

The sun was already starting to push the early-morning temperature past a hundred by the time Perry got to the end of dusty, rutted Homestead Road. A big Pahrump fire truck was parked askew, its chrome bells gleaming in the sun, and a fireman was casually hosing down the burned-out skeleton of the Chicken Ranch.

Now, in full daylight, long after the fire had consumed itself, the picture it made was not nearly as dramatic. It looked like a big charred spot on the earth, filled with blackened and twisted metal girders. As the water played on it, the gray-and-white aluminum ash mixed with soot, then ran into muddy pools that soaked into the sand. The Pahrump Fire Chief poked through the rubble, delicately probing for hot spots. Deputy Steve Blackwell, who had gone off dispatch duty at 8 A.M., was standing at the end of the road looking forlorn. Perry thought it was odd: There were no more than three cars for miles around, his included. Yet this sheriff's deputy named Blackwell, a big boyish-looking man with a close-cropped military haircut, claimed he had been posted there to direct traffic. Not very bright, Perry thought. And extremely nervous to boot.

"Where's the Sheriff?" Perry asked.

Blackwell was literally shaking. He could scarcely speak, he was stuttering so badly. "R-r-r-responding to an au-au-auto accident," Blackwell managed to say.

"Where are all the girls?" Perry asked.

"G-g-g-girls?" Blackwell asked.

Perry jerked his thumb over his shoulder toward the scorched patch of desert. "From the whorehouse," he said.

Blackwell pointed down the road. "F-first trailer you come to."

Perry got back into his car and drove out Homestead Road, letting the brief blast of air-conditioning wash over the soaked front of his white shirt until he saw the trailer. It was a double-wide set back from the road. The front yard was desert sage and sand, and up on the front porch were quails in wooden pens. Perry could see a goat tethered to the side of the trailer.

Perry knocked on the front door. Fran and Jerry Kotecki, an electrician and his wife, answered the door looking distraught. Perry asked about the girls of the Chicken Ranch and was told that the only one still there was the Chinese girl, Suzi, and she was asleep in the back bedroom. Perry was allowed in and walked back through the cool air of the trailer to the back bedroom. Suzi was heavily sedated, spoke only in broken English, and was not much help to Perry.

Mrs. Kotecki explained that Suzi had broken out through her bedroom window when the trailer went up in flames and had scraped the skin off the entire length of her left leg. She was very scared and very lucky to be alive. She had been taken by ambulance to Doc Cecil, one of two doctors in Nye County, who had treated her leg, given her a sedative and sent her back to the trailer to rest.

Perry thanked the Koteckis and said he thought he'd better see the other girls at the sheriff's station. He walked through the dark rooms of the trailer and out the front door into the blinding sun. It took a moment before he could see anything. When his eyes began to find focus, he saw a white car in the gravel driveway. The car's door was dominated by a large gold star with the words NYE COUNTY SHERIFF'S DEPARTMENT in the center.

Leaning against the car, waiting for the FBI agent to appear, was Sheriff Jay Howard and Sheriff's Lieutenant Glen Henderson. Nothing Perry had ever seen in Philadelphia had prepared him for them. Howard, red-faced and potbellied, was wearing a tan sheriff's uniform along with a cowboy hat tilted on his head. Henderson, a massive man with a king-of-the-mountain face, had tobacco stains all over the front of his tan shirt. His sheriff's badge was pinned to the edge of his cowboy hat, which had some kind of writing scrawled all over it.

As Perry walked slowly across the sand, the two men stood against the patrol car, their thumbs hooked into their belts, and silently stared at him. As soon as Perry got close to them, Henderson began to talk.

"It hadda be done by a pimp," Henderson bellowed. "It hadda be a pissed-off pimp."

Perry introduced himself to Nye County's finest, and all the while the men were shaking hands Henderson never stopped talking. "It hadda be a pimp," he said over and over again. "It hadda be a pimp. It hadda be a pissed-off pimp."

CHAPTER

Twelve

The Chicken Ranch burned down on Saturday morning just before dawn. By Monday morning Walter Plankinton was busy letting everyone in Bill Beko's county know he was going to be around for a long time to come. He hired a bulldozer to push the pile of twisted steel and charred aluminum to the back of his twenty acres. He bought two new twelve-foot trailers, hauled them to the site, and was already planning a new Chicken Ranch that would rise like a phoenix from the ashes of the old one. He bought a Cyclone security fence topped with barbed wire, and an electric gate, and had them installed around his twenty acres. Then, to make sure everyone in Nye County took notice, he scheduled a gala opening ceremony for the following Thursday. If God could create the world in seven days, Walter Plankinton could create the third Chicken Ranch in five.

That done, Plankinton escalated his fight with Bill Beko's county by spending the week talking to every television and radio and newspaper reporter who would listen. Inasmuch as the burning of the Chicken Ranch was the biggest story in Nye County at that moment, and would be for a long time to come, they were all willing to listen.

"I know what a black man felt like in the middle of Alabama years ago," he told a Las Vegas *Sun* reporter, "when the boys in white hoods rode through the town with torches." He told the Las Vegas *Review-Journal* that the "Tonopah Mafia" was "morally responsible" for the fire, which he repeatedly referred to as "the attempt at mass murder."

The *Review-Journal* asked Sheriff Jay Howard for a response to that charge. "Now, that's got to be the most ignorant thing I've ever heard," the Sheriff said. "That is a completely ignorant remark." Howard told the reporter that he was not going to get into a fight with Walter Plankinton. "You'd like that," he said. "It sells papers. Well, I'm not about to fight with him in the papers. He's not the best-liked person around here, you know."

Then Howard went on to tell the *Review-Journal* that "everybody was jumping to conclusions" when they reported that a masked man had pushed open the Chicken Ranch door, knocked down the white-haired grandmother who was working as a maid, then set the trailer on fire. "That's very likely what happened," Howard said. "I'm not implying it isn't. But we have no concrete proof yet. All we have is what the little doll who answered the door said."

On June 15, 1978, five days after the fire, Plankinton did just what he said he would do. He opened the new Chicken Ranch where the old Chicken Ranch had burned to the ground. He opened it on the very same spot with five of the very same girls. Seven of the girls who had almost been killed in the blazing walls of those aluminum house trailers had left Nye County the morning after the fire. But five others—including Suzi, who had come so close to losing her life—had decided to come back. The life of a whore in the desert was always a risk, they said; they were willing to take this one for the chance to go back to earning $1,000 to $2,000 a week.

The mariachi band was already playing when Walter

Plankinton arrived with the champagne. The working girls followed, making their entrances in slinky evening gowns of royal blue and emerald green. The television newsmen from Las Vegas were not far behind. As far as they were concerned, this was the best kind of news of all: it had sex, it had intrigue, it had small-town color and big-time crime written all over it. As far as Plankinton was concerned, two minutes on the six-o'clock news was gold; you couldn't buy advertising like that. You couldn't buy revenge like that, either, not without committing a felony.

The mariachi trumpet player blew Taps over the pile of twisted metal that had been the second Chicken Ranch, while Plankinton announced that he was dedicating the debris as "a monument of one man's fight against dictatorship, tyranny, and intolerance." The television cameras ate it up. Then the Chicken Ranch working girls, wearing stiletto heels to match their evening gowns, formed a chorus line and tried to perform a Rockettes routine to the music of the mariachi band.

Finally, when the television crews had gone off with tape for the evening news, Plankinton, and his girls, and the mariachi band, stepped up to the front door of the new trailers. There they held the solemn ceremony that, in the brothel business, is the equivalent of having the First Lady break a bottle of champagne over a ship. Sherri, Plankinton's "tall, beautiful redhead," the first lady of the house, pulled up her long clinging royal-blue dress, slipped down her lace bikini panties, and peed on the front steps.

The Chicken Ranch was back in business.

CHAPTER

Thirteen

The Monday morning after the fire, FBI agent Jim Perry was plotting neither celebrations nor revenge. He was taking the elevator from the second floor of the United States Courthouse in Las Vegas to the fourth floor, to begin planning the federal investigation of the Chicken Ranch fire with Chief Assistant U.S. Attorney Larry Leavitt. In Philadelphia, Perry had been involved in the kind of big-time political-corruption cases that no one in the small, insular state of Nevada had ever even attempted. Ever since Perry had arrived in Las Vegas he had been looking for someone in the U.S. Attorney's Office who had the makings of a good corruption prosecutor. By the time of the Chicken Ranch fire he had decided it was Leavitt.

A cool, controlled, dispassionate man, Leavitt had the look of a classic prosecutor. Although he was only forty, he was prematurely gray and balding. He had been born and raised on the North Side of Chicago and graduated from the University of Illinois with a degree in philosophy. He came west to Berkeley, California, intending to get his Ph.D. and spend the rest of his life teaching philosophy on a university campus. Then, in 1964, the student revolution

struck. Leavitt went out on the streets, and soon decided
to switch to law.

Leavitt had arrived at the U.S. Attorney's Office only
three months before, after spending six years as a prosecutor in the Clark County District Attorney's Office. He
had just finished prosecuting one of the most sensational
murder cases in Las Vegas history—the murder of union
boss Al Bramlet by two men whom Bramlet had hired to
firebomb several Las Vegas nightclubs—when he was offered the job of chief prosecutor for the U.S. Attorney.

In many ways Perry and Leavitt were as different as two
men could be. While Leavitt was growing up on the streets
of Chicago, Perry was growing up on a South Dakota farm.
While Leavitt was protesting the Vietnam War at Berkeley,
Perry was flying 525 F-4 Phantom bombing missions over
the skies of Vietnam. But the two men had one important
thing in common: they both wanted to work political corruption. This morning they both wanted to do what no
other law enforcement officer in Nevada had ever done:
investigate Bill Beko's county.

The fact that the case was arson did not help them. Arson
was a state offense, and they were empowered to investigate only federal offenses. They decided that their way into
this case was through RICO, the Racketeering-Influenced
and Corrupt Organization Act, which allowed the federal
government to prosecute two or more state offenses if they
were committed through a pattern of racketeering by an
enterprise engaged in interstate commerce.

That Monday morning Perry and Leavitt had very little
to go on. Perry had already interviewed the Chicken Ranch
girls, but they were little help. The only real lead came from
Maria and Suzi. Suzi was convinced the high-school boys
who were the last to leave the Chicken Ranch that night
had come back to burn it down. Maria remembered that
one of the boys was named Danny. He said he worked at a
Safeway in Henderson, just south of Las Vegas. He had
brought his brother to the Chicken Ranch because it was
his brother's eighteenth birthday and he was still a virgin.

Perry found the boys and spent most of the day interviewing them. They said they had known nothing about the fire until they read about it in the papers. The only thing they could tell Perry was that as they left the Chicken Ranch at four-thirty in the morning they passed another car coming in the opposite direction. By the end of the day Perry was convinced they had nothing to do with the fire.

"They're young," he said to Leavitt when he got back that afternoon. "They're scared to death. And all their stories jibe."

Before Perry left for home that Monday, he took one call about the case. It was from an informant who said he had just talked to Ralph Petrillo, owner of a girlie magazine. Petrillo said he had met a guy named Kenny, a big guy built like a bouncer. This Kenny said that he did not believe Walter Plankinton would be around much longer.

Tuesday was a much better day. Another man called, this one a friend of Plankinton. He said he had heard from a former sheriff's deputy, John Nocito. Nocito said that an ex-con named Bo Hyder was telling people that Bill Martin had tried to hire him to burn down the Chicken Ranch and beat up Plankinton. Martin's name was interesting. As owner of the Shamrock Brothel up the road from the Chicken Ranch, Martin would have been hurt the most by Plankinton's business. Bo Hyder said that the deal to burn out Plankinton fell through because Martin wouldn't give Hyder money up front. The informant told Perry that he could find Hyder in Tonopah, at a bar on Main Street called the Pastime.

That morning Perry also called the FBI office in Jacksonville, Florida, to see if anybody had ever interviewed those two former sheriff's deputies, Larry Massoli and Frank Homstad. He had requested the interview last April, and had never heard back from anyone.

"What the hell did you people ever do about that interview?" Perry asked a secretary who answered the phone.

The secretary put Perry on hold for a few minutes. When she came back, she read him the interview. Massoli, she said, had told their agent that an old Nye County sheriff's lieutenant named Glen Henderson once warned him that Bill Martin "and some of his boys were going to burn the Chicken Ranch down."

"Wow!" Perry said. He couldn't believe his good fortune.

Perry went straight up to Leavitt's office to tell him the good news. If Plankinton was telling the truth and Peter Knight had asked him for a percentage of the Chicken Ranch take, it was a pretty safe bet that Knight—and Beko before him—had demanded the same of other whorehouse owners. Maybe Bill Martin had been paying off Nye County officials for years. That would go a long way toward explaining why, when Martin decided to burn out Plankinton, the Nye County Sheriff and District Attorney had no choice but to protect him. If they turned on Martin and investigated the arson, Martin could turn on them and reveal the payoffs.

Perry and Leavitt were amazed at how quickly the outline of this case was falling into place. If they could convict Martin for the arson, they might be able to "flip him"—the FBI's term for turning a suspected felon into an informant. Then Martin might be able to lead them straight to Peter Knight and Bill Beko.

"The more I hear about this county, the more it smacks of some story out of the old South," Leavitt said to Perry. "This rural place untouched by civilization, where the men who run it are lords unto themselves."

They immediately decided to round everybody up, slap them under oath, and find out just what the hell was going on in this crazy desert county. They issued subpoenas for Martin, Henderson, and Hyder to appear before a grand jury the following week. They decided to fly Massoli and Homstad in from Florida to testify that same day.

By Tuesday afternoon, less than three full days after the fire at the Chicken Ranch, Jim Perry was on his way to Nye County to deliver subpoenas.

Perry pulled up in front of the Pastime Bar in his gray
Plymouth Fury and stepped out into the hot June day. The
Pastime sat on Main Street, just a few blocks from the Nye
County Courthouse. The front of the Pastime was a long
solid wall of volcanic rock with a small doorway cut into
the north corner. The inside of the bar was like any number
of southern-Nevada taverns. It was as dark as a starless
desert night, the exact opposite of the world of unrelenting
sunlight outside. It smelled of beer and dry mold and those
peculiar olfactory signatures of tobacco and sweat that men
leave behind in places where they drink by themselves, in
darkness in the middle of a sunlit world.

Perry and Pete Krusing, an FBI agent he had brought
with him, stood in the doorway for a moment before their
eyes adjusted. When their eyes began to focus, they found
themselves facing one of the most frightening-looking men
they had ever seen. He was in the middle of the room,
playing pool by himself. He looked as if he could pick up
any of the dozen solitary cowboys at the bar and throw the
cowboy, like a rag doll, across the room. He had a big face,
high cheekbones, and a long handlebar mustache. A red
bandana was tied around thick brown hair that hung to his
waist. Except for the click of the pool balls, the bar was
silent, and when Perry and Krusing stepped inside even
that sound stopped.

God, Perry thought to himself, this place is so quiet, they
obviously know we're the feds. As he stepped up to the bar
he looked over at Krusing, who was a young attorney from
Wisconsin. He could tell that Krusing was just dying.

"Is Bo Hyder here?" Perry asked. Without saying a
word, the bartender pointed to the man standing at the pool
table.

Hyder didn't even look up. He slowly laid his cue stick
on the rail of the pool table, where the only balls remaining
were the ivory cue ball and the black eight. Hyder lined up

the shot and fired the cue ball into the side pocket, as if he'd meant to do so. Then he stood without moving, staring at the big green felt expanse with nothing but the eight ball on it.

Perry walked over and showed Hyder his badge. "Federal Bureau of Investigation," he said. There was a moment's hesitation. The dozen cowboys at the bar continued to stare at Perry and Hyder with that dim, implacable awareness of men who drink in the middle of the afternoon in taverns in the wilderness—they would have stared with equal intensity at a television set if one had been on.

Hyder and Perry began the first of a series of negotiations. Perry wanted to sit near the door so that he could get out quickly if he needed to. But Hyder wanted to sit at the back of the bar in a booth near the jukebox. Finally Perry gave in and led Hyder to the back and sat down.

"We're investigating the fire at the Chicken Ranch," Perry said.

"Fuck you," Hyder yelled. "I've been in the pen, man, and I'm a member of the Aryan Brotherhood. I'm not talking to anyone."

"There are a lot of ways you can go with this, Bo," Perry said. "You can come down and cooperate with the grand jury, or you can go back to jail."

Hyder kept yelling at Perry, and Perry just kept talking quietly, offering him his options. Then Perry noticed a woman standing by the bar, watching them. She was probably only in her early twenties but had the appearance of an old, beaten-down woman, with great sagging breasts and sloppy clothes. She kept edging closer and closer as the three men talked, until finally she was about five feet from the booth. She just stood there watching and listening. Perry realized that it was Hyder's wife, that word had already gotten out that they were there holding Bo. He turned to the woman and said, "Look, we won't arrest him." The woman walked off without a word, and suddenly Hyder changed. He opened up and began to talk. In doing so, he gave Perry his first glimpse into Bill Martin's world in Lathrop Wells.

Hyder had been convicted of grand theft in California in 1969, he said, and had served fifteen months in San Quentin. In 1971 he was convicted on seven counts of forgery and one count of burglary. He served another eighteen months. He came to Nye County in October 1977 because he had an uncle who was retired and living in a trailer down the highway from Lathrop Wells. Two days after he got into town he went to work for Bill Martin. He pumped gas and helped out as a bouncer at the Shamrock when there was trouble. And every Wednesday or Thursday he would load the cash from the Shamrock into Bill Martin's car before Martin set out for Las Vegas.

It was not long before Hyder began bitterly referring to Martin as "God." He had his own little world there in Lathrop Wells, Hyder explained to Perry, where he acted like he was God. He hired only people he could easily control, Hyder explained, alcoholics, ex-cons, drifters, people who had no other place to go. He put them to work for starvation wages—$1.75 or $2 an hour—and let them run a tab at the Coach House Bar. Martin had paid Hyder $88 for a six-day work week. "He works like a loan shark," Hyder said. "He adds up bar debts, gets ahold of you so you can't leave. He's good at intimidation. He likes to play with people's minds."

One night in February, Hyder said, he was called in to see Martin in his office behind the bar at the Coach House. "Martin said he was aware that I had a record," Hyder told Perry and Krusing, "that Glen Henderson had told him about it. I figured he was letting me know that I'd better do what he wanted or he'd set me up and have me busted again. Then he said, 'You know, that son of a bitch in Pahrump has been going too far. He has to be taught a lesson.' He told me he wanted Plankinton's arm broke, and his leg broke, and the whorehouse burned down. He offered me fifteen hundred dollars to do it.

"Knowing Bill Martin the way I knew him, I said, 'OK, man, you guarantee me seven hundred fifty up front, and promise me a lawyer, and seven fifty when I get back.' And he didn't say anything. I left the office, and the only other time I talked to Martin about it was a few weeks later. He was sitting at the bar and he'd been juicin' a little bit. He asked me if I'd thought about accepting his proposition. I told him I wouldn't do it."

Perry found Hyder's story interesting. So interesting, in fact, that he wanted some friends of his to talk to him. When Hyder was finished, Perry handed him a subpoena to appear before the Federal grand jury.

"Remember, Bo, you have to appear," Perry warned him. "You have to answer that subpoena."

"Don't worry," Hyder replied. "I'll be there."

Jim Perry and Pete Krusing got up from the booth, walked past the cowboys at the bar and out into the sun on Main Street.

"Howdy boys, what're you doing here?"

As Perry's eyes adjusted to the brightness, he saw that it was Sheriff Jay Howard, leaning against his white county car with the big gold star on the driver's door.

"We're here to investigate the Chicken Ranch arson," Perry said. Perry wanted to conduct this investigation very high profile; he wanted the men who ran Nye County to know he was there.

"Well," Howard said, "I just wanted to let you know that I've talked to Bo Hyder, and Bo Hyder is a liar."

In the hills above Main Street and the center of town, Tonopah is crisscrossed by narrow, winding gravel roads. Jim Perry drove Pete Krusing through this maze in the air-conditioned Plymouth until he came to an old wooden house that sat up on a rise, overlooking the entire town. It was as if the house had been placed there for no reason other than surveillance. When the Plymouth pulled up in front, it was immediately surrounded by pit bulldogs, bred through centuries for their ability to bite something and hold on to it.

A good-looking, amiable young man came out and held the dogs while Perry and Krusing got out of the car. The man with the dogs—his "security," he called them—was John Nocito, the former sheriff's deputy who was the original source of Hyder's story. Nocito was the kind of man who loved to be able to tell an investigator what he wanted to know about someone in Tonopah, then turn around and tell that very same someone that he was being investigated.

Nocito sat Perry and Krusing down and told them that Bo Hyder had indeed told him the same story Hyder had just told the two FBI agents. Then Nocito told Perry and Krusing one more piece of the story that Hyder had told Nocito but had failed to tell the FBI. After Hyder refused to burn down the Chicken Ranch, Martin also offered money to a friend of Bo's to burn it down.

"His name is John Deer," Nocito said. "Bo likes to call him Big John Deer. He works the construction site near Lathrop Wells."

Perry and Krusing spent the night at the Silver Queen Motel, not far from the Pastime, on Main Street. After Perry had checked into his room, he called Leavitt at home to tell him about Hyder.

"You shoulda seen the scene at that pool table," he said. "I will never forget that as long as I live! I mean, the guy's standing there, and, God, the place was so quiet, and he doesn't even look up, he shoots on an eight ball and the cue ball goes in the side pocket and doesn't even hit the eight ball. And the only ball left is the eight ball. I'll never forget it!"

"Will he testify?" Leavitt said.

"He swears he'll come. I don't know."

"Well, it's a start," Leavitt said. "It's a start."

• • •

Perry and Krusing left for Lathrop Wells the next morning. When they got there, they turned off I-95 and headed down 373 toward Death Valley. By the time they reached the construction site they were looking for, the Plymouth was covered with a fine layer of white sand.

As Deer approached the FBI agents, Perry could see why Bo Hyder called him "Big John Deer." He was only five feet eight inches tall, but he was as powerfully built as a mountain lion. He had dark thinning hair, long thick sideburns, and huge dirty hands. He shuffled as he walked toward them, and stared at the ground. He looked very unhappy and very scared.

Jim Perry introduced himself and told Deer they were investigating the arson at the Chicken Ranch brothel. Then he told Deer he had heard that Bill Martin offered to pay Deer to burn the Chicken Ranch down. John Deer insisted that he knew nothing. He knew nothing about Martin, nothing about a fire, nothing about Hyder. He knew nothing about anything that went on in Lathrop Wells.

Although they didn't believe a word of it, Perry and Krusing thanked him and left. About ten miles back toward Lathrop Wells, they turned off 373 onto the back roads of the Amargosa Valley. With a huge cloud of white dust surrounding the FBI car, they slowly made their way to find Glen Henderson. As they pulled into Henderson's driveway, the cloud enveloped the strange little scene that stood like an apparition out in the middle of the desert.

On their left was a small white rusting trailer with a warped and worn plywood porch and an old refrigerator sitting out in front. On their right was a second old trailer and a wooden flagpole. An American flag was flying from the top of the wooden flagpole, and in the middle of the flagpole a bugle hung from an old piece of rope. Just below the bugle was a wooden sign nailed to the flagpole announcing that this was indeed Fort Henderson.

Perry and Krusing shook their heads at each other and began to laugh. There, between the two trailers, was the fort itself, the small wooden shack, no more than ten feet wide on a side, that Glen Henderson had built when he was assigned to patrol Lathrop Wells and the Amargosa Valley. On the door of the shack was a large piece of buckled and peeling plywood that had been cut into the shape of a sheriff's badge. On the scabby wooden badge were painted the words NYE COUNTY SHERIFF'S OFFICE.

The FBI agents walked up to the shack and opened the front door of the drafty room. A picture of Bill Beko was mounted above the door, the way pictures of kings are mounted in the houses of subjects in small Middle Eastern kingdoms. In the dark room Perry saw several beat-up tables and chairs, a worn desk, a ramshackle filing cabinet, and, in the corner, an old black Franklin stove.

Like another piece of dilapidated furniture, Glen Henderson lay upon a filthy cot, his great belly protruding into the air. Perry and Krusing had to bite their lips to keep from laughing aloud. At their approach, Henderson struggled to his feet and, supporting himself with a cane, hobbled across the room.

"I'm not well," he told Perry and Krusing. "I've got diabetes. And arthritis. My hip's acting up. I can't hardly move." Then he told Perry how much he'd always liked the FBI.

There was an unwritten code that Perry had learned years ago that he knew he had to follow. Despite the fact that he and Leavitt were about to drag Henderson before a grand jury, Henderson was still another law enforcement man. So Perry was very proper and polite. He simply handed Henderson the subpoena and explained that Henderson would have to appear before a federal grand jury in Las Vegas on June 22, 1978, at 9:30 A.M., in relation to political corruption in Nye County and the burning of the Chicken Ranch brothel. And Glen Henderson just kept on saying how sick he was. And how much he liked the FBI.

• • •

Perry and Krusing left and drove back toward the highway until they approached the Lathrop Wells corner. There they saw a bright-orange Union 76 ball mounted high in the air on metal poles that sat in the center of a long gravel parking lot littered with wrecked and abandoned cars. At the south end of the parking lot was the Shamrock, a long, low nondescript building with plain wooden walls and a bright-green front door. Along the roof of the Shamrock were a string of Christmas lights and a wooden sign on which someone had carefully hand-painted a picture of a nude blonde with a wineglass in her hand.

At the north end of the parking lot was the Coach House Bar, a small white stucco building with a false front of rough wooden planks. Perry pulled into the parking lot, parked in front of the Coach House Bar, and went inside to find the one man who, Perry was convinced, held all the answers to what was going on in this desert county.

The Coach House Bar was just like the Pastime: a small dark room where men went to drown their sorrows in the middle of a sunlit world. Perry and Krusing stood still for a few seconds while their eyes adjusted to the darkness. Then they walked over to the bar.

"We'd like to see Bill Martin," Perry said.

"He's not here," the barmaid, Pam, said. She was big and British and pretty in a dumpy sort of way.

"Where is he?" Perry asked her.

"I don't know where he is," she said.

What a bitch, Perry thought to himself. "Look, we're the FBI," he said, "and we're going to start knocking on all the doors unless you find him."

Pam turned on her heel and disappeared through a door at the back of the bar. A few minutes later Martin walked out to greet Perry and Krusing. He wore brown slacks and a gold knit shirt, and his wavy, graying hair was combed straight back from his forehead. He strode out with the air of a man in complete control. He might have been a New York City cop again, helping out the authorities. He smiled a sour little smile, laying a cold hand in each man's hand in turn. Then he motioned them into a small dark room at the side of the bar, as if he had called them to the meeting.

Perry was as polite to Martin as he had been to old Glen Henderson. Martin was the man Perry and Leavitt hoped to "flip" one day. Perry wanted to keep things as cordial as possible under the circumstances. "This is a subpoena to appear before the federal grand jury on June twenty-second at nine-thirty A.M. in Las Vegas," Perry said, handing Martin the legal document. "The nature of the grand-jury subpoena relates to political corruption in Nye County and also the burning of the Chicken Ranch brothel."

Perry then asked Martin for his full name, any aliases, his date of birth, his birthplace, his height, his weight, the color of his hair and eyes. He asked if Martin had any arrest record, and Martin proudly said he had none. Then Perry asked Martin one last thing. He asked Martin to give him the names and addresses of any close associates. Martin gave him only one: Kenneth Kolojay, of Lathrop Wells, Nevada.

Late Sunday night in Tonopah, four days after Jim Perry had returned to Las Vegas, Bo Hyder walked to a phone booth on Main Street. He dialed the operator and asked her to get him the FBI office in Las Vegas. Hyder tapped impatiently on the wall of the phone booth as the telephone rang and rang. Finally, the agent on duty at the FBI office in the federal courthouse answered. Hyder told him he was a witness for Jim Perry. He was scheduled to testify before a grand jury on Wednesday, Hyder said, and he had to talk to Perry right away.

Police work, like politics, makes strange bedfellows, and there were none stranger than Bo Hyder and Jim Perry. While Hyder had spent that Sunday playing pool and sipping blackberry brandy in the darkness of the Pastime, Perry had spent the day attending services at the Good

Samaritan Lutheran Church, where he was on the church council, and watching the Chargers–Broncos game on television with his son. When the telephone rang in the cozily furnished family room of Perry's suburban ranch house, Perry and his wife, Caroline, were sitting in the room watching the eleven-o'clock news, while the kids were in their rooms, getting ready for sleep.

"Listen, Perry," Hyder said. "There's a rumor going around Tonopah. Before I have a chance to testify, I'm supposed to be killed."

"Jesus," Perry said. "Where did you hear it?"

"It's around all the bars," Hyder said. "Everybody's heard it."

Perry was angry, frustrated. He didn't know what to do. This wasn't Philadelphia; you couldn't get into your car and get to Hyder in twenty minutes. This was the goddamned Nevada desert. Hyder was two hundred miles away.

"Bo, I know this isn't what you want to hear," Perry said. "But the only thing I can suggest is that you call the Sheriff's Office and ask for protection."

"Fuck you, Perry," Hyder said. He shook his head angrily and slammed down the receiver of the telephone. Hyder turned away from the phone booth. As he did, he heard a loud crack. It broke the still desert air, then bounced off the rocky hills of Tonopah from which so many men had taken their fortune eighty years ago. Hyder had been around enough trouble in his life to know that sound. It was the sound of gunshot.

Hyder looked around the dark, deserted street of the old mining town. The only lights came from the gas stations at the end of Main Street, and from the front of the old Mizpah Hotel. The only sound came from the occasional static of cowboys' voices mixed with the words of a song from a jukebox when somebody opened the door of the Mizpah or the Pastime or the Rex Café.

Hyder ran to his battered old Chevy pickup and drove

up the winding back roads of Tonopah until he reached the trailer of the one friend he knew who had a telephone. As soon as he got inside, he called Perry again. It was almost midnight now, and the ringing telephone woke Perry and his wife and kids.

Perry didn't know what the hell was going on up there. Maybe Martin only wanted to scare Hyder with a gunshot. Then again, maybe Martin meant to kill him. Either way, Perry wasn't going to take any chances. Hyder was an essential element in the grand-jury investigation of the Chicken Ranch arson. He had to have Hyder safe for testimony on Wednesday at nine-thirty in the morning.

"Get your ass down to Las Vegas," he told Hyder. "We'll put you up in a hotel here."

Hyder raced home to get his wife, then asked an old friend to ride with them "for protection." The three crowded into the front seat of Hyder's battered old pickup truck and, taking swigs from a pint bottle of blackberry brandy that he kept under the driver's seat, made their way to Las Vegas.

CHAPTER

Fourteen

The United States Courthouse in Las Vegas is a long, low building of slate-gray glass and concrete that sits on Las Vegas Boulevard, in the heart of downtown, away from the lights of the Strip. It is an alien world in Las Vegas, a world of muted colors and muted voices, of walnut conference tables and thickly padded leather chairs and white dress shirts and three-piece suits.

Glen Henderson was the first to arrive at the courthouse for the grand-jury hearing on Wednesday morning. Wearing old khaki slacks and a yellow knit shirt, supporting himself with the same cane he had used the day Perry served him with the subpoena, he walked through the wide glass doors of the courthouse. Inside the lobby he could smell the odor of ammonia, and chrome and marble polish that is characteristic of most government buildings. It was a far cry from the smell of alkali dust and tobacco juice that pervaded Fort Henderson. Henderson took an elevator to the fourth floor and walked down a hallway to the grand-jury waiting room. Wheezing with the effort, he lowered his immense body into a chair.

A few minutes later Larry Massoli and Frank Homstad

walked up the same wide steps of the courthouse. They had
flown in from Florida the night before, at government ex-
pense, and had spent the night at Caesar's Palace. They
were happy to be back in Las Vegas, happy to be there to
testify against Bill Martin and Glen Henderson. Massoli
and Homstad took the elevator to the fourth floor and
walked down the same hallway, toward the grand-jury
waiting room.

They had not seen Henderson since they left Nye County
for Florida a year earlier, after Henderson told them that
Bill Martin and his boys were going to burn down the
Chicken Ranch. When they opened the door and saw Henderson slouched there, they were startled.

"Hiya, boys," Henderson bellowed, not missing a beat.
"What're you doing here? Gee, it's good to see you. How
is Florida? You two sure got a nice tan."

Massoli and Homstad were followed into the room by Bo
Hyder, who had shaved his head for the occasion. Gone
was the waist-length hair tied back in a bandana. He looked
like an assassin out of a movie now. He sat beside Glen
Henderson and did not say a word. If he had been scared
by the shot fired at him three nights ago, he was not about
to let it show.

This strange crew sat together until nine-thirty, when
Larry Leavitt walked in and silently crossed the room to
another door at the far side of the small waiting room.
Leavitt carried himself with the quiet confidence of a man
who has spent much of his life in a courtroom. He took
great pride in the fact that his face never revealed what he
was thinking. Which at this moment was: What a motley
group of people to take before a federal grand jury. Where
in American jurisprudence could you find a case like this,
he thought, except in the state of Nevada?

Inside the grand-jury room, twenty-three jurors were
seated in four rows of padded chairs facing a long conference table, where the foreman, the deputy foreman, and
the secretary sat. Leavitt greeted the jurors and explained

that this morning they were going to hear testimony concerning a fire that had occurred at the Chicken Ranch brothel in Pahrump, Nevada, two weeks ago, at four-thirty in the morning, when a masked man threw a flammable liquid into the brothel, where fourteen people were living. He did not describe the horrible scene inside those trailers, as those fourteen people were running, screaming for their lives. He knew that, if he did that, he could be accused of unduly influencing the grand jury. But he hoped the jurors would envision the scene for themselves. Then Leavitt brought Larry Massoli and Frank Homstad and Bo Hyder in one by one and had them repeat the stories they had told the FBI. By the time all three men had finished testifying and left the room, it was almost noon.

Leavitt opened the door and nodded to Glen Henderson, who hobbled into the courtroom on his cane and sat at the end of the long conference table. Leavitt sat at the other end, facing him down the length of the long walnut table. They were a bizarre pair. There was Leavitt, the former philosophy major, at one end, in his crisp white shirt, navy tie, and carefully tailored tan three-piece suit. And there was Glen Henderson at the other end in dirty old khaki slacks and a bright-yellow short-sleeved shirt stretched tightly over his huge beer belly.

As soon as Leavitt looked at Henderson, he realized that he had trouble on his hands. Henderson performed like a charmer. Here was a salt-of-the-earth sheriff from out on the range, come to entertain the big-city folk. Throughout the testimony, Henderson had a twinkle in his eye. Several times he even made the jurors laugh.

Leavitt asked him point-blank, "Did you ever tell either Deputy Massoli or Deputy Homstad that if they got any calls about a fire occurring at the Chicken Ranch brothel they were to disregard them and go to the other end of the valley?"

"So help me God," Henderson said, "I never made a statement like that."

You wily old devil, Leavitt thought to himself. He was

going to make sure there would never be any doubt in the mind of anybody who read the transcript of this testimony that Henderson was sitting here, under oath, flatly denying this.

"Are you saying categorically that you know you never told them anything like that?"

"I never did."

"Did you ever tell them to disregard any calls concerning any trouble in Nye County?"

"No, sir," Henderson said. "No, sir."

"You can say that categorically and without reservation?" Leavitt asked. For the first time there was the slightest trace of anger in his voice.

"I sure can, sir," Henderson said. "I never made a statement like that in my life."

After a break for lunch, Leavitt escorted Bill Martin— who had arrived at the courthouse with his attorney—into the grand jury room. Martin crossed the room with the same cockiness with which he had greeted Jim Perry a week before. He studied the faces of the jurors in the room, walked to the end of the conference table, and sat down. He had that unmistakable air of someone cooperating with the prosecution, helping them out. Mr. Innocent, Leavitt angrily thought to himself.

"Mr. Martin," Leavitt asked, "are you acquainted with an individual named Bo Hyder?"

"Yes, I am."

"Directing your attention to the latter part of January and the early part of February 1978, did you ever have a conversation with Bo Hyder relative to burning down the Chicken Ranch?"

"No. This man is a known—" Martin stopped himself, then nodded to Leavitt and said, "Go on."

"What were you about to say?" Leavitt asked.

"I was going to volunteer some information for your information," Martin said smugly, "but perhaps I had better not."

"Go ahead," Leavitt said. Leavitt knew that if he tried

to stop Martin, he could be accused of grand-jury abuse. Besides, he wanted to let Martin say whatever he wanted. He knew that if he let Martin talk long enough, the odds were Martin would give Leavitt something Leavitt could one day use against him. So Leavitt sat there, stone-faced, and let Martin go on.

"Sometimes you have to work with whatever tools you have available to you," Martin began, as if he were a professor addressing a college class. "You, I mean, not me. This man is not a very reputable character. He is a narcotics addict, a drunk. The man is weak, completely weak. He is an ex-convict. He is an informer. . . . This man is so unreliable that it is unthinkable to me that anybody would even consult with him about a thing like that. He is always under the influence of drugs or alcohol, one or the other."

"How much daily contact did you have with him when he worked for you?" Leavitt asked.

"He was around all the time. He is totally unreliable, totally untrustworthy, completely drunk. He blew up one of our tow trucks. He took it out and just burned it out."

Leavitt loved it. That smug bastard, he thought to himself, he doesn't realize he's doing just what I want him to do. When Martin finally wound down, Leavitt asked him two more questions.

"Have you ever told anybody that you wanted to do any kind of harm to Walter Plankinton?"

"No, sir," Martin said.

"Have you ever offered anybody any money to burn down the Chicken Ranch?"

"No, sir," Martin said.

CHAPTER

Fifteen

During that hot summer of 1978, while Jim Perry and Larry Leavitt were trying to find a break in the Chicken Ranch case, the Republican candidate for sheriff of Nye County, Joni Wines, set out in her silver Honda Accord to visit every one of the seven thousand people who now lived there.

Most of those people had no idea of the explosive issues swirling around them. Perry and Leavitt, obligated by law to conduct grand-jury investigations in secret, had not told the Las Vegas *Sun* and the Las Vegas *Review-Journal* reporters who roamed the federal courthouse what they knew so far about the case. Walter Plankinton had not yet gone public with his charge that Peter Knight had asked him for a percentage of the Chicken Ranch take; all he had told reporters was that "the Tonopah Mafia" was out to get him. As a result, the only thing most voters in Nye County knew was that a loudmouthed whorehouse owner was complaining about the way the Sheriff was handling an arson investigation.

Joni Wines, more politically naïve than most, did not even know that. The only thing she remembered about the

Chicken Ranch fire was that a neighbor told her she had seen the smoke from ten miles away. So it never occurred to Joni Wines to make the Chicken Ranch an issue in her campaign. She simply set out to convince the voters she could bring more efficiency and respectability to the Sheriff's Department than that afforded by the back-slapping, beer-drinking incumbent.

She drove over two hundred miles to Gabbs in the northernmost part of the county, where she met workers going into the magnesite mine. She met the shift going in at 4 P.M., went back for the group going in at 11 P.M., then slept for a while in the tiny back seat of her car and awoke to a wind-up alarm so that she could be back out there in time to shake hands with the workers on the 6 A.M. shift.

She took her daughter Kelly and her six-year-old granddaughter Lauren and drove two hundred miles to Warm Springs, population twenty-five, which sits just above the nuclear test site east of Tonopah. She asked the lady at the Warm Springs Café when the silver miners went to work, and the lady said 5 A.M. So she and her daughter slept in the car all night to wait for them. In the morning Joni Wines got up, combed her hair, brushed her teeth, and shook hands with the silver miners as they went into the Gila Mine.

She tried to drive the 280 miles to Sunnyside, which is not even on the map. She wanted to meet the six people there who were registered to vote. She went once with her husband, and the roads were washed out. She went again with Kelly and Lauren, but the Honda had two flat tires and they were stranded for six hours in the desert. So Joni Wines finally wrote each of the six voters a personal letter soliciting their votes. She got five out of six.

While Joni Wines was driving across the county, speaking to every potential voter she could find, Jim Perry was doggedly tracking whomever he could find who might provide information concerning the Chicken Ranch fire. Perry and Leavitt were still convinced that Bill Martin was the key to this case. If they were able to convict Martin, he might take Bill Beko and Peter Knight down with him. So Perry went back to Lathrop Wells to have a talk with Beverly Nichols, Bill Martin's girlfriend.

At the Coach House Bar, the British barmaid, Pam, told Perry that Nichols was in the house behind the Shamrock Brothel. Perry walked around to the small frame house. If the agents in Philly could see me now, Perry thought, shaking his head. The house sat on the very edge of the open desert, surrounded by a corrugated-tin shed, steel propane tank, and a dozen wrecked and rusted cars. It looked like the office of a junkyard. Perry knocked on the door. A short dark-haired young woman answered the door, and Perry identified himself.

"Wait just a minute," the woman said. She closed the door and turned the lock. When she opened it again, she asked if Martin could sit in on the interview. Perry refused. It was just the sort of thing Bo Hyder had told Perry that Martin (or "God," as Hyder called him) could do so well: intimidate someone without saying a word.

Beverly Nichols closed the door to the house behind her, took Perry to the Coach House Bar, and told him her short, unhappy life story. It took exactly three sentences. She was twenty-six years old, three-quarters Oklahoma Cherokee, with a husband and two children back in Death Valley Junction. She had left them in 1975 to move to Lathrop Wells. She had been with Bill Martin ever since.

Then Beverly Nichols gave Perry a few details to flesh it out: She and Martin moved into the small frame house behind the Shamrock, and he started spending most of his time there. He would go to his house in Las Vegas every Wednesday or Thursday. She said Martin stayed in Las Vegas until the end of the eleven-o'clock news every Friday evening, and then he would drive back out to Lathrop Wells. Beverly gave Perry no hint that she knew about Martin's wife and children.

She said she knew nothing about the Chicken Ranch fire.

Bill had arrived back in Lathrop Wells about one o'clock the morning of the fire. Then she and Bill had spent the night the way they spent most of their nights, sitting in the Coach House Bar, drinking until dawn.

July Fourth came and went and Perry was still getting nowhere. After the holiday, he and Krusing drove out to the new Chicken Ranch to interview the girls who had almost lost their lives the night of the fire. They were still badly shaken as they talked about that night, reliving the suddenness of it all, when the lights went out and they found themselves trapped in those six aluminum trailers as the walls of the trailers began to melt. Suzi said she still had nightmares in which she was trapped in her room again. In the nightmares she could smell the thick black acrid smoke and see the almost Day-Glo colors of the orange and red flames.

They tried to help Perry. But only Rita, the buxom redhead who was the mother of the mother-and-daughter team at the Chicken Ranch the first night it opened, had anything to say. After Plankinton's arrest that night for opening the original Chicken Ranch inside the Pahrump town boundary, Rita said, she had gone to work at the Shamrock. One night during dinner, several months before the fire, Martin told her, "Some people should stay where they are." Rita took that to mean that if she stayed at the Shamrock she would be safe, but if she went back to work at the Chicken Ranch her life would be in danger.

As soon as Perry got back from the Chicken Ranch, he started his search for Kenneth Kolojay, the man whose name Martin had given him as a "close associate." The only Kolojay listed in either the Nye County or the Clark County telephone book was a Shirley Kolojay. She lived in a small ranch house on Decatur Boulevard, on the west side of Las Vegas. Perry drove out that afternoon to see her.

When she opened the door, Perry told her he was trying
to find a man named Kenneth Kolojay. The woman burst
into tears. She had married Kenneth Kolojay ten years earlier in Illinois, she told Perry. They had a five-year-old son,
Todd. They had divorced five months ago. She still loved
Kenny, she said.

Perry asked Shirley Kolojay if she ever heard from
Kenny. She said that she did. Perry asked her to tell him to
get in touch with Perry or Assistant U.S. Attorney Larry
Leavitt. Shirley said she would.

Two weeks later, on July 20, a young man who looked like
a Las Vegas nightclub bouncer walked into the waiting
room of the U.S. Attorney's Office. He had sandy brown
hair, a pugnose, and a fat neck and face. A knit shirt
stretched tightly across his massive shoulders and chest.
He told the receptionist his name was Kolojay and he was
here to see Larry Leavitt.

Leavitt was amazed to hear that Kolojay was in the waiting room. So he's going to play this the way Martin is
playing it, Leavitt thought to himself, he's going to act like
he's only too happy to cooperate. Leavitt tried to reach
Perry, but Perry was out on another case. So Leavitt let
Kolojay sit out in the waiting room for ten or fifteen minutes just for fun. Then he walked out and, with great cir-
cumspection, shook hands with the blue-jean-clad bouncer,
and invited him into his office.

Leavitt offered Kolojay a seat in one of the two straight-
backed old leather chairs that sat opposite his desk. He saw
Kolojay glance over to his left, at the one personal touch in
the office, two sepia-toned turn-of-the-century photographs
of London's Clapham Common and the Arles River in
France. He could see Kolojay almost saying to himself, So
what else would you expect?

Leavitt took a seat in what he liked to call his "slightly
cock-eyed" government-issue swivel chair, making sure he

leaned backward instead of forward, otherwise the chair would tip him forward and he would slide right under the desk. He pulled out a yellow legal pad and, with the stern look of the prosecutor on his face, started to question Kolojay.

Kolojay told Leavitt he had worked as manager of the Shamrock Brothel for Martin starting in February 1978. He said his job involved buying supplies and doing paperwork. The only thing he knew about the Chicken Ranch, he said, was what he'd seen when he was a customer there. Kolojay was trying to act cooperative, but he was having a hard time hiding his contempt.

Leavitt asked Kolojay if he had ever told anyone that he thought Walter Plankinton wouldn't be around much longer.

No, Kolojay said, he had never talked to anyone about Plankinton.

Leavitt asked Kolojay if he had ever been to the office of a girlie-magazine owner named Ralph Petrillo.

Yes, Kolojay said, he had gone there to place an ad for the Shamrock.

Had he told the publisher that Plankinton wouldn't be around any longer? Leavitt asked.

No, Kolojay said. He was certain that when he saw Petrillo no mention of Walter Plankinton or the Chicken Ranch was ever made.

Leavitt was better at concealing his emotions than Kolojay. He was sure that Kolojay was lying to him. And he was sure that Kolojay knew that he knew. And there was nothing he could do about it. He was furious, but he thanked Kolojay for his cooperation, walked around his desk, and escorted him out of the office.

As soon as Kolojay was out the door, Leavitt picked up the phone and called Perry to tell him what Kolojay had had to say. This time he reached him.

"He's a young punk," Leavitt said bitterly. "He was trying to act cooperative. But he wasn't as good at it as

Martin was. He kept trying to smile at me, but there was always a slight sneer on his face.''

"This goddamned case," Perry said. "This goddamned case."

Perry was starting to get a lot of pressure from his supervisor to stop making these four-hundred-mile round trips out to the middle of the desert. There was more important work to be done in Las Vegas, his supervisor said. But Perry and Leavitt wanted to break this case. They knew there were important issues involved. Fourteen people had almost died in that fire in those trailers that night, and not one public official charged with enforcing the laws in Nye County seemed to give a damn.

They decided to meet for lunch at Jo Jo's Restaurant, a few blocks from the courthouse on Las Vegas Boulevard, where they ordered a noontime breakfast of fried eggs, sausages, and black coffee and sat down to commiserate with each other.

CHAPTER

Sixteen

By the fall of 1978, three months after the Chicken Ranch fire, a certain calm had returned to Nye County. The Chicken Ranch, the Shamrock, and the other brothels in the county were operating in relatively peaceful coexistence. Plankinton was raking in the money, and if Martin wasn't raking in quite as much as he felt was rightfully his, he was certainly getting by.

Jim Perry and Larry Leavitt were getting nowhere with their investigation. And District Attorney Peter Knight was telling Las Vegas reporters that the FBI's investigation of the Chicken Ranch arson was turning out "exactly" as he thought it would. "It's just too bad," he said, "that a lot of federal time and money is being spent investigating charges made by crackpots."

But the calm was not to last for long. While Sheriff Jay Howard had been laughing at Joni Wines from his traditional place in the bars and at the summer picnics he attended with a beer can always in one hand, Joni Wines had been driving all over the county, slowly and quietly building a following. She didn't have much of a platform, but then no candidate for Nye County sheriff—from the seventy-eight-year-old retired butcher who was sheriff when Bill Beko became district attorney to the current incumbent —had ever had one.

She impressed people, instead, with her quiet determination. They had never seen a candidate who was willing to go door to door just to meet them. And while there was a fair amount of grumbling in this frontier county about electing a white-haired lady as their sheriff, there was also a fair amount of grumbling that ''she couldn't be any worse than what we have now.''

By the time Jay Howard realized what Joni Wines was doing, he saw that the situation called for drastic measures. On October 26, Jay Howard made headlines in Nye County newspapers by telling the editors that Joni Wines had lied about her qualifications for office. He said she had lied about working with juveniles from the Douglas County Probation Department near Lake Tahoe, and had lied about running Harrah's Recreation Center there. She had also lied, Howard insisted, when she said she had worked as an investigator for the Tahoe Bureau of Investigation.

When Joni Wines saw the Friday paper, she was frantic. She called the editor of the Pahrump Valley *Star* to find out what the deadline was for a reply. She was told she had until Tuesday to get it in before the election. She immediately picked up the phone and called friends at the detective agency where she had worked. She also called the Mayor of Carson City, who knew she had worked with juveniles from the Probation Department. She called everyone who could prove that she was not lying, and asked them to write letters.

''Please get them in the mail today,'' she begged. ''I have to have them by Tuesday.''

Two arrived in Monday's mail. The other two arrived on Tuesday. Joni Wines took the four letters and drove to the trailer that housed the offices of the Pahrump Valley *Star*. The paper's owner and editor was Kathy Ledford, a tall, attractive blond woman who had divorced her husband and moved her teenage daughter to the desert "to get her out of Las Vegas." She had been looking for some way to make money when she started her fledgling four-page weekly— now the third weekly in Nye County—just a year earlier.

She had already been in Nye County long enough to know it would be to her advantage to support the local sheriff, who had lived in the county thirty years, over this outsider from Lake Tahoe. Ledford took one look at the letters corroborating Joni Wines's side of the story and shrugged.

"Well," she said, "I know I have to put them in the paper. But when I do, Jay's goose is cooked."

And it was.

On Tuesday, November 7, Election Day, 1978, the incumbent Sheriff, Jay Howard, and his challenger, Joni Wines, spent the day wandering in and out of the cinder-block Pahrump Community Center, where everyone from around the valley was coming to vote. At six o'clock Joni Wines and her lady friends, who had spent the summer and the fall campaigning for her—"the ragtag little ladies," Howard called them—left the Community Center to drive over to the Cotton Pickin' Saloon to have some dinner.

As Joni Wines, wearing the chocolate-brown polyester pants suit that she wore for most special occasions, and her friends walked out to the Community Center parking lot, they saw Jay Howard and some deputies sitting on the hood of a white sheriff's patrol car. The hot wind was swirling the dust from the parking lot around them. When the women got close to the patrol car, Howard leaned his head back, opened his mouth, and began braying like a jackass, "Hee-haw, hee-haw, hee-haw." At five-twenty the next morning he was officially declared one by the people of Nye County, who voted Joni Wines into office as their new sheriff.

Joni Wines did not really win the election. Jay Howard lost it. Almost 3,000 of the 7,000 residents in the county

voted in the election, and Joni Wines won by only 139
votes. It was the town of Gabbs in the northern part of the
county, where Howard had a reputation for rolling drunks
and rustling cattle, that put Joni Wines over the top. She
won Gabbs by a vote of 226 to 64.

For three days after the election the telephone in her
Pahrump trailer never stopped ringing. One of the calls was
from Frank Homstad in Panama City, Florida. Joni's good
friend Lola Binum, who had first dared her to run for office,
had called to tell him the good news. Lola had always figured that Homstad and Larry Massoli had left Nye County
because of some kind of trouble in the sheriff's department,
although she had no idea the two men left because they had
been ordered not to respond to an arson. She told Homstad
that now that her friend, Joni Wines, had been elected sheriff, Homstad should call her and ask for a job. So Homstad
did call and Joni Wines told him he could have a job in
January, when she took office.

Homstad then called Larry Massoli to tell him about the
offer. He told Massoli he should also call Joni Wines. But
Massoli wasn't as lucky. Every time he called he got a busy
signal. And when he finally did get through, he reached
Joni's husband, Blaine, who by now had lost his temper
with the new public life his wife was suddenly leading.
Blaine curtly told him he would pass along the message.
But Joni Wines was too busy preparing to become sheriff
of Nye County to call Massoli back.

It was the Thanksgiving weekend of 1978 when Joni Wines
began to learn what it was really going to be like to try to
seize power in a county composed of less than a dozen
insular communities spread out over eighteen thousand
square miles of desert, a county that had been run by Bill
Beko for almost a quarter of a century.

Joni Wines's twenty-three-year-old daughter Kelly, who
had campaigned with her, was followed by sheriff's deputies and harassed when she tried to buy beer in a grocery–

gas station. The same deputies followed one Wines supporter everywhere he went for one entire day. They wrote down license numbers and gave cars tickets and generally made a nuisance of themselves whenever they could.

They were sure they could get away with it. They never thought that this little white-haired grandmother would stand up to them. But Joni Wines was a paradox of naïveté and pertinacity, artlessness and candor. As the men who ran Nye County were about to find out. Joni Wines wrote a letter of complaint to Ray Shamblin, the Pahrump sergeant who had been on duty the night of the Chicken Ranch fire. "Under no circumstances," the letter said, "will I keep anybody in the department who feels that this is the way to perform his job."

On Thanksgiving morning Joni Wines answered the phone, and there was Jay Howard on the line, woofing at her in a seething rage.

"Regarding this letter down here, you thinking your friends are being harassed," he said, "nobody in my department is doing that, and I want you to know that you're to keep your goddamned ass out of the department until January. I have given orders to everyone in every sheriff's station that you're not to have anything to do with them till January."

"Thank you," Joni Wines said. "That's what I would have expected out of you." She slammed down the telephone.

The following Monday she got an even more telling lesson in what her new life as sheriff of Nye County was going to be like. That Monday she drove north to the Amargosa Valley with Pat Edenfield, her campaign manager, and drove off the Amargosa highway onto a rutted, dusty dirt road to the trailer of another of her lady supporters. They had decided to plan an all-day barbecue on the site of the Mecca Club, an old wrecked white stucco-building that sits in the middle of a sagebrush-strewn parking lot on the highway between Death Valley Junction and Lathrop Wells.

The purpose of the barbecue was to pay off Joni Wines's $3,500 in campaign debts. The longer they talked, the more concerned Joni became about the propriety of raising money that way. She wanted to make sure she wasn't breaking any laws. The hostess said she knew exactly whom to ask: Lathrop Wells Sheriff's Lieutenant Glen Henderson. He was a lawman. He talked to Judge Beko. He knew about these things. They dialed Fort Henderson.

"I'll look into it for you," Glen bellowed into the telephone.

An hour later he called back. "I've talked to somebody on this," he told them, "and this here thing is completely illegal. But I think I can work something out. I think there's someone here that might lend you the money."

On their way home, Pat Edenfield and Joni Wines began worrying about what Henderson had said.

"It doesn't sound quite right to me," Joni Wines said.

"Do you know an attorney?" Edenfield asked.

The primitive nature of politics in Nye County—and even more especially of Joni Wines's own political machine —was evident in the fact that she had run for sheriff and had won and still did not have her own lawyer. She did know one, though. There had been a man in Lake Tahoe whose children had grown up with hers. She had heard he'd moved to Las Vegas. His name was Charlie Waterman. The next day Joni Wines called him and explained her problem.

"Funny you should call," he said. "I just had a call from a couple of fellas in Lathrop Wells. They would like to give you the whole amount."

"Wow," Joni Wines said. "That's an awful lot of money for two people. I wouldn't want to accept it unless there were no strings attached."

Joni Wines never heard from Waterman again. It wasn't until months later that she learned that Charlie Waterman was Bill Martin's attorney.

CHAPTER

Seventeen

There were to be many curious twists and turns to this story before it had finally played itself out, but two weeks after that telephone call between Joni Wines and Charlie Waterman, in the MGM Grand Hotel not far from Waterman's office, there occurred one of the most curious twists of all.

On Saturday night, December 9, in one of the restaurants on the first floor of the MGM Grand, just off the ornate 423-foot-long casino with its elaborate red-flocked wallpaper and huge crystal chandeliers, a pale tired-looking man in his middle thirties with the gaunt, bony look of the Okies who came to the Central Valley of California handed one of the waiters a stolen credit card to pay for the dinner he and his two companions had just eaten. When the waiter failed to return with the credit card and the bill, "his two companions melted," as a cop would later say, but the man who had used the stolen credit card was so slow witted he stayed to wait for it.

When the waiter finally returned, he was accompanied by a security guard, who turned the man over to the Las Vegas police. The police booked him, fingerprinted him, and punched his name into a computer terminal that was tied into the National Crime Information Center in Washington. The computer spat out: "LV CINI Smith, Raymond Ladale, white male adult, wanted CA 5002, murder, and conspiracy to commit murder, no bail."

CA 5002 was a code for the Police Department in Modesto, California. A Las Vegas police detective picked up the phone and called Modesto. He was immediately switched to Detective Jack Smith. Smith told the Las Vegas cop that the man he had just picked up had been named as the middleman in the October murder of a German couple named Ingrid and Reiner Junghans. He had been implicated by a sometime pimp and sometime counterfeiter whom they had already arrested for the murder, Elbert Easley.

Modesto is on the other side of the Sierra Nevada from Nye County, and news does not travel much over that forbidding mountain range, even in the age of electronic communications. So the story may have made four or five lines in the Las Vegas *Sun,* but it certainly didn't make the Pahrump Valley *Times* when the bodies of a thirty-six-year-old businessman and his pretty blond twenty-six-year-old wife were found in their Mediterranean-style town house on the northern edge of that California town. The killer had tied their wrists and ankles with bailing wire. He had stuffed small rubber balls into their mouths to keep them from screaming. He had then taken an ice pick and stabbed the man and his wife a total of one hundred times.

The Modesto police had arrested Elbert Easley on November 1, 1978, and charged him with the murders. They had been tipped off that Reiner Junghans' business partner had paid Easley $4,000 to kill the couple. The day of Easley's arrest, the police also pulled in Easley's girlfriend, a young prostitute named Lorrie Ross. At first Lorrie refused to talk. So the detectives told her, "Go ahead, keep refusing, you'll soon find yourself charged as an accessory to murder." And that was all it took. Lorrie told them everything she knew about the murder-for-hire. Then, to make sure they still wouldn't book her, she told them about another crime Elbert had been hired to commit.

She said that Easley had spent part of May and part of June 1978 in Nevada. Easley told her that he went there to take a job at a whorehouse. He told her he had been a bodyguard for the girls. Lorrie said that sometime in June of 1978 Easley called her from the Kings Canyon Motel in Fresno. He had just come back from Nevada and wanted to see her. When she went to the motel, Easley said he wanted her to come back to Nevada with him. To convince her to come, he reached into his pocket and took out a small package wrapped in aluminum foil. He counted out seven hundred dollars in ten- and twenty-dollar bills.

"I asked him how he got the money," Lorrie told the Modesto detectives. "And he said he did a job for a friend. He said he burnt a whorehouse down."

On November 2, 1978, a week before the Nye County sheriff's election, Modesto Police Detective Jack Smith obtained a search warrant for the apartment that Elbert Easley and Lorrie Ross had just rented. In the apartment he found a large black bag, which Elbert called "my bag" and almost always carried with him. Inside the bag Smith found a round decal with a large green shamrock on it. Written in bold letters across the shamrock were the words "Best Lay on the Highway—Lathrop Wells." Along with the decal was a letter from the United States Probation Office. The letter gave Easley permission to travel to Lathrop Wells, Nevada, from May 22, 1978, to August 22, 1978.

In a kitchen drawer in the apartment, Smith found a fifty-dollar Western Union money order and a Western Union telegram. They had both been sent to Easley from Bill Martin, in Lathrop Wells, Nevada. Written on the money order and the telegram was the same message: "You have a job over here."

On Monday, November 6, 1978, the day before Nye County elected Joni Wines sheriff, Modesto Police Detective Jack Smith called the Metro Police Department in Las Vegas and asked if they had a case of someone burning down a whorehouse there. The officer on the desk told Smith that they had nothing like that, but he was sure that someone had burned down a whorehouse in the county north of them. He told Smith to call Nye County.

Smith then called the Nye County Sheriff's Department and talked to the officer in charge. So much was going on in Smith's office in those early days after what had become known in Modesto as "the ice-pick murders" that Smith forgot to get the Nye County deputy's name. Smith said he had a man named Elbert Easley in custody and thought he might be a suspect in a whorehouse arson in Nye County. The officer he talked to said they did have a fire in a whorehouse, but they had a good idea who did it and they knew it wasn't Elbert Easley. He told the Modesto detective that they weren't interested.

On Tuesday, December 12, 1978, three days after Las Vegas police picked up Easley's accomplice, Raymond Smith, at the MGM Grand, Modesto Police Detectives Ron Ridenour and Steve McDonough flew to Las Vegas to interview Smith. McDonough and Ridenour were obsessed with the details of this bloody murder case and this cold-blooded little pimp named Elbert Easley. McDonough loved to tell stories about what they had found out about Easley, about how he had absolutely no respect for human life. Only a half hour after he had stabbed the young German couple a total of one hundred times with an ice pick, he stopped at a coffee shop and had a hamburger and a milkshake. He would murder his own mother if the money was right, McDonough said. They loved telling stories of the bloody murder scene, stories of the way it took them only sixteen days to trace the murderer.

And so in the course of what McDonough would later describe as "just shooting the bull," he told two of the Las Vegas detectives that this Elbert Easley had told his girlfriend that he'd burned a Nevada whorehouse down.

"Have you had any cases like that around here?" McDonough asked them.

"No, we haven't," one of the detectives said. "But you know, I had a night teacher in a criminal-justice class I was taking, a detective named Gene Alesevich. He told us he worked for a lawyer whose client had his whorehouse burned down several months ago."

CHAPTER

Eighteen

Wearing a long, flowing dress in a silver-, white-, and pink-flowered pattern, Joni Wines stood in front of the wide oak judge's bench in the Nye County Courthouse on New Year's Day and was sworn into office by Judge William P. Beko as the sheriff of Nye County. Not one of the men and women who witnessed the ceremony in that packed courtroom had any idea that by the end of the year this little round woman with white bouffant hair would have torn Nye County apart.

Certainly the last one to think so that morning was Bill Beko. For Joni Wines was still naïve in the ways of politics and government. Just a few weeks before she took office, she had done what everyone else in Nye County government had done before her: she had gone to consult "the man on the hill." After talking to Glen Henderson about how to pay off her campaign debts, she called Judge Beko for his advice. She told Beko she thought it was a bad idea to hold the fund-raiser, and that she was going to get a bank loan instead. Beko was very understanding.

"Why don't you come to Tonopah?" he said. "I know a banker and we'll arrange a loan."

So Joni Wines drove the 165 miles to Tonopah to the silver-domed courthouse on the hill. She climbed the wide wooden steps at the front of the courthouse to the second floor, walked past the gilt-framed portrait of James W. Nye in the hall, and knocked on Judge Beko's office door.

When Judge Beko came out to greet her, she was surprised at what a tall, stately man he was, with such thick handsome white hair. He escorted her into a large sunny office and offered her a chair in front of his old wooden desk that held a nameplate carved out of a small log and a small white bust of Socrates. Behind his silver-frame glasses, his eyes were silent and impassive, as if he was carefully studying her. But he spoke in a smooth, soothing voice, and he couldn't have been more friendly.

Two weeks later she was back in Beko's office. She had asked old Pete Bertolino, who had been in the department two years, to be her undersheriff. It was said he could track a man across the desert as well as the Shoshone Indians who first came to this forbidding land. When she asked him to accept the position, however, Bertolino said, "Well, you'll have to talk to the man on the hill."

So Joni Wines went up to Judge Beko and told him she would like to appoint Bertolino. And Bill Beko, who told anyone who asked that since being appointed judge he stayed out of Nye County politics, said, "Excellent! Excellent!"

Bertolino accepted.

Then Joni Wines told Judge Beko that Jay Howard had ordered her to stay out of the sheriff's offices. She wanted to look at procedural manuals and budget figures so that she could prepare the next year's budget. If she had to wait until January 1 to do that, she said, she would have a very difficult time.

Judge Beko picked up the phone on his desk and called Art Sorenson, who was undersheriff to Howard. Beko told him to come up to the office. Sorenson came up the back stairs of the courthouse and entered the Judge's office. Beko introduced him to Joni Wines.

"Art, I'd like to borrow your procedures manual and your budget figures."

"Yes, sir," Sorenson said and went back downstairs and got them. He brought them into Judge Beko's office and handed them to Beko.

Beko handed them to Joni Wines, saying to Sorenson, "I'm borrowing them from you, and Mrs. Wines is borrowing them from me."

Joni then told Judge Beko that she intended to fire some deputies when she took office. She had drafted a letter for that purpose, which she wanted to show to him.

"I think it's too blunt," Beko said. "Let me give you one."

And Judge Beko typed out a very diplomatic but firm letter for the new sheriff to use in firing Jay Howard's deputies.

The last time Judge Beko gave Joni Wines his advice and counsel was a few days after he had sworn her into office. Sheriff Wines had assigned Frank Homstad, who had come back to Nye County from Panama City, Florida, to work in the Pahrump sheriff's station, where he had to report directly to Glen Henderson. Homstad—who had always been far less aggressive than his buddy Larry Massoli—had decided to try to keep his mouth shut and forget about the testimony he had given against Henderson to Larry Leavitt and the federal grand jury. But old Glen Henderson hadn't. When Henderson saw Homstad walk into the sheriff's station, he started bellowing at him to stay the hell out of Lathrop Wells. And Homstad started screaming back that if that was the way he wanted it, then Henderson could stay the hell out of Pahrump.

Realizing that there was bad blood between them, but not understanding why, Joni Wines decided to separate the two men. She assigned Henderson to cover only Lathrop

Wells and Amargosa, and began looking for a new lieutenant to cover Pahrump. As soon as word got out that she
was looking for a new lieutenant, Judge Beko paid her a
visit.

It was the first time he had come down to her office and
the only time he insisted on anything. He wanted her to
hire John Adams, a man who had worked for Beko as a
Juvenile Court probation officer, as the lieutenant in charge
of Pahrump. Judge Beko made four trips to the new Sheriff's office to tell her what a good man Adams was. What
he didn't tell her was that Adams was his good friend and
golfing partner and frequently joined Beko and Peter
Knight out on a Las Vegas golf course.

"Wow!" Jim Perry said.

Perry was sitting in his office on January 19, 1979, when
he got a call from Tom Huddleston, the state fire marshal
in Carson City. Huddleston said he'd just gotten a call from
Walter Plankinton's attorney, Leonard Smith. Smith said a
private detective who worked for him, a man named Gene
Alesevich, had come up with the name of a possible
Chicken Ranch arson suspect from the Modesto, California, police. His name was Elbert Easley. He had reportedly
bragged to a girlfriend about burning down a whorehouse
in Nevada. Huddleston told Perry that Smith hadn't called
Perry with the information because he was afraid Perry was
no longer interested in the case.

Smith couldn't have been more wrong about Jim Perry.
Perry immediately called Modesto Police Detective Jack
Smith. Smith told Perry the story of how they had pulled in
this little pimp for the murder of a German couple and then
pulled in his girlfriend. She told them that four months
before Easley was paid $4,000 to commit the Modesto mur-
ders he was paid another $1,000 by some other men to burn
down a whorehouse in Nevada. Easley was as cold as they
come, Smith said. He was as capable of setting fire to a

building with fourteen people inside as he was of committing the ice-pick murders. Smith was sure Easley fully expected those fourteen people in that whorehouse to die. "We have Easley in custody in the local jail," Smith said, "and he's not admitting to anything."

Perry didn't have much time. He and Leavitt were really rolling on their first political-corruption case. They were about to indict Tex Gates, the head of the Clark County Business License Bureau, for taking kickbacks from two men who operated ticket booths in the lobbies of the Strip hotels. But this Chicken Ranch case had gotten under Perry's skin. He and Leavitt still wanted to find out what was going on in that miserable county out in the middle of the desert. He didn't want the state fire marshal getting in and taking over the case.

Perry thought about going straight to see Easley, but decided that as long as Easley wasn't talking he should build his case first. He sent a request to the Sacramento FBI office to interview the girlfriend, Lorrie Ross, in Fresno. An agent was put on the case. It took him a month before he located Lorrie Ross in a run-down apartment in the dry, hot central-California valley town of Fresno, about a hundred miles south of Modesto, where she had been living with Easley when the police arrested him.

Lorrie Ross told the FBI agent that she and Easley were living together in April of 1978. During that time Easley was in touch with an old friend named Jack Tatum. Easley had met Tatum when he was serving time at the federal penitentiary at McNeil Island, Washington, for counterfeiting. Easley talked to Tatum about finding a job, and Tatum told Easley that his brother ran a brothel in Nevada and there was a chance that he could get Easley a job there.

Lorrie said she and Elbert had a fight and broke up on April 23, 1978. Soon after that Easley went to Nevada. Lorrie wasn't sure where he went, but she thought it was a place called Lexington Wells or Lathrop Wells.

During May and June, Easley traveled back and forth

from Nevada to California. One of the times he came back to Fresno, he asked Lorrie to meet him at the Kings Canyon Motel. That, Lorrie said, was when Easley asked her to come back with him to Nevada, showed her the $700 in cash wrapped in aluminum foil and told her he had gotten the money for burning down a whorehouse in Nevada.

Lorrie also told the FBI agent that Easley said Jack Tatum's brother had "a great deal of influence" with the top lawman in the area where the whorehouse was and that they were "very good friends." Easley had been advised by this top lawman to leave the state after burning down the whorehouse, which was why Easley had returned to Fresno.

While Lorrie Ross was talking to the FBI, and Jim Perry was rekindling the fire under the Chicken Ranch case, Tom Huddleston, the state fire marshal, was talking to the Las Vegas *Review-Journal*. On March 9, 1979, a story with the byline of reporter Clyde Weiss appeared with all the details of the Easley arrest: the fact that among his belongings were a telegram and a money order from Bill Martin, owner of the Shamrock Brothel, and a receipt for a Western Airlines ticket from Las Vegas to Fresno three days after the fire. The story lamented, "Repeated efforts to reach Martin for comment have been unsuccessful."

In Tonopah, the day the story appeared, Joni Wines picked up the phone and called her new Pahrump lieutenant, John Adams, whom Bill Beko had convinced her to hire. She asked him to look into what the Sheriff's Department had done about investigating this fire at the Chicken Ranch and to look into what he could do about all these new leads on the case.

Adams told the Sheriff that her department had not investigated the fire because the department did not have the expertise to investigate it then and did not have the exper-

tise to investigate it today. The best they could do, Adams
said, was leave it to the state. And Joni Wines, still abys-
mally naïve about the ways of government and the law,
simply accepted Adams' explanation.

At the same time, two hundred miles south of Tonopah in
the office of Walter Plankinton's attorney Leonard Smith,
a California attorney named Roger Hanson was standing
with Smith and Plankinton reading the same front-page
story about Easley.

"Hey," Hanson said, pointing at the picture, "I know
that man."

"You what?" Plankinton and Smith said. They couldn't
believe what they were hearing.

Hanson was a defense attorney specializing in appeals
before the Ninth Circuit Court of Appeals in San Francisco.
Smith had worked with Hanson on a case two years before,
so when he needed an attorney to prepare Plankinton's
appeal of his sentence to serve sixty days in the Tonopah jail, he asked Hanson to file it for him. Now here
was Hanson telling them he knew the pimp named Elbert
Easley.

He had defended Easley's sister, Hanson explained,
after she had been sentenced in 1973 to life without the
possibility of parole for the shooting, kidnapping, and attempted robbery of a barmaid near Bakersfield, California.
Hanson had handled her appeal. After he had won a new
trial for her, she had ended up serving only five years. The
Easley family had never forgotten it. When their son, Elbert, was arrested in Modesto for the ice-pick murders, the
family had asked Hanson to represent him. Hanson had
refused because he knew that it would be a long trial and
that the Easleys could not afford to pay him.

That was all Leonard Smith and Walter Plankinton had
to hear. As they looked over the story in the Las Vegas
Review-Journal, Plankinton, Smith, and Hanson decided

that they might as well solve the Chicken Ranch case themselves.

A guard stood behind Elbert Easley as he faced Roger Hanson and Leonard Smith in the small, windowless visiting room at the Stanislaus County Prison in Modesto, California. Easley kept shaking his head and squeezing his eyes as if he couldn't quite get the world into focus. He stared at the two attorneys for long periods of time, as if looking through them and the wall behind them, out into the big open mountain ranges of California.

Easley was a small, fragile-looking man wearing a loose-fitting blue prison uniform and with long, thick black hair that he proudly combed so that it looked like Elvis Presley's. He had the same face as the thousands of Okies who had come to California before him. It was a face that told of poverty, poor health, and poor nutrition, a face with a cold, thin, cheerless mouth and a sharp narrow nose.

Hanson began by letting Easley talk about his murder case. It was a good way to get a convict to open up: talk about his chances of getting out, getting off, let him work out his reasoning in his head so that he feels comfortable, loquacious. When he had talked about his case for a while, Hanson let him know what they wanted.

"Come on, Elbert," Hanson said. "We just want to know the truth. We know what Lorrie said about you and the whorehouse fire. We just want the truth."

Hanson and Smith held their breath waiting for Easley to reply. They had all their hopes for the Chicken Ranch case riding on this interview. They were sure they were going to solve the case today.

Easley shook his head, squeezed his eyes. "Lorrie," he said in his thin, lifeless Oklahoma twang. He said it as if remembering a place he'd gone where he ought not to have gone. "She's a congenital liar. Lorrie's a confused little girl. The Modesto cops showed Lorrie pictures of all kinds of dead people. The cops trapped her. You can't believe a word Lorrie says.''

Roger Hanson tried to push Easley, but there was simply no pushing a man like that. It was like trying to push the desert wind. It just went through your fingers.

"Who's Bill Martin?" Hanson asked. "What did Martin hire you for? Was Martin involved in burning down the whorehouse? Did Martin give you the seven hundred dollars?"

Easley stared straight ahead and shook his head back and forth, back and forth, until Hanson stopped.

"What the hell do you expect me to do?" Easley finally asked Hanson angrily.

"I want you to make a statement about the fire."

Easley shook his head again. "I'm going up to San Quentin for this murder," he said. "And I won't survive up there if they know I've been a snitch."

It was just a name from a dingy little hooker, and for all Jim Perry knew it might end up the way everything else in this case had ended up, but he figured he might as well give it a try. Perry stepped up to the computer console in the FBI offices on March 21, 1979, and punched in the name that Lorrie Ross had given them, Jack Tatum.

James Luther "Jack" Tatum, the computer told him, was a fifty-six-year-old con from Oklahoma, six feet tall, only 155 pounds, with a rose tattoo on one arm. He had spent much of his life, from the age of twelve, in federal and state prisons. He had ten felony convictions for burglary, theft, counterfeiting, destruction of property. He had been charged once with arson in a case out of Sacramento, but the charges had been dismissed due to insufficient evidence.

The computer also confirmed what Lorrie Ross had said, that Tatum had served time at McNeil Island Federal Prison in the state of Washington. Tatum had been sent

there for counterfeiting by a Judge Roger Foley, whose
courtroom happened to be two floors above Perry's office
in the federal building in Las Vegas. Tatum had been released on parole June 16, 1975.

"Not bad," Perry said to himself. "Not at all bad.
Maybe there's some hope for this case yet."

Perry went straight to the probation office upstairs and
had the supervisor check Tatum's file. On April 10, 1978,
Tatum's parole file had been transferred from the probation
office in Sacramento to the one in Las Vegas, because
Tatum had taken a job in Lathrop Wells as a gas station
attendant for a man named Bill Martin. Martin confirmed
the employment on May 12.

The next report Perry found in Tatum's file was almost
too good to be true. Tatum's new parole officer reported
that on May 22 another ex-con, who had also served time
at McNeil Island, was transferred to the Las Vegas parole
office for supervision, because he was also going to work
for Martin. The second ex-con was named Elbert Easley.

Perry walked down the back stairs of the courthouse to
the U.S. Attorney's Office and, without checking first to
see if Leavitt had anybody with him, pushed open Leavitt's
office door and started reeling off the information about
Tatum and Easley before he was even inside the room.

"It's beginning to look good," Perry said.

"Now we'll see what our friend Peter Knight has to say
about our crackpot investigations," Leavitt drily replied.

Leavitt and Perry sat down to talk about what to do next.
They had some leverage with Tatum. He was out on parole
after spending most of his life in federal penitentiaries. He
might just be willing to tell them about Elbert Easley and
Bill Martin.

They were scheduled to go to trial on the Tex Gates case
in only a couple of weeks. And they were working on another hot political-corruption case: the prosecution of three
men who had unsuccessfully attempted to bribe Harry
Reid, the chairman of the Nevada Gaming Commission.

They would probably go to trial on that soon after they finished Gates. They wanted to try to find Tatum first.

Perry went back to his office and dialed the number the probation officer had for Tatum. It was in Roseville, California, a little town outside Sacramento. Perry told Tatum he wanted to fly to Sacramento to interview him about an investigation into an arson at the Chicken Ranch brothel in Nye County, Nevada.

"That'll be fine," Tatum said in a slow Okie drawl. He was as cool and calm as he could be. "I'm livin' at my sister's house and workin' at cuttin' firewood and pannin' for gold. I can meet ya anytime."

Perry made a date to meet Tatum at the federal parole office in Sacramento a week later. But when Perry arrived at the office, Tatum wasn't there. Perry got a map of the Sacramento area and drove out to Roseville to find the house where Tatum and his sister lived. But no one was home.

"You son of a bitch," Perry said to the empty house.

He drove back to the Sacramento airport and caught the next flight for Las Vegas. At home that night, from his family room, he kept calling Tatum. Through the six-o'clock news, through Caroline's dinner, through *Dallas* and *The Dukes of Hazzard,* Perry kept calling. Finally, in the middle of the eleven-o'clock news, Tatum's sister answered. She said that Tatum wasn't there. She also said her brother was "deathly afraid of Bill Martin."

Perry stayed in touch with Tatum's parole officer. The next time Tatum reported in, he said he was living in Shoshone, California, a little desert town only fifty miles from Lathrop Wells, on the edge of Death Valley. Perry called Tatum again. And again Tatum was cool, calm, and friendly. He said he was helping a guy named Harrison build a house there. He agreed to meet Perry the next day, at noon, at the Shoshone post office.

The next morning Perry drove ninety miles across the blistering desert in his gray Plymouth to the post office in

Shoshone. Jack Tatum wasn't there. He got back into the Plymouth, turned off the air-conditioning and opened the windows so that the Plymouth wouldn't overheat. Then, sweating in his neat blue blazer, he drove slowly around the miserable little desert town, stopping every few blocks to ask anyone he saw if they knew a man named Harrison who was building a house in town. And everyone told Perry that no one had built a house in Shoshone in the last fifty years. Which was the way it went out in the desert, chasing men and clues.

A few days later, Perry was back in his office when he got a call from the receptionist. Jack Tatum was waiting outside to see him. Perry was due in the Tex Gates trial in an hour. He had just enough time to give Tatum a piece of his mind. Perry walked out into the FBI waiting room and read Tatum the riot act, yelling and screaming and demanding to know why he'd had to chase Tatum all over California.

Tatum didn't even blink. "I came here because I want to cooperate," was all he said.

Perry calmed down and looked at the man standing before him. No wonder he acted the way he did, Perry thought. He had the dead-eyed stare of a man who had spent his whole life in prisons, where men turn themselves into fortresses in order to survive. It was the stare of a man who is not going to give anybody the satisfaction of knowing he could be injured by anything they might do to him.

Tatum was a tall scarecrow of a man with a long narrow face and a sharp, pointed nose. It was the same kind of nose that Barbara Perri said she saw on the man who pushed her on her back before setting fire to the Chicken Ranch. He was bald except for a hank of yellowed wavy hair that he wore long at the base of his skull. His street clothes hung loose on his lean body as if he'd been dressed by state and federal authorities for so long that he could no longer remember how to find clothes that fit him.

Tatum told Perry that he'd met Martin several years ago and worked for him after leaving McNeil Island in 1975. Around May 1, 1978, Tatum said, Martin called and asked him to come back to work for him in Lathrop Wells as a maintenance man. While he was there, Easley came to work for Martin, too. Tatum remembered that Easley lived in a bunkhouse in back of the Coach House Bar and built Martin a carport and was drunk most of the time.

Tatum denied ever having talked with Easley about getting him a job at the Shamrock. He denied ever having been to the Chicken Ranch brothel. He denied knowing anything about the arson. And worst of all for Perry, he said he thought Easley hadn't arrived in Lathrop Wells until July 1978, a month after the Chicken Ranch fire.

Perry was frustrated. This case was like being on a goddamned roller coaster. Every good lead they'd gotten had turned into a dead end. But Perry had lived with this case almost two years now, too long to be willing to give it up as dead. Perry left the FBI office and walked up the back stairs of the courthouse to the third floor, where he was scheduled to go into trial with Leavitt on the Tex Gates case. In the few minutes they had before court was convened, he briefed Leavitt on the interview with Tatum.

"I know this case, though," Perry said. "This is not the end. I'll bet you something or someone is going to turn up again."

He had no way of knowing that, as he and Leavitt walked into the courtroom, someone already had.

CHAPTER

Nineteen

She wore shiny yellow polyester slacks with a skimpy spaghetti-strap top and matching yellow jacket. Her hair was dyed a deep henna red and fell in thick curls around her face. Her small cupid's-bow mouth was thickly painted with red lipstick. Her eyebrows had been tweezed in a high unnatural arch and her frightened eyes coated with brown eye shadow and smudged eyeliner and black mascara. Her thin heart-shaped face was layered in heavy makeup. And there was a line at her neck where the makeup ended and you could see the pretty milk-white freckled skin of a young red-haired girl.

She stood at the only pay telephone in the Exchange Club, in the narrow, dimly lit space between the backs of the slot machines and the restroom doors. The Exchange Club was a small coffee shop and casino in the center of Beatty that Nye County District Attorney Peter Knight had inherited from his parents. She picked up the phone and dialed the operator and asked for the Sheriff.

When one of Joni Wines's deputies answered, she told him that she was a girl from the Shamrock Brothel and that she had run away because she was afraid for her life. In the old days, one of the deputies from Beatty, just thirty miles up the road from Lathrop Wells, would have put in a call to Glen Henderson and told him that there was trouble with one of the bimbos from the Shamrock. Then Henderson would have put in a call to Bill Martin, who would have sent one of his men up to Beatty to put the girl into his car and take her back to the brothel. It was a comfortable kind of arrangement in which the working girls in Nye County had as much in the way of civil liberties and constitutional rights as a stray dog in a city pound.

But this was no longer the old days in Nye County. Joni Wines's deputy, Chuck Davis, brought the girl to the small sheriff's station on the other side of the town's major crossroad and told her that they would indeed help her. They sat her down at a desk in the brand-new cement-block station and gave her about twenty minutes to calm down before they asked her to begin telling her story.

Her name was Beverly Burton. Although she did not know the exact details of Heidi's death—it was suspected that one of Bill Martin's men had run her car off the road at ninety miles an hour—Beverly and every other working girl knew the general outlines of what could happen in Nye County if you were nothing but a whore and crossed the wrong people. And she felt she might end up like Heidi if she wasn't given protection.

Beverly's story read like something out of a twisted fairy tale. She had grown up in Monroeville, Pennsylvania, just outside Pittsburgh. She left high school after three years to live with a trucker from Oklahoma named Bernie Ray Burton, and four days after her eighteenth birthday, in August 1977, she married him. Six months after the wedding, Bernie left their Virginia Beach, Virginia, home one morning and didn't come back. Beverly went home to her mother. She was sitting in the Colonial House, an all-night diner in New Kensington, Pennsylvania, near her mother's home just north of Pittsburgh. She was crying over a cup of coffee when a man named Jimmy Gentile and his buddy Ernie sat down next to her and asked how they could help her.

"I told him that I had to find my husband," Beverly told

Chuck Davis, "and he told me he had a friend in Las Vegas who could locate people through their Social Security numbers. He told me to meet him at the Colonial House the next night, and he could arrange for me to fly to Las Vegas to meet this friend."

She was taken to a one-story white building on Fourth Street in Pittsburgh, an old-style speakeasy-type gambling club. She remembered that the name "Westmoreland" was written in big black letters on the front of the building. When she and the men arrived, a man checked them out through a little peephole before letting them inside. While they were there Ernie telephoned someone named Frank Isaac in Las Vegas and told Beverly that all the arrangements were made. Then he took her to the airport, bought her a ticket to Las Vegas, and put her on the plane.

When she arrived in Las Vegas, Beverly was met by a man called "The Arab," the same Frank Isaac whom Ernie had telephoned from Pittsburgh. He took her to a fortress-like house with bars on the windows and the door. He kept her there for two days. Then on May 2, 1978, he told her they were going on a picnic to Lake Mead. Beverly happily went along, taking with her only the shorts and blouse she was wearing. Instead of taking her to Lake Mead, "The Arab" took her to Bill Martin's Shamrock Brothel.

"When I got there," Beverly told the sheriff's deputy, "I was taken inside and met by Nick di Candia, who's an old friend of Bill Martin's from New York who works there. Nick told me that Bill Martin had paid Frank Isaac two hundred dollars to bring me there and that I had to stay and earn enough money to pay Bill Martin back. It was the first time I had heard that I was supposed to be a prostitute, and I was pretty hysterical the whole day." Davis realized that if what Beverly said was true—if she had been "transported across state lines for immoral purposes," as the federal law read—then they had a nice little white-slavery case to take to the FBI in Las Vegas.

Beverly said that Nick di Candia locked her in a laundry

room that night so that she couldn't escape. The next day she met a man named Ken Kolojay, who told her his real name was Todd Christopher. "Ken at first was nice to me and told me he would help me get out of the deal I was in," she said. She sounded as if she was remembering a lonely time somewhere in her life that she regretted. "He went and talked to Bill Martin about me, but then he came back and told me that I'd have to stay and work as a prostitute."

The following day Kolojay explained her duties to her. She was to dress in a bikini bathing suit or a see-through negligee—salesmen would come by the Shamrock and sell the clothes to the girls. When a customer came in, all the girls were to go out to the parlor for a lineup. If the customer picked Beverly, she was to take him back to the room and negotiate as much money as she thought he had on him. Before undressing, she was to collect the money, go into the kitchen, deposit it in a wooden box there, and then return to the room to service the customer. She would pay Bill Martin $10 a day for room and board, then split her money fifty-fifty with the house.

Beverly took in $3,600 in her first week there. She should have been able to collect $1,800, pay back the $200 to Martin for her room and board, and leave right away. Except for one catch. The catch was that Kolojay took away her money. "I didn't get any of it," Beverly told Chuck Davis. "He paid for my incidental expenses and my weekly doctor's visit, and that was all the money I saw.

"I kept trying to get away from the Shamrock, but I was stopped by Kenny from leaving. He threatened me. He hit me and beat me and called me his slut and said I was his whore. Once a few months ago when he was high or drunk, he pistol-whipped me. He wouldn't hit me when people were around, but he would drive his car out in the desert and beat me.

"He would constantly threaten me not to try and leave and threaten my life if I tried to leave. He knew where my sister and mother lived, and he threatened me that if I ever left Lathrop Wells and he couldn't find me, he would get to my sister or my mother and harm them.

"Last January I tried to get away by getting a ride with a truck driver, but Kenny followed me and grabbed me and took me back to Lathrop Wells. On the way back he told me that if I didn't go back to work as a prostitute, he would have it set up with the sheriff in Pahrump to arrest me. He said he would tell the sheriff that I had robbed the Shamrock and the sheriff would lock me up. I know that Bill Martin and Kenny are very close to Glen Henderson at the Sheriff's office. I know that they would do anything for Bill Martin or Kenny."

Two weeks before her interview with Chuck Davis she tried again to leave the Shamrock. She kept trying to catch the bus on the highway, but every time she did so, Kolojay would catch her and bring her back. "Tonight I was drinking in the bar of the Coach House with Kenny," she told the deputy. "We were drinking Kahlua and milk at the bar, and we started fighting. So I ran out of the Coach House with just what I was wearing and started walking down the highway. And Kenny ran out and got in his Lincoln and he started chasing after me and trying to run me down. I was screaming and trying to stop cars on the highway to pick me up, and he was backing the Lincoln up again to try to run over me, and a man in a Jeep stopped, and I jumped in, and he drove me to Beatty and let me out at the Exchange Club, where he told me I could call the police."

The sheriff's deputies questioned Beverly late into Sunday night. Then they took her around the corner to the Wagon Wheel Motel and checked her into one of the dozen run-down cabins for the night. At six o'clock the next morning they drove her to Las Vegas to tell her story to the Metropolitan Police Department's Vice Squad. Then, because her story involved white slavery, they drove her over to the federal courthouse on Las Vegas Boulevard and took her to the FBI office.

Leavitt and Perry were sitting in Leavitt's office when they got the call from FBI agent Joe Murray. He told Leavitt that a couple of Nye County sheriff's deputies had just walked into the FBI office with a young hooker from the Shamrock Brothel who said she needed help.

"What did I tell you!" Perry yelled. "What did I tell you!"

They had only a couple of minutes before they had to go back into court on the Tex Gates case, but they wanted to get a look at this girl before Murray interrogated her. Leavitt told Murray to bring her up to his office. When Murray arrived with Beverly a few minutes later, he was carrying a Polaroid snapshot of her that an FBI clerk had taken when she was first brought in. He handed the snapshot to Leavitt.

She was still wearing her shiny yellow slacks and skimpy spaghetti-strap top and she stared straight ahead, just as she did in the snapshot, mute and expressionless. Leavitt asked her a few questions. She mumbled as if she was on drugs. Whatever personality she has, Leavitt thought, is locked up inside her. All you can see is a seasoned, streetwise coldness.

She reminded Leavitt of why he was in this business. When he had been in law school at Berkeley he told his friends he could never, ever be a prosecutor, because he could never participate in putting another human being in prison. It took only three months in the Clark County District Attorney's Office to change all that. He started to see the victims of crimes and talk to them and their families. He quickly, as he liked to say, reordered his priorities.

Leavitt thought he would never forget how troubled Beverly looked. He had been married and divorced twice and had spent most of his life in and out of relationships. The one lasting relationship in his life was with his daughter, Laura, now a college student in Santa Cruz, California.

Laura was the same age as this girl standing before him. After she and Murray left the room, Leavitt slipped the snapshot into his desk drawer, as if it might serve as some sort of talisman.

While Perry and Leavitt went off to trial, Murray listened to Beverly tell the same story she had told the Nye County sheriff's deputies the night before. When she had finished, Murray asked her if she knew anything about the Chicken Ranch arson.

To Murray's surprise, she nodded yes.

"Right after the fire," she told the FBI agent, "Kenny told me that if I was ever asked about where he was at the time of the fire, I was supposed to say he was with me at the Shamrock the whole time. He would always say to me that I was always to tell anybody who asked that I was with him the night the Chicken Ranch burned."

CHAPTER

Twenty

On Tuesday, April 10, 1979, Beverly Burton returned to the FBI office in the federal courthouse to sign the official statements the FBI had taken from her. While she was there, she agreed to testify before Larry Leavitt and the federal grand jury in the courthouse on Thursday, April 12. At the end of the day on Tuesday two FBI agents walked her the half-dozen blocks from the courthouse through downtown Las Vegas' Glitter Gulch to the room they had rented for her at the high-rise Union Plaza Hotel. They told her to relax on Wednesday, take it easy, sit out by the pool. On Thursday morning they would call her and make arrangements to meet her and escort her back to the courthouse for the grand-jury hearing.

On that morning FBI agent Joe Murray called her room at the Union Plaza Hotel. He got no answer. He gave her time to get out of the shower and called again. There was still no answer. Murray was an old-timer in the FBI's Las Vegas office and he was excited about this white-slavery case. Barely able to control his anger, he left the FBI office and, through the growing heat of a Las Vegas morning, raced across town. He took the elevator to Beverly's room. It was empty.

He walked back to his office and called the Shamrock
Brothel. Murray was pissed, but he was not going to let
Kolojay know it. He was the kind of agent who did everything by the book. He asked Kolojay if Beverly Burton was
there. Kolojay, sounding absolutely victorious, said yes.
Murray told Kolojay he was investigating certain statements and allegations made by Beverly Burton about her
employment at the Shamrock. He would be in Lathrop
Wells tomorrow, Good Friday, to take statements from
both of them. As he slammed down the phone Murray
thought, She better have something awfully interesting to
say about standing up a grand jury.

There are two main places in small, sagebrush-strewn desert towns where men and women gather. One is the
churches. The other is the bars. On this Good Friday afternoon as Joe Murray arrived in Nye County, where the bars
outnumbered the churches three to one, there were a fair
number of people in both. Murray pulled his unmarked car
off the highway at the Lathrop Wells corner and drove
across a huge gravel parking lot. To his left was the Union
76 gas station and the Coach House Bar. To his right was
the Shamrock.

Wearing jeans and a tight-fitting knit shirt that showed
off his muscular upper body, Kolojay greeted the FBI
agents at the Shamrock's Kelly-green front door. He
tried to be polite, but found it impossible to conceal the
edge in his voice as he escorted the agents into the
brothel. The smell of stale smoke and cheap cologne
permeated the plush red wallpaper and motel sofas in the
parlor. A huge jukebox stood mute and blinking in the
corner.

Making mental notes of everything they saw so that they
could report back to Perry and Leavitt, the agents followed
Kolojay through the room into the kitchen. As they passed
one hallway they could see a row of doors opening into

small bedrooms. A few girls wandered around wearing nothing but cheap string bikinis and vacant stares.

They came into the kitchen and sat at an enormous table. Along one wall of the kitchen were the small wooden boxes with slots where the girls put the money they took from their customers. Jim Murray told Kolojay that the FBI was conducting an investigation regarding allegations made by Beverly Burton that she had been kept at the Shamrock against her will and forced to work as a prostitute. Then Murray read Kolojay his rights.

Kolojay nodded. He understood his rights, he said, and he would be happy to cooperate. He said that Beverly was at the Shamrock today. She was working as a prostitute. She had never, Kolojay said, been kept against her will.

Murray asked Kolojay if he knew how Beverly had come to work at the Shamrock in the first place. Kolojay said he had no idea. Murray kept questioning Kolojay, but it was to no avail. Kolojay was a stone wall. He had no information about anyone at the Shamrock doing anything unlawful, he told Murray. In fact, he volunteered, the Shamrock had a good working relationship with the local Nye County sheriff's deputy.

Murray told Kolojay that he would like to interview Beverly Burton. Then Murray warned him that Beverly Burton had been subpoenaed to testify before a federal grand jury in Las Vegas. The law, Murray drily told him, provided harsh penalties for anyone who harmed a federal-government witness. Kolojay nodded and slowly heaved his massive body up and away from the table until he was standing. He went to get Beverly Burton so that Murray could see for himself that she was at the Shamrock voluntarily.

A few minutes later a new Beverly Burton walked into the Shamrock's kitchen. She was not the same frightened, subdued girl Murray had seen two days before. She was cold and quiet and street tough, and the line where the makeup of the desert whore left off and the skin of a young girl began was blended in at her neck, so that it was impossible to tell which was the the real person.

Murray asked why she had come back to the Shamrock.

"I wanted to come back and go to work," she said, staring straight ahead.

Murray asked if anyone had forced her to return.

"No. I came back on my own." She spat out the words. "I don't want to talk to you. Or anyone in the FBI. Or anyone in the government anymore. I don't want to give anyone any more information. If you want to talk to me anymore, I will hire a lawyer to represent me."

There was nothing more Murray could do, except hope she changed her story back again before she got on the stand before the grand jury. For he was certain Leavitt would still want to put her up there under oath and see if she would deny making her original statements.

What Murray didn't know was that she already had done just that. On the previous day, alone and afraid, Beverly picked up the telephone next to her bed in the Union Plaza Hotel, dialed the Shamrock, and asked to speak to Kolojay. She was like the other girls in the desert whorehouses who spent all their time talking about "sick love"; she wasn't strong enough to live for long without her pimp. She had convinced herself, somehow, that Kenny loved her. She even carried a snapshot of his five-year-old son, Todd, around in her purse. She told Kenny that she was in Las Vegas and that she had talked to the FBI.

"Get yourself back up here," Kenny told her.

So Beverly dutifully walked out of the Union Plaza and walked to the on ramp of I-15 that runs north out of Las Vegas. She stood there, with the harsh sun reflecting off her shiny yellow jacket and her henna hair, until a trucker stopped and said he'd take her back to Lathrop Wells. As soon as she arrived back, Kenny told her that Bill Fox, a deputy who worked in the Amargosa Valley under Glen Henderson, was coming over to the Shamrock to take a new statement from her.

Beverly sat with Kolojay and Fox at the same table where she sat with the FBI agents today. She made a whole new set of statements to Fox, who duly took them down for her to sign. She told him that the Nye County sheriff's deputies in Beatty and the FBI agents in Las Vegas had forced her to sign the statements she gave them after she ran away from the Shamrock. She said that none of the things she had told the Nye County Sheriff's Department and the FBI about Martin and Kolojay and Henderson were true.

That Good Friday night, Nye County Sheriff Joni Wines was in her trailer home in Pahrump, planning to spend the weekend with her family, when the phone rang. It was a message to call Don Barnett, the Nye County Commissioner against whom Walter Plankinton had once run for office. Joni Wines was given the number of the Lathrop Wells sheriff's station, which didn't surprise her. She knew that Don Barnett was one of Glen Henderson's best friends.

When she got Barnett on the phone, he was so angry he sounded as though he was spinning. He was furious that the Sheriff's Department had interfered in the Beverly Burton affair.

"I will not allow you to hold these kinds of investigations in this county!" Joni Wines remembers his shouting.

"Don, the girl came to us for help," Joni Wines said. There was a hardness to her voice Barnett had never heard before. Joni Wines may have been naïve about how to raise funds to pay off a campaign debt. She may have been naïve about how to hire a sheriff's lieutenant. She may have been naïve about how to conduct an arson investigation. But she was not so naïve that she couldn't recognize a young girl crying out for help.

"I don't care!" Joni Wines remembers Barnett's hollering. "We're not going to do it. We're not going to ruin the

reputation and good name of people in this valley! If I have
to go all the way to the state to stop you, I'm going to do
it."

Then Don Barnett hung up and dialed the sheriff's station in Beatty. He told the deputies there—who had dutifully reported Beverly Burton's statement that Glen
Henderson and his deputies "would do anything for Kenny
and Bill Martin"—to get off the backs of the deputies in
Lathrop Wells. By late that night Barnett's anger had managed to fan the brushfire disagreement among the Nye
County sheriff's deputies into a full-blown conflagration.
The Beatty cops swore they were telling the truth when
they reported what Beverly said about Bill Martin and Glen
Henderson. Henderson's Lathrop Wells cops swore that
the Beatty cops had forced Beverly to lie about them.

Joni Wines consulted her undersheriff, Pete Bertolino.
Together they decided to bring in state polygraph experts
to administer lie detector tests to the deputies about their
involvement in the Beverly Burton affair. That would settle
once and for all who was telling the truth and who was not.

On Easter Sunday Joni Wines and Pete Bertolino met the
state polygraph experts at the Beatty station. She told the
deputies that she wanted to settle the matter and asked if
anyone would object to taking a lie detector test. The
Beatty deputies were so eager to prove they were in the
right that they flipped coins to see who could go first. The
deputies each made an appointment to take a polygraph
test the following week.

Then Joni Wines and Pete Bertolino and the polygraph
experts went on to Lathrop Wells to get a similar agreement
from Glen Henderson's men. When they walked into Henderson's shack, both Henderson and Bill Fox were there.
Joni Wines explained why she was there and suddenly
everyone started screaming at once. Fox was incensed at
the suggestion that he take a lie detector test. Fox's out-
burst was so vituperative that Joni Wines decided then and
there that she would fire him, even though he later took
and passed the polygraph test.

Henderson was even more adamant. He'd been in the department nineteen years and nobody had ever questioned his word before. He said he'd resign before he'd take it. Even when Pete Bertolino took him out for an hour to talk, Henderson just kept bellowing that he would not consent to take the polygraph test. He'd resign rather than submit to the indignity. Joni Wines warned him that he might be fired if he refused. At which point he became as belligerent as Fox had been. He let loose a string of expletives—largely involving the repetition of the words "pig" and "fucker"—the likes of which Joni Wines had never heard.

Glen Henderson never came back to work in the Nye County Sheriff's Department. He told old Pete Bertolino that he was taking sick leave and vacation leave that would last until the end of May. Then, on the morning of May 31, Henderson left his little white house trailer and walked across the sand to Fort Henderson, which had served as his command post in the Amargosa Valley desert for twelve years. He went inside the cluttered one-room shack, where Bill Beko's photograph looked down on him from its place of honor, pulled all the telephones out of the wall, and in one swift movement of his powerful arms, threw them out into the sand. Then he slammed the door behind him and closed up Fort Henderson forever.

The message said it was an emergency. "The little girl from Bill Martin's place who caused all the trouble last week" wanted to see her. It was Easter Monday morning, and Joni Wines had stopped in at the Beatty sheriff's station on her way to Tonopah when she got the message. So she called the Shamrock. To her surprise, she had no trouble being put through to Beverly Burton. Beverly told her that she wanted to straighten everything out immediately. It was urgent. Joni Wines agreed to see Beverly at the Beatty sheriff's station. But she said she didn't want Kenny Kolojay to bring Beverly there; she'd send a matron and a deputy to get her.

While the matron and the deputy were on their way to Lathrop Wells, Beverly arrived in Beatty in Bill Martin's white Corvette, driven by Kolojay. He sat outside the sheriff's station in the expensive sports car, where everyone could see him, while his whore—the girl he called "my slut"—talked to the lady Sheriff.

Joni Wines waited until the police matron had returned and had her search Beverly before they talked. And Beverly loudly complained that her rights were being violated. She was wearing skin-tight jeans and a cheap crinkly cotton blouse, and was chain-smoking. She was doing a fair job of acting tough, holding a cigarette alternately between her lips and her fingers. Although she was trying hard to act street smart, Joni Wines could see that she was scared to death. Whatever had been done to this girl, it had been done by people with an awe-inspiring power to convince.

The three women sat at a table and Joni Wines announced that she was going to tape the conversation. That started Beverly on a new round of protests about her rights, but Joni Wines sat there, quietly insistent, until Beverly gave in. She turned the tape recorder on and asked Beverly what she wanted to tell her. The tape recorder sat there, the tape ominously turning. As Beverly's eyes grew wider and wider, the only sound you could hear was the tape hiss. Beverly sucked on her cigarette. For a moment her streetwise act hung between her and the Sheriff. She said she was there to complain about the way she'd been treated by the sheriff's deputies in Beatty when she first came to them. The tape turned and turned. And then the streetwise act crumbled and Beverly began to weep.

"Please, turn off the machine," she said.

Joni Wines clicked it off. "You're with friends," she told Beverly. "Just tell us how we can help you."

Beverly began sobbing. "I'm so frightened," she said. "I don't know what to do."

"You're with friends," Joni Wines said. "We will do anything we can to help you."

Then Beverly told her that Kolojay had sent her to complain about the deputies. "I didn't want to go back to Kenny, but I was afraid of him, afraid of him hurting me or my family. I knew that he had the phone numbers and addresses of my family, and I was afraid. So I came here when they told me to, and he and Bill Martin told me what to say. They told me what to say today and at the interview in the kitchen of the Shamrock with the Lathrop Wells deputy."

Joni Wines told Beverly that she was afraid her life would be in danger if she returned to the Shamrock. She convinced her to let them take her to Las Vegas. She said they'd arrange to have her flown back to her family in Pennsylvania.

While Kolojay sat out in front of the sheriff's station in Bill Martin's white Corvette, Joni Wines had a patrol car pull into a vacant lot behind the station. Beverly and the matron and a deputy sneaked out a side door, ran down an old path to the car, and headed for Las Vegas. Joni Wines gave them a half hour's head start, then had a deputy go out to the white Corvette and tell Kolojay that they were keeping Beverly in custody for the night.

On the long ride to Las Vegas, Beverly didn't say a word. She just sat in the back seat like a beaten young girl. When Bill Martin's blue-and-orange Union 76 sign appeared above a spot of shimmering desert, signaling the approach of the Lathrop Wells corner, Beverly slid down in the seat until she disappeared from view. She didn't raise her head again until they had passed the Coach House and the Shamrock Brothel. Then she kept a watch out the rear window, glancing back at the highway from time to time, to make sure no one was gaining on them.

Beverly had been safely back at her mother's house just outside Pittsburgh for only twelve hours when she picked up the telephone and dialed the number of the Shamrock

Brothel and asked to speak to Kolojay. "I was a very mixed-up girl at that time," Beverly would say years later. "I did a lot of irrational things." She was back at the Shamrock Brothel again within twenty-four hours.

Ten days later FBI agent Joe Murray received a letter in his office at the federal courthouse in Las Vegas. It was written in a childish script on legal-size blue-lined yellow paper and was postmarked Lathrop Wells, Nevada:

> I felt I better write you, hoping it's not to late. I've told so many lies about Kenny and other people. See I love Kenny and always have. The night this all started, Kenny and I had an arguement and he told me he didn't love me any more, and asked me to leave. I wanted him so bad that I would have done anything to keep him. I was so upset when I went to beatty I had no intentions of signing any statements, they did talk me into it and had me doing things I would have never done on my own the next thing I knew it was at Metro and then to you. This has gone to far. I could end up in trouble for all the damage I have done, I do fill my rights were violated several time, by the state for making me go home, and by Sheriff Wines in beatty for making me go to Vegas.
>
> I came here on my own knowing it was for prostitution and I can prove it. I was never held against my will from any one.
>
> Kenny has never hurt me in any way and he's never held me against my will either.
>
> I've never seen Fox or Henderson do anything wrong, or anyone else for that matter.
>
> I can't believe this has gone so far only, a few lies from me and the beatty cops got me blowing this totally out of proportion.
>
> This is the Gods Truth, and I will Swear this Under Oath!
>
> Sorry doesn't seem to fit But Lord knows I will be.
>
> One last statement.
>
> Joni Wines had no right telling me if I went back with

Kenny I would never get out alive, and not letting me go with him that night!

BEVERLY ANN BURTON

You will not here from me again or talk with me again until you see me in Court.

CHAPTER

Twenty-one

That Easter Sunday fight over Beverly Burton marked
the beginning of the fight for Joni Wines's political life. On
June 8, 1979, former Nye County Sheriff's Deputy Bill
Fox, whom Joni Wines had fired eight days earlier after he
screamed at her for suggesting that he take a lie detector
test, filed a petition with Judge Beko's court in Tonopah
asking the court to declare the Nye County Sheriff guilty of
"malfeasance, malpractice and nonfeasance in office" and
order her removal from office. The petition was based on a
Nevada state law that allows any citizen to charge any
public official with malfeasance in office, and orders that
the official be removed from office if malfeasance is proved.

Fox's petition listed twenty-nine counts of alleged mis-
conduct (each one of which was published in the Pahrump
Valley *Times*) including Joni Wines's actions from the day
Beverly Burton walked into the sheriff's station in Beatty
through Easter Sunday, when the confrontation in the
Lathrop Wells sheriff's station occurred over the polygraph tests. The petition also included a bizarre list of allegations ranging from the charge that she defamed Bill Fox
to the charge that she allowed a reporter from the Los

Angeles *Times* (who, unaware of the trouble brewing in
Nye County, had simply come to do a cute story on this
white-haired lady sheriff) to "drive her sheriff's vehicle at
unlawful speeds, from 80 to 90 miles per hour."

The most serious charge involved Glen Henderson's version of the events surrounding Joni Wines's attempt to pay
off her campaign debts. "During November of 1978," the
petition read,

> Petitioner and his immediate supervisor, Lieutenant
> Glen Henderson of the Nye County Sheriff's Depart-
> ment, were visited by Joni Wines at the Lathrop Wells
> station of the Nye County Sheriff's Department, at
> which time and place Joni Wines stated that she had a
> bill totaling "about $3,000" on her charge cards and
> needed to pay them off so she could "start office clean."
> Joni Wines further then and there stated that she "had
> heard" that someone in Lathrop Wells could give her
> the money and she asked how she could get it.

Judge Beko disqualified himself from hearing the case,
since he was cited by Bill Fox as someone who had personal knowledge of the facts disputed in the petition. Judge
Stanley Smart, who had ruled for Walter Plankinton in the
Chicken Ranch public-nuisance suit, was assigned to come
to Tonopah to hear the case. A date for the court hearing
was set for June 28.

On that day the room was filled with the good old boys
of Nye County, come to seek their revenge. Friends of Bill
Martin, Glen Henderson, and Bill Fox packed the gallery,
while a small group of Joni Wines's supporters sat in the
front of the room. Those who did come to watch were
amazed at Joni Wines's strength. Every time Fox's attorney fired a question at Joni, her best friend and former
campaign manager, Pat Edenfield, held her breath, afraid
of what would happen next. But Joni held up under the
volley of questions. And soon Pat Edenfield was saying to
herself, My God, she's going to win this.

The arguments in the case went on for two full days, and at the end Judge Smart ruled from the bench without even taking a recess to consider his decision. He told the crowded courtroom that there was "insufficient evidence of malfeasance in office" on the part of Sheriff Wines. The only possible malfeasance, Judge Smart told the packed room, was letting someone operate a sheriff's vehicle in violation of the speed limit, and he did not think that was sufficient reason "to undo what the voters of Nye County had done when they elected Mrs. Wines as sheriff."

That afternoon a victorious Joni Wines went back to her office on the first floor of the Tonopah courthouse and typed up a statement for the Nye County newspapers. It was a statement that would only serve to escalate the fight with the allies of Bill Martin and Glen Henderson.

> TO MY NYE COUNTY FRIENDS:
> You and I have just been through a traumatic, humiliating, and often disparaging ordeal together, an ordeal where my integrity, competency, judgment, and performance as your sheriff have been challenged and set to ridicule. There should now be no doubt that I will not tolerate dishonest, illegal activities, insubordination, conduct unbecoming an officer, indiscretion, immorality. I will continue to strive for equal law enforcement and protection for all.

While Joni Wines was being vindicated in Nye County, over five hundred miles away in Monterey, California, Elbert Easley was being convicted of the first-degree murder of Ingrid and Reiner Junghans, the couple who had been found with rubber balls stuffed into their mouths, their hands and feet bound with bailing wire, their bodies stabbed one hundred times.

Since the Assistant District Attorney, Michael Land, was demanding the death sentence, Easley's trial had been divided into two parts. In the first part the jury had to decide whether Easley murdered the Junghanses. In the second part, the penalty phase, they had to decide whether the sentence should be death. The jury found Easley guilty of first-degree murder. That day the judge ordered the penalty phase of the trial to begin one week later.

In the penalty phase, Easley's prosecutor had to prove that Easley had so little respect for the law that he should be put to death. To this end Land sent Modesto Police Detective Ron Ridenour to Nye County to serve subpoenas on Walter Plankinton, Frank Homstad, and the former Chicken Ranch night maid, sixty-two-year-old Barbara Perri, asking them to testify about the fire at the Chicken Ranch. If Land could show that Easley had set fire to a brothel full of sleeping women, he could certainly show that Easley had no respect for law or for human life.

The day before the penalty phase of the trial was scheduled to begin, the judge postponed the hearing for a week due to his court schedule. As soon as Modesto Police Detective Ridenour heard about the postponement, he called Plankinton, Homstad, and Perri. He found Homstad and Perri. But he couldn't find Walter Plankinton, because Plankinton was already on his way.

For an assistant district attorney in a murder case like Easley's, one of the most aggravating jobs is lining up witnesses to testify. Usually, you have to beg them to agree to come. And then you have to make all the arrangements for them: book the airline reservations, meet them at the airport, put them up in a hotel. But that was not the case with Walter Plankinton.

The next morning Plankinton walked into the District Attorney's Office, a suitcase in his hand. "I'm ready to testify," he said.

"Oh my God," Michael Land said. "I must apologize. I thought you knew about the postponement. I'm so sorry you made the long trip."

But Plankinton wasn't sorry at all. He was more than happy to turn around, drive the five hundred seventy-three miles back to the Chicken Ranch, then turn around again and drive back the following week just to tell his story.

That was when Land realized he had "opened up a whole Pandora's Box" in Nye County. Plankinton was convinced that once the District Attorney introduced evidence in court concerning the Chicken Ranch fire, Plankinton's story would suddenly be given new validity, and justice would somehow fall in alongside him. Plankinton said he'd be happy to return the following week. In fact, he'd bring Nye County Sheriff Joni Wines with him.

If he was nothing else, Walter Plankinton was a smart in-fighter, and he knew just when to strike. He had been quietly watching the fight over Beverly Burton with Joni Wines on one side and Bill Martin and Glen Henderson on the other. Plankinton knew that his enemies had now become her enemies. He guessed it was time to go to the new Sheriff with his story of the Chicken Ranch arson and its political ramifications within her county.

His guess was exactly right.

It was only a few weeks earlier, after Glen Henderson retired from the department and boarded up the door to Fort Henderson, that Frank Homstad had decided it was safe to tell Joni Wines all he knew about the Chicken Ranch case. Joni Wines not only wanted to find out more about Elbert Easley and Bill Martin and the Chicken Ranch arson, she was also eager for an excuse to get away from the hostility she was starting to feel as she made her way around Nye County. She talked to her husband, Blaine, and convinced him to take a week's vacation. Then, telling only her secretary where she was going, she left on the long drive over the Sierra Nevada and across northern California to the Monterey courthouse to watch and listen.

• • •

Prosecutor Michael Land began the penalty phase of Easley's trial by bringing Modesto Police Detective Steve McDonough to the witness stand to testify about the evidence he had found in Easley's "black bag" linking him to Bill Martin and the Shamrock Brothel.

Then he had Barbara Perri, the little white-haired Chicken Ranch maid, testify about the night she answered the door to find a man wearing a blousy shirt and a floppy brown hat, with dark material covering most of his face. She told the jury how this man had pushed her on her back, thrown gasoline or kerosene all over the front parlor of the Chicken Ranch, then set the room on fire.

Land then called Frank Homstad to the witness stand and had him relate the story of the day Glen Henderson and Bill Martin told Homstad and Larry Massoli not to answer any call concerning trouble at the Chicken Ranch. Finally, the prosecutor called Walter Plankinton.

This was the moment Plankinton had been waiting over a year for. Land took Plankinton through the events from the time he arrived in Nye County until the time he went to visit Peter Knight at the Nye County Courthouse. Then, for the first time, Plankinton publicly told his story of that meeting.

"I was making a tour through the courthouse to introduce myself to various people employed there," he said in his country-boy twang. "I walked in and introduced myself as Walter Plankinton. And the District Attorney, Mr. Knight—Peter Knight—indicated that he had been wanting to talk to me, that he had heard that I was interested in establishing a brothel in the Pahrump area. And I indicated I may or may not be.

"Mr. Knight made a statement to me at that time, and that was that if I had an interest in establishing a brothel in that area, I would have to get the permission of the people who counted, as he put it. I didn't quite understand what he was talking about at that point. He went on to state to me that it was—that that was a close proximity to Las Vegas, the closest of any brothels, and that was a very sought-after spot, so to speak.''

"His conversation went on to indicate that the district attorneys in small counties in Nevada made somewhere around $20,000 a year, and that it always had been the plum of those district attorneys throughout the out counties, or cow counties, as they're called, to get a piece of a brothel, or some remuneration. The man went on to tell me that they felt it was a franchise type of arrangement, whereby it would cost approximately seventy-five thousand dollars up front and five percent off the top.''

Plankinton paused for dramatic effect. His voice began to rise. "At that moment, I became extremely upset, angry at him, and I told him that I'd never paid a crooked politician a dime in my life, and he sure as hell wasn't going to be the first. His answer to that was, well, that, 'Mr. Plankinton, if you decide to run a brothel in Nye County without getting the permission of the people around here who count, the only place you'll run one is from the inside of my jail.'

"At that moment I terminated the conversation and we drew swords and . . .''

Plankinton stopped his testimony at that point, a catch in his throat. "As everybody in Nevada knows,'' he continued with difficulty, "we've been at it ever since.''

The Las Vegas *Sun* carried a front-page story of Plankinton's testimony the next Sunday morning. The story included the accusation that Nye County District Attorney Peter Knight had asked Plankinton for a $75,000 bribe. As soon as Knight had seen the paper, he fired off a letter to Plankinton (with copies, of course, to the Nye County papers) challenging him to a lie detector test.

WALTER PLANKINTON:

I hereby accuse you of being an unmitigated liar in all respects where you have indicated that I, at any time, solicited funds from you for "a piece of the action" or any other thing in return for an evident promise to allow you to operate a brothel in Nye County.

I have spoken this date with George Wendell, of the Department of Investigation and Narcotics of the State of Nevada, who is in charge of several experienced polygraph operators. I have asked Mr. Wendell if he would be willing to administer polygraph examinations to each of us. Mr. Wendell has indicated his willingness to conduct such polygraph examinations. . . .

Walter Plankinton indicated his unwillingness to take such a polygraph examination.

On the second day of the death-penalty hearing, the prosecutor called Easley's girlfriend, Lorrie Ross, to testify that Easley had told her he'd been paid $700 to burn a Nevada whorehouse down. Then Prosecutor Land called Barbara Perri, the white-haired Chicken Ranch maid, back to the witness stand.

"Mrs. Perri," Land began, "did you have lunch today with Detective McDonough and others?"

"Yes," she said in her sweet, grandmotherly voice. She was the perfect witness for this job: she seemed so earnest, so anxious to tell the truth.

"Do you recall if Detective McDonough asked you anything about whether you could identify anybody?"

"Yes, he did."

"What did he say?"

"He asked me about his nose. I said that the man who pushed me down's face was real slight, was slender. That he had a pointed nose that was . . . I said a scarecrow was prettier than he was."

"Now, when you said that," Land went on, "did you

say anything about the person seated in the courtroom, Elbert Easley?"

"Yes," Barbara Perri said. "From the nose, this part of his nose and face, even though it was covered up."

"The nose of Elbert Easley," Land persisted, "and the sharpness of his face—does it resemble, in your mind, that picture that you have of the assailant as you saw the assailant on June the tenth?"

"Yes," Perri said.

"Is this the first time, to your knowledge, that you have ever seen Elbert Easley?"

"Yes."

"When you saw Elbert Easley for the first time, today, did you at that time recognize the nose and the face as that which you saw on June the tenth?"

"I did."

Michael Land looked up toward the judge with a half-smile on his face. "No further questions, Your Honor."

That night Easley's court-appointed attorney, John Grisez, called Bill Martin at the Coach House in Lathrop Wells, Nevada, and asked Martin to come to Monterey to help exonerate his former employee, Elbert Easley.

Martin was very cordial, very cooperative, as he always was with officers of the court. He said he "would have no problem testifying," but that he wanted to talk to his attorney first. A few hours later Charlie Waterman called Grisez. He said he had to do some legal research on the question of how he should advise Martin and that he would get back to Grisez that evening. By the following morning Grisez hadn't heard from Waterman or Martin. Just before he went back into court, where the life-or-death fate of his client would, quite literally, be decided, he called Martin.

"I'd like to help the guy," Martin said. "But I don't want to get involved." Then Martin added that if Grisez subpoenaed him he'd make himself "unavailable."

• • •

The Monterey Superior Court jury sentenced Elbert Easley to die in the gas chamber at San Quentin. As soon as the bailiff read the sentence, Easley's mother, Ethel, a wizened lady with a Dust Bowl weariness to her face, left the courtroom and sat on one of the wooden benches in the corridor. Plankinton, having decided to take justice into his own hands, followed her out and approached her.

"Mrs. Easley," he said, "I think that Elbert has a lot of information I'd like to hear about the fire at my brothel, and I'd like Elbert to tell the truth and testify about that fire. If Elbert would tell the truth about the fire, I would be in a position to arrange to pay fifteen thousand dollars to Roger Hanson to handle the appeal of Elbert's death sentence."

Ethel Easley said she would talk to her husband and have him talk to Roger Hanson. Lee Roy Easley talked to Hanson to make sure the deal was all right with him. Then Lee Roy went to see his son in prison.

"Boy," he said, "you tell the truth. 'Cause you're in a spot now."

Elbert said nothing. He just stared into empty space in the middle of the prison visiting room. His father finally shook his head and stood up and left.

But the following day Easley telephoned his father. "Get ahold of Roger," he said. "I have some information for him."

CHAPTER

Twenty-two

From the day that Joni Wines drove back to Nye County from the Easley murder trial, her fate and the fate of the Chicken Ranch arson case would be inextricably tied together. During the trial Joni, who only then fully realized the role Larry Massoli and Frank Homstad had played in the case, had called Massoli in Panama City, Florida, and asked him to come back to work for her.

From the way Massoli reacted, you'd have thought he'd gotten a call to the holy wars. On Tuesday he gave a moving company $125 extra to come out that day. By Tuesday afternoon he and his wife and kids were in his Trans Am heading west on I-10 for Nye County. On Friday he reached Las Vegas, left his family at his mother-in-law's, and kept right on driving another four hours north to Tonopah to get his badge and gun and uniform and be sworn in as deputy sheriff of Nye County, Nevada. Without stopping to rest, Larry Massoli worked the night shift, then reported to Joni Wines on Saturday morning.

"I want you and Frank to work as investigators for the department," Joni Wines said. "I want you to work on the Chicken Ranch arson."

For Larry Massoli, a man who believed against all odds

in justice, fairness, truth, and honesty, it was the assignment of a lifetime. In a sense it was a holy war for him. It
so clearly pitted right against wrong. The forces of wrong
had forced Massoli to flee his home in Nye County, and
now he was back to set matters straight. What made it
all the more exhilarating was the fact that he had absolute faith in the supremacy of right over wrong. He knew
he couldn't lose once Joni Wines had handed him the
scepter.

Massoli had been back in Nye County only three days
when he called Plankinton's attorney, Leonard Smith, and
made an appointment to meet Smith and Gene Alesevich,
the private detective who had been so instrumental in finding Elbert Easley.

"I can't be bought," Massoli said in his pitch to Smith.
"I can't be bullied. I will make sure any information you
give me will get into court."

Smith listened to him. He liked the fact that Massoli had
left Nye County over this case. Smith decided he could
trust him. He told Massoli that Plankinton could get Easley
to talk. He didn't tell Massoli it was costing Plankinton
$15,000.

"The only thing Easley needs," Smith said, "is a guarantee that Leavitt won't prosecute him for the arson."

Larry Leavitt and Jim Perry were "really cooking," as
Perry liked to say, that summer of 1979. They had won the
Tex Gates political-corruption case. Then they had gone
right back into trial on the attempted bribery of the chairman of the Nevada Gaming Commission. And they had
won that one too. When the second trial was over, Perry
took his family to his father's farm outside Aberdeen,
South Dakota, where he spent two weeks horseback riding
and helping his father with the farm, the way he had done
as a boy. Leavitt, ever the opposite of Perry, went off to
sip piña coladas on the wide white beaches of Puerto Va-
llarta with a new girlfriend named Barbara.

Leavitt had been back at work for only two days when he got the call from Larry Massoli. Leavitt asked Massoli to come over to his office. The meeting did not go well. Massoli did not like the cool, dispassionate way Leavitt conducted himself. Leavitt did not like Massoli's almost religious fervor about this case; it made him nervous. Still, Leavitt was thrilled that they might actually get Easley's confession. He said yes, he would agree not to prosecute Easley.

For the next two days Larry Massoli and Frank Homstad were like two overgrown kids, making plans for the biggest adventure of their lives. Massoli called Leavitt and Perry and told them he was going to interview Easley on Saturday at the Modesto jail. Perry did not want to let Massoli and Homstad go alone; he wanted to go with them. He had been on this case even longer than Massoli had; he had as much of a proprietary interest. But Perry had to meet with an undercover agent on a new political-corruption case. He tried to get Massoli to postpone the meeting. But there was no way Massoli was going to postpone it.

Massoli then called Gene Alesevich, who had the same kind of crazy zeal about this case that Massoli had. Alesevich was in the middle of throwing a fit because Leonard Smith had suggested he might just confuse matters by his presence.

"Here we are going for the kill," he yelled, "and they won't let me go." Alesevich borrowed $100, got on a plane, rented a car at the Modesto airport, and was the first to get to the Modesto jail. Hanson missed his flight from southern California and had to take the bus. Massoli and Homstad, unable to find money in the Nye County Sheriff's Department budget for their plane fare, drove the five hundred miles in a patrol car.

• • •

"Walt, Walt," Alesevich hollered into the handset. "You should give us the biggest comp at the Chicken Ranch. All twelve broads, all twelve broads."

When Massoli and Homstad finally arrived at the Modesto jail, the first thing they saw was Alesevich talking to Plankinton on a pay phone while Hanson stood outside the phone booth holding a ten-page confession in his hand.

The confession was written in Hanson's own sprawling print on yellow legal-pad paper. Easley had dictated it and signed it. It read:

I, Elbert Easley, freely discussed the following facts with attorney Roger S. Hanson this 28th day of July, 1979, in the Modesto Jail, Stanislaus County, Calif.:

1. Jack Tatum sent a telegram to me, his son Levi Tatum actually sent the telegram.

2. After I was over there working about a month and 3 or 4 days before I participated in burning down Chicken Ranch I was told by Jack Tatum that Bill Martin wants it burned down.

3. Jack Tatum brought up the burning of the Chicken Ranch. I had met Jack Tatum in prison at McNeil Island Federal Prison. Tatum called me at the hospital where my daughter was dying and where she eventually died. Jack Tatum left his phone number, and I asked my parole officer Jan Arnold if I could go over to Nevada for 90 days, something like a probationary period. Jack Tatum promised me $100, but only $50 was sent. I asked him to put "You have a job over here" only for purposes of showing my parole officer that I had employment.

4. I went back and forth from Nevada to Calif 2 or 3 times while I was working there. I built his (Martin's) car port 2 or 3 times, and I tore it down because he was not satisfied with it. When some of his other employees left, Martin turned them into police, asked them to look for them.

5. I was doing maintenance work, but I wanted to work around the whores. Jack Tatum accused me of

fooling around with his daughter-in-law (Diane, Levi's wife) sexually. I told him I was leaving. Ken Colajay (sp?) said I could leave if I left my tools. I had 98 lbs of tools, he only sent me 58 lbs of tools when I left.

6. Jack Tatum told me that they really wanted to kill Walt Plankinton but finally decided to burn the whorehouse down.

7. A couple nights before it was burned Jack Tatum wanted me to drive him to the Chicken Ranch, keep engine running while he burned it down. He discussed this plan with me. Ken Kolojay was present.

8. Jack Tatum mixed coal oil (kerosene) and gasoline in a can. Ken Kolojay borrowed a Chrysler from some one from Las Vegas and Ken Kolojay and Tatum and I went in the Chrysler to the Chicken Ranch.

9. I saw Bill Martin give Jack Tatum an envelope full of money after the job was done to burn the Chicken Ranch down. If all trailers were burned successfully, the money was $15,000, after it was burned. I was present when Bill Martin paid Jack Tatum the money asking him if he was sure it was burned totally. Jack said it was, and Bill Martin paid him the money. All I got was $1,000, cash.

10. The Chrysler was blue and was borrowed in Las Vegas (light blue, a 1969 model).

Kolojay had been to Japan, some airline was supposed to build a casino at the Lathrop Wells site of the Shamrock. It was supposed to have oriental whores. The trailer house that we stopped at is 5 or 6 miles from Rt. 95 near Lathrop Wells. A friend of Kolojay provided the Chrysler, drove it all the way to within a few (1 or 2 miles) miles of Chicken Ranch. No one had on any orange blouse/shirt that the woman was wrong. Jack Tatum is about 55 years of age. I stayed in the car all the time. Jack & Ken Kolojay went to whorehouse door came open, Jack forced door open, Kolojay threw gas/ oil mixture into the whorehouse. Jack ignited it. There was no "bomb," he just used a match. The gas/oil was spread on the sofa which made a good fire.

One week before Jack Tatum went to Chicken Ranch,

Jack bought pussy, I talked to a whore. I considered
hanging douche bag in toilet, starting the fire that way,
but decided against doing it that way.

On the last page of the confession Easley had drawn a
map describing the route they had taken from Lathrop
Wells to the Chicken Ranch and back. On the map Easley
marked the location of a trailer where they had stopped
because their car was overheating. He said they had had to
repair a leaking radiator hose. A couple who occupied the
trailer had helped them. On the sketch Easley wrote, "got
black tape fixed hose and carburator" and "man and wife
in trailer house 40–50 years of age."

Hanson and Massoli took the confession into the jail
commander's office and had him make a copy. Then Massoli and Homstad got into the Nye County Sheriff's patrol
car and started back across the Sierra Nevada to complete
the thousand-mile round trip. When they arrived on Sunday morning, they took the confession straight to Joni
Wines.

Joni Wines and Larry Massoli decided to drive into Las
Vegas early Monday morning to give the confession to
Leavitt. Before they did that, however, they also decided
to give it to the Las Vegas *Sun*. Massoli did not trust Leavitt; he was convinced they would have to use the press
to pressure Leavitt to prosecute this case. Wines was
convinced that once the people of Nye County had heard
about the confession, they would see that she'd been right
about Bill Martin and Glen Henderson and Bill Fox all
along.

So Wines and Massoli spent most of that 100-degree August evening on the telephone with a young Las Vegas *Sun*
reporter, Scott Zamost, walking him through the entire
story of the Chicken Ranch arson from the day in July 1977
when Bill Martin and Glen Henderson warned Massoli and

Homstad not to respond to the fire, until the time convicted murderer Elbert Easley confessed.

Joni Wines made sure she gave the *Sun* plenty of quotes. "Arrests and indictments are imminent," she said, not having the faintest idea what Leavitt would need to get a federal indictment. "This is a major break in the case. With all the rumors that have come to me in the past year, I'm glad something has come to light."

Monday morning the Las Vegas *Sun* hit the streets with Joni Wines's revelations and Bill Martin's and Kenny Kolojay's replies. Rather than putting an end to the Nye County brothel wars, Easley's confession just seemed to get them going full tilt.

Martin called Easley "a two-bit fucking murderer" and told the *Sun* that Plankinton had deliberately set the fire at the Chicken Ranch to collect insurance money. "As far as Mr. Easley," Martin said, "there's no doubt in my mind that he's lying about everything. I don't think anything of the confession. There's nothing to it. Anybody could dream up a story like this. It's really a very bad story. It's really unbelievable. . . . We really don't care what Walter Plankinton does or did, but let's put this on record—we're gonna start."

Kenny Kolojay said, "I don't even care if they indicted me. Why should I? I didn't do anything. I don't lie for anybody for money and I don't do jobs for money like that. I am not a corrupt person. It's really a scandal. It really stinks. Bill Martin wouldn't lower himself to talk to a person like Easley."

Kolojay offered to take a polygraph test to prove his innocence. He told Zamost, the *Sun* reporter, that he had spent the entire night of the fire with a prostitute at the Shamrock whose name was Beverly Burton. He volunteered to have Beverly talk to Zamost. When Zamost accepted the offer, Beverly got on the phone and dutifully stood by Kenny's story.

Henderson remained sequestered in his trailer next to the

former Fort Henderson. He wasn't talking to anyone. However, Jay Howard offered to exonerate himself and his old employee. "That's the craziest thing I ever heard," Howard said. "As far as I'm concerned, Henderson is as straight as a string." The reporter asked Howard why he had never been able to make any arrests in the Chicken Ranch arson case. Jay Howard, who no longer had the right to wear his gun and his gold sheriff's star, looked him straight in the eye.

"How could there be any arrests?" he bellowed. "You're talking about something that happened in the middle of the desert!"

Larry Leavitt had been out of bed only a few minutes when he heard the Las Vegas *Sun* hit the lawn in front of the large Spanish-style house that he was sharing with his girl-friend, Barbara. It was not a half mile from a rambling ranch house where Bill Martin had moved his wife and children several years before. He staggered out to get it, then tossed it on the kitchen table while he made himself some coffee. When he finally opened up the paper, he found his entire Chicken Ranch arson case laid out before him. There was even a line in the story that said Larry Massoli had spent the previous night trying to contact Assistant U.S. Attorney Larry Leavitt to get him "to seek indictments against the men Easley implicated."

"Goddamn that Massoli!" Leavitt said. "Goddamn him! This is just the kind of thing I was afraid he might do. He might as well have handed the grand-jury file over to Martin and Kolojay. Now they can try to get to Easley!" Leavitt was storming about the kitchen now. "Listen to this," he yelled at Barbara. " '*He tried to contact Assistant U.S. Attorney Larry Leavitt to get him to seek indictments.*' That bastard. Here I have this guy on Death Row whose credibility is about as vulnerable as the credibility of any-one you can imagine in the history of jurisprudence, and

he's talking about indictments. I'm not about to indict anybody on Easley's testimony alone. I've got to have more
corroboration."

When Joni Wines and Larry Massoli arrived in Leavitt's
office four hours later with the Easley confession, Leavitt
was ready for them. He sat them down in front of his old
wooden desk and, like a stern father, read them the riot act
about leaking this story to the press.

But it was too late for lectures. Wines and Massoli were
utterly convinced that once the people of Nye County
knew the truth about the Chicken Ranch arson, all Joni
Wines's troubles would end. They had no idea that her
troubles would only be beginning.

CHAPTER

Twenty-three

"This is a warning. This is your last day."

On Tuesday night, July 31, the day after Easley's confession appeared in the Las Vegas *Sun,* Joni Wines was alone in her Pahrump trailer when the telephone rang. A deep, disembodied male voice left that warning.

Joni Wines felt the skin crawl on the back of her arms and neck. The line went dead, then the dial tone came on. She felt a metallic taste on the back of her tongue, as if lightning had just struck nearby. She replaced the receiver and tried to rest, but sleep was a long time in coming.

Wednesday morning, August 1, the phone rang again and the same man said, "This is a warning. You don't have long." It was a cold reminder of where she was and what she had done. It gave her pause to wonder why she had come this far. She had spent most of her life raising children, hers and other people's, in Lake Tahoe. Now here she was, out in the desert with an official pistol and badge, like some crazy lady in an old Western movie. It was also a chilling reminder of how useless her weapons were if someone in this valley really wanted to harm her.

Wednesday night the phone rang again and the same man said, "This is your last day."

Thursday night Joni did not want to stay home alone in her trailer. Her husband Blaine was in Las Vegas at his job as shift supervisor at the Sahara's keno counter. She went to dinner at the Calvada Coffee Shop in Pahrump with Pat and Bruce Edenfield, her best friends and former campaign managers. When dinner was over, they walked out into the starry, clear desert night and got into their cars.

The Calvada was set far back from the main highway. Joni pulled her car out of the parking lot into the Calvada's long driveway, and the Edenfields pulled out behind her. Suddenly, a pair of headlights screamed out of the darkness from behind them on a dirt road that ran almost parallel to the driveway. As they passed, the Edenfields could see they were the lights of a Ford Mustang.

As Joni's car pulled out onto the main highway, the Mustang suddenly cut across the open desert and turned onto the highway behind the Sheriff's car. The Mustang accelerated, its engine whining out in the echoless desert air, and pulled into position to sideswipe Joni's car off the road and into the sand. It was an old trick in the desert, a trick that had probably been used on Heidi, the prostitute from the Shamrock. At highway speeds a car's wheels would bog down in the sand, and the car would tumble end over end as it left the pavement.

Bruce Edenfield laid his hand on the horn of his car and didn't take it off again until the white Mustang had passed Joni's car. Joni managed to stay on the road, and Bruce raced ahead to get the Mustang's license number. Then Joni and the Edenfields drove straight to the sheriff's station less than a mile away.

The next day the deputies brought the man in. He had once worked for Bill Martin, but claimed he'd been in Nye County for only two weeks. He said he'd never heard of a lady sheriff in his life. He just thought she was some dumb broad driving too slow, and he was trying to pass her.

Maybe it was coincidence. Maybe it was just a strange concatenation of unrelated events. But between the phone calls and the assault with the automobile, Joni Wines had been severely shaken. She never drove alone on the long desert highways of Nye County, Nevada, again.

Larry Leavitt took the Polaroid snapshot of Beverly Burton out of his desk drawer and laid it on top of the piles of yellow legal pads and grand-jury transcripts on his crowded desk. He pulled a Carlton—the cigarette he was always talking about giving up—out of a pack, lit a match, and leaned back in his old leather swivel chair to study the snapshot. Tomorrow morning, Friday, August 3, Leavitt would once again present the case of the Chicken Ranch arson to the federal grand jury of the District of Nevada. His first witness would be Beverly Burton.

Leavitt prided himself on his ability to handle witnesses; it was the one part of being a prosecutor Leavitt was rather smug about. When he had first seen Beverly he had tried to be paternal, tried to let her know that he and Perry would always be available to help her. He had been the understanding father then. Now, as he stared at the washed-out colors of the Polaroid, he decided it was time to be disapproving. No matter how much empathy he felt for this sad young girl staring vacantly up at him from the snapshot, now was the time to get tough.

She showed up in his waiting room the next morning wearing skin-tight jeans and a tank top through which every curve of her nipples and breasts was clearly visible. She looks like a street rat, drawn and haggard, Leavitt said to himself. Without giving her any time to relax or get her bearings, without offering her so much as a cup of coffee or explaining the grand-jury procedure to her, he marched her straight down the hallway to the other end of the building and, "boom," as Perry liked to say, sat her down before the twenty-three grand jurors.

Then Leavitt did something he had never done with a grand-jury witness before. Instead of sitting at the opposite

end of the long walnut table, as he had sat opposite Bo
Hyder and Bill Martin and Glen Henderson, he sat on the
edge of the table so that he was looming over her, two feet
from her face, as he fired questions at her, one after the
other.

Leavitt had a stack of contradictory statements she had
made, first to the Nye County sheriff's deputies in Beatty,
then to the FBI, then to the Nye County sheriff's deputies
in Lathrop Wells, then to Sheriff Wines back in Beatty
again. Leavitt dragged her over that testimony line by line
and grilled her on every point.

"Didn't Kenny tell you he was going to town the night
of the Chicken Ranch fire?"

"No," Beverly said. "Because he didn't go to town.
Those few nights I know. I know when the newspapers
came out about the fire, and I know he was there that
night."

"Isn't it a fact," Leavitt demanded, "that Kenny Kolojay told you to say that?"

"No."

"I remind you," Leavitt said, staring down at her, "you
are under oath."

"Yes, I know," Beverly shot back.

"During that twenty-four-hour period, did Kenny Kolojay ever leave your side?"

"No. He never left the Shamrock."

Beverly Burton wouldn't break. Leavitt was tough. But
Beverly was tougher. Or more afraid. She was in the grand-
jury room for an hour. When she had finished, she and
Leavitt walked back to the U.S. Attorney's Office, two
silent combatants, neither one saying a word.

Leavitt had learned long ago never to give up on a witness. And he was certainly not going to give up on this one
and wake up one morning to read in the Las Vegas *Sun* that
her body had been found on the highway north of Lathrop
Wells. While Beverly walked to the receptionist's window
to collect a voucher for her $35-a-day witness fee, Leavitt

walked toward the door to the inner office. Before he opened that door, he turned to her and said just one thing.

"When you're ready to tell the truth, call me."

"Have you seen this?"

It was eighty forty-five on Friday morning, August 17, and Leavitt was already late for an eight-thirty meeting when Perry walked through his office door, waving the morning edition of the Las Vegas *Sun*. Leavitt shook his head "no". He had only glanced at the paper in his rush to get to work, thereby unwittingly sparing Barbara another early-morning soliloquy. For in it was an exclusive interview with Kenneth Kolojay, who charged that Walter Plankinton had offered Easley $10,000 for his confession "in exchange for help in lessening his sentence."

"I always thought there was something a little weird about that deal," Leavitt said, quickly lighting a cigarette while he read through the entire article. "I've never known a con like Easley to give away something for nothing."

"What do you think?" Perry said. "How much will it hurt us?"

"We'll ask Plankinton about it," Leavitt said. "But I wouldn't get too worried. The way to go is to be completely up front about it. Tell the jury right away. Get it out in the open." Leavitt started laughing. "In fact, I might actually enjoy letting somebody else be the fall guy for a change. It's always the government that cuts a deal with some clown like Easley. At least this time I won't have to hear about 'what a scandal' it is that the government—'the government!'—would make a deal with a convicted murderer."

In the same way that turning over a rock in the desert will bring out all manner of strange creatures, so did turning over the case of the Chicken Ranch arson. The crazies came out to help Joni Wines and Larry Massoli solve the crime. One old lady called and insisted that the only time she could meet Sheriff Wines was at 3 A.M. in her trailer out in the desert. She sat and talked for hours, at the end of which she announced that her only solid accusation concerning illegal activities in Lathrop Wells, Nevada, was that she had received a registered letter in 1972 that had been opened before it was delivered. Another old lady produced a Mexican marriage license that showed her to be Dwight David Eisenhower's wife.

Finally, a week after Sheriff Wines was nearly run off the highway, a telephone call paid off. Pat Copeland, one of Joni Wines's original supporters—whom Jay Howard had dubbed the "ragtag little ladies"—called to say she had John Deer at her Amargosa Valley trailer. He was scared to death, she told them—he kept saying, "Someone's going to die before this investigation is over"—but he was willing to talk. If they could get over there at eleven o'clock that night, when Bill Martin and his men in Lathrop Wells wouldn't see them, Deer would tell them what he had refused to tell Jim Perry a year before: that Bill Martin had asked him to burn down the Chicken Ranch.

Larry Massoli immediately called Jim Perry in Las Vegas. Perry said that he and another agent, Mike Hanley, would be at the Copelands' trailer, just down the highway from the Lathrop Wells corner, at eleven. Then Perry walked upstairs to Leavitt's office to tell him the good news.

"You have to give Joni credit on this one," Perry said. Perry knew how pissed off Leavitt was with Wines and Massoli. "This one's all hers."

Leavitt didn't say a word. But he knew Perry was right. These were the kind of people that Perry and Leavitt, the outsiders from Las Vegas, could never hope to get.

Just before eleven that night Perry's unmarked gray Plymouth approached the Lathrop Wells corner. The only lights at the desert crossroads came from the Union 76 sign, the spotlight on the Coach House Bar, and the Christmas lights strung around the roof of the Shamrock. At the corner Perry turned left onto Highway 373, heading toward Death Valley, and drove a few miles until he came to Copeland's land, a desert junkyard where ancient cars and trucks, washers and dryers, and other machinery the function of which Perry could no longer discern, at least not by moonlight, stood rusting out under the starry sky. Perry wound his way through the maze created by these skeletal remains until they came to a small green trailer with shades drawn and a light on inside.

Outside the trailer the temperature had still not dipped below 100 after the day's 120-degree high. Inside the trailer the air was icy cold and stale. The air-conditioner compressor thunked off and on at regular intervals, shaking the walls of the trailer. Pat Copeland nervously opened the trailer door and led Perry and Hanley to two huge men who sat at a kitchen table, flies buzzing about their heads. As Perry and Hanley walked over to shake hands, one of the men, Pat Copeland's truck-driver husband, Bill, stood up and began shouting at the FBI agents.

"I want none of this!" he yelled. "Once you talk to anybody in this case you might as well talk to the whole world, because it's gonna get back to everybody else in this damned county that you talked!"

He stormed past Perry and Hanley, slammed the kitchen door, and walked out into the desert night. While Perry went over to shake hands with Deer, Mike Hanley stood guard at the door. There was something about the heat and the hour of the night and the fear he could feel in this trailer, out on this dirt road, in the middle of nowhere. Hanley was afraid Copeland was going to come back with a shotgun and blow them away.

When he realized Copeland was not coming back, he walked over and joined Perry and John Deer at the small table. Deer looked as frightened as he had a year ago when Perry met him at the construction site just down the highway. He told them that around February 1978, four months before the fire, Bill Martin called him into his office behind the Coach House Bar and asked him to burn down the Chicken Ranch. Deer said he refused.

Then he told them that he had worked for Martin for nine years and that he was sure Martin paid off Glen Henderson regularly. Deer said he himself had been Martin's bagman as early as 1970, when Martin told him to take an envelope of cash to Henderson's trailer. Deer said he had seen a ledger book in Martin's office with a list of names and dollar figures next to them. He was sure it was a record of payoffs to Nye County officials. But he couldn't recall any of the names. It had, after all, been nearly a decade.

Perry served Deer with a subpoena to appear before the grand jury in Las Vegas in two weeks. And such was Deer's fear of Bill Martin and the network of friends Martin had in high places that he agreed to testify at the federal courthouse only after Perry promised to sneak him into the building through a freight elevator.

Leavitt had told Perry to call him when he left Lathrop Wells. He didn't care how late it was, he said. He'd stay up and watch a late movie. So Perry stopped at the first gas station past the Lathrop Wells corner and used the pay phone to call Leavitt, who was watching *The Maltese Falcon* for the fourth time.

"It was just what we thought all along," Perry said. "Deer's sure Martin's been paying off Nye County officials."

"Bogart would be proud of you," Leavitt said. "Now if we can just indict Martin and then get him to flip."

They met in Leavitt's office the first thing the next morning. If they could prove the white-slavery case they had with Beverly, they could indict Martin under RICO—the Racketeering-Influenced and Corrupt Organization Act—which would allow them to prosecute any enterprise that engaged in interstate commerce in a pattern of racketeering activity. The enterprise would be the Shamrock. The interstate commerce would be the out-of-state customers. The racketeering activity would be the arson and the white slavery.

They decided to track down Nick di Candia, the first person Beverly had met when she arrived at the Shamrock. It was di Candia, Beverly said, who told her Bill Martin had paid Frank Isaac $200 to deliver her there.

Perry found di Candia in Glendale, Nevada, fifty miles northwest of Las Vegas, mixing drinks behind the town's only bar. He was a friendly little white-haired man with a New York accent. He didn't look like someone who had run a whorehouse; he looked like someone's grandpa. He told Perry he had met Martin in the fifties in New York City, and in 1958 Martin had called him to come to Lathrop Wells to help him build a whorehouse. He had worked for Martin off and on until March of this year.

Perry asked if he knew Frank Isaac, the Las Vegas man who had delivered Beverly to the Shamrock. Di Candia said he knew him as "the Arab." He said that all he knew about Isaac was that he had cheated Martin in a business deal some years earlier. Perry asked di Candia if he had ever paid money to Isaac to bring prostitutes to the Shamrock. Absolutely not, di Candia said.

Then Perry asked him about June 10, 1978, the night of the Chicken Ranch fire. Di Candia said he remembered the night well. He was called out late that night to work on a water leak at the whorehouse. He asked Ken Kolojay to help him fix the leak, and he distinctly remembered that they worked on the leak until 2:30 or 3 A.M. When they were finished, he cooked breakfast for Ken and himself. Then they went to bed about 3:30 or 4.

"Do you know where Kolojay slept that night?" Perry asked him.

"Absolutely," di Candia said. "He slept with a prostitute named Beverly Burton. In Room Number Six. We all got up around nine that morning, and that was when we heard that the Chicken Ranch had burned."

Four days later, Perry got a call from Kolojay. He said he wanted to prove his innocence. Perry was sure he had talked to di Candia.

"Kenny, pal," Perry said, "there's only one way to do that. Testify before the grand jury."

"Great," Kolojay said.

Perry immediately went up to Leavitt's office, had a subpoena drawn up, and delivered it to Kolojay at his ex-wife's house, where he had told Perry he was staying.

Perry had heard all about Kolojay from Leavitt. "He looks like a nightclub bouncer," Leavitt had said. And sure enough, that was exactly how the young punk who opened the door looked. Perry introduced himself and handed Kolojay the subpoena. He told Kolojay he would have to appear at the federal courthouse to answer the subpoena on Thursday, September 6. Then Perry decided to push his luck a little. He asked Kolojay if he could come inside and talk.

"Sure, come on in," Kolojay said, trying to be friendly.

Perry reminded him of the interview in the Las Vegas *Sun* right after the Easley confession, in which Kolojay had said he would like to take a polygraph test.

"Would you still like to take one?" Perry said.

That was all it took to set off Kolojay. He started screaming. "I'll take one only if Easley and Tatum take one!" he yelled. "Easley's a goddamn liar! I had nothing to do with the Chicken Ranch fire!"

Perry just sat there and kept quietly firing questions at a very angry Kenny Kolojay.

"Where were you the night of the fire?"

"I worked with Nick di Candia until three in the morning on some broken water pipes," he said. He had the alibi down pat. "Then I went to bed with Beverly Burton. The next morning we heard from a trick that the Chicken Ranch had burned."

"Did you talk to Nick di Candia within the last day or two?"

"Yes."

"Did you talk to di Candia about your whereabouts on the night of the fire?"

Kolojay blew up. He stood up and started walking toward the door, screaming at Perry that he'd tell everything else to the grand jury.

Twenty-four

Nye County had operated without public scrutiny since the silver miners came to settle there almost a hundred years before. With now only nine thousand people spread out over eighteen thousand square miles, it was a place where people minded their own business and let their neighbors clean their dirty laundry in private. "If you mind your own business, and don't get into things," one Pahrump woman liked to say, "you won't find a dead body in your backyard."

Now, in the rush of publicity surrounding not only the Chicken Ranch investigation but also the existence at its center of a white-haired lady sheriff—a grandmother, at that—Nye County was being opened up to unprecedented public scrutiny. While Larry Leavitt was in Las Vegas trying to lay the groundwork for some indictments in the case, Joni Wines was sitting in her courthouse office in Tonopah doing just what Leavitt had forbidden her to do: talking to the press.

The Las Vegas *Sun* had been giving Scott Zamost a lot of space for the story since Wines had given him the Easley confession. Suddenly a whole slew of reporters were fol-

lowing in his footsteps. The Los Angeles *Times* came back.
The Reno *Gazette–Journal* called. As did AP, UPI, and the
National Star. When it was time for recriminations, Joni
Wines would blame Larry Massoli for courting the reporters, and Larry Massoli would blame Joni Wines. The truth
of the matter was that they were both courting the nation's
press, and having the time of their lives.

The stories were invariably written by young reporters
who dropped into Nye County from New York or Los
Angeles and were appalled at the lives the people led in this
Godforsaken desert. So as they sang the praises of this
brave new lady sheriff, they also sang a sad ballad about
her dangerous desert county. Joni Wines told the *Star* that
there were "two major crime syndicates" in the county,
when of course she had no solid evidence of that. "It's a
case of many things having gone on in the past while many
backs were turned," she said. "And because I have opened
investigations—bringing in the FBI—many people are
upset."

And when men and women from Pahrump and Lathrop
Wells and Beatty made their weekly 120- or 180-mile round
trip to Las Vegas to buy their groceries, there was the
August 14 issue of the *Star* next to the checkout counter
with a story about "crime-plagued Nye County, Nevada."
Above the story was a picture of Joni Wines pointing a .38
out a patrol car window and the headline "PISTOL PACKING
GRANNY SHERIFF DECLARES WAR ON TOUGH COUNTY'S
RUTHLESS CRIME BOSSES."

The anger of the county rose up day and night like heat
waves. Joni Wines had won election as sheriff of Nye
County by a scant 139 votes. There were 1,536 people in
the county who had wanted her to be sheriff. But there
were 1,397 who hadn't. And she was about to lose the
support of many of the other 1,536. All the goodwill she
had generated when she drove all over the highways of the

county, asking for votes and shaking hands, was quickly disappearing. She had been elected largely because, unlike the beer-drinking, potbellied Jay Howard, she looked as though she would not be an embarrassment to the county. Now she and that noisy whorehouse owner Walter Plankinton were causing the county more embarrassment than anyone else in its hundred-year history.

Suddenly the people no longer cared if some stupid whorehouse had burned down. They no longer cared if the Sheriff's Department hadn't responded, or if a few good old boys happened to hold office and be, as one said, "as crooked as a baloney tree."

It was their county, it was their home, and they didn't want to read about it in the newspapers. They had settled this unforgiving land, had endured its hardships, and had claimed the right to live there alone, in peace. Barren and inhospitable as this scrap of desert was, it was theirs, and they weren't going to let anyone give it a bad name. As far as the people of Nye County were concerned, it was them against the world now, and they were beginning to wonder, to put it in rancher language, if Joni Wines was "inside pissing out or outside pissing in."

In those first weeks after the Easley confession, the meetings of the Nye County Board of Commissioners—which Joni Wines and Larry Massoli attended—turned into free-for-alls. Glen Henderson's good friend Commissioner Don Barnett got into a shouting match with Massoli.

"You're accusing people in the papers!" Barnett yelled. "You're accusing people of political corruption when nothing has been proven!"

"If the shoe fits, wear it!" Massoli yelled back. "If you're honest, you don't have anything to worry about. If you're a crook, I'll get ya!"

"Glen Henderson is one of the finest cops in the world!" Barnett said.

"He's a crooked son of a bitch!" Massoli replied. "And I'm gonna put him in jail. And any friend of his, too."

At which point Barnett started swearing at Massoli and Massoli threatened to arrest him for swearing in a public meeting.

By the next Commissioners' meeting, tensions had reached such a fever pitch that Joni Wines refused to attend. Instead, she sent a letter to District Attorney Peter Knight and the Commissioners.

GENTLEMEN:
AS YOU KNOW, I AM DEEPLY INVOLVED IN A SERIOUS, TIME-CONSUMING INVESTIGATION, AN INVESTIGATION I CONSIDER TO BE OF TOP PRIORITY. SURELY YOU GENTLEMEN, ALSO ELECTED BY THE PEOPLE TO DO A JOB, CAN UNDERSTAND THAT.

The letter was the last thing anyone in Nye County wanted to hear. But Joni Wines was too caught up in the spotlight to notice. A week later both *Us* and *New West* magazines called. They said they wanted to do stories for their October issues. And Joni said, of course, they should come.

Us came first, with two reporters and a photographer. The photographer asked if they could go outside to shoot some pictures. And Joni suggested that they drive over to the old one-room Pahrump schoolhouse. Then he said he wanted Joni to look like a uniformed sheriff instead of a white-haired housewife in a pantsuit. So Joni found a blazer that looked like a uniform jacket and pinned her sheriff's star to it. And borrowed a shirt and tie from one of the deputies.

Then the photographer asked for guns. There was laughter, kidding. The photographer spotted Frank Homstad's souvenir World War II Thompson submachine gun, which Homstad had mounted on his office wall. The photographer took it off the wall and put it in his car. And the next thing

Joni Wines knew, she was standing in front of the school-house holding the Thompson submachine gun in her hands and laughing, while Massoli, Homstad, and another deputy cracked jokes in the background. There was a soft click as the shutter snapped open and then snapped closed again. It was only for a thousandth of a second, but it would also be forever.

CHAPTER

Twenty-five

Elbert Easley had been held in custody for only ten months by August 23, 1979, but confinement had already begun to take its inevitable toll. When he appeared to testify before Larry Leavitt and the federal grand jury, his complexion was pasty, his body thin, his face unshaven. Dressed in blue prison clothes, he looked as if he'd been racked by a wasting disease, by a cancer. He was, in fact, a man condemned to death.

He had chains around his ankles, around his waist, around his wrists. He had raw open wounds covering both bare arms, and he could move his hands only six inches from his body, bound now as he had bound his victims. Only he was still free to talk. About ten o'clock that morning he went into the grand-jury room with Leavitt and told his story, just as he had told it to Roger Hanson before.

The next day Perry took Easley out in the bright sunlight to retrace the route he and Tatum and Kolojay had taken the night of the fire, to see if the ride might jog Easley's memory.

The one thing Perry and Leavitt wanted to find was the couple who lived in the blue-and-white trailer where Easley said they had stopped on the way back from the Chicken

Ranch, when the old Chrysler began to overheat. They knew they had to find a respectable witness to corroborate the story of this Death Row murderer, and they hoped the couple who lived in the trailer could help them.

It was one of those intensely hot days in the desert when the heat boils up off the sand and it looks as if you could run forever in any direction and not get caught. It was a delicious taste of freedom for Easley, an intoxicating experience after his confinement, after his day-to-day proximity with the certainty of his own death.

Perry, in the company of a U.S. marshal and another FBI agent, drove Easley out Homestead Road to the Chicken Ranch. Perry planned to ask him where his route led from there. But as soon as the car pulled up in front of the brothel, Easley began begging.

"Please," he said, "please let me buy some pussy. Just this once."

Perry felt truly sorry for him, not just that his need was so raw, so naked and unashamed, but that his sense of reality was so distorted that he could imagine Perry might release a condemned murderer, shackled hand and foot, to get laid at the Nevada whorehouse that had replaced the very one he had once burned down.

Perry ordered the marshal to turn the car around and follow the route Easley said they had taken back to the Shamrock. They had driven almost the entire route when finally, about eight miles south of the Lathrop Wells corner, Easley spotted the trailer. They turned the FBI car up the driveway and drove by a row of water spigots and hoses that looked as if they were left over from an old trailer park. When Easley saw the spigots, he was sure he had found the right place.

He remembered all the details. He said the car had died by a tree and the owner had asked them to move it away from the tree because the steaming water was spurting out of the radiator. Then he remembered that the man had come out with a roll of black tape and helped them repair the broken hose.

They pulled the car back on the highway and drove to the Lathrop Wells corner. They pulled into the parking lot in front of the Coach House and the Shamrock. Easley was really enjoying himself now, showing the FBI agents around, telling them where everything was in Bill Martin's little town. Finally, a man Perry had never seen before walked out of the Shamrock and told Perry to "get the hell out of here."

It was after six-thirty on Monday evening, August 27, when Larry Leavitt got into his dark-brown Mercury Cougar in the courthouse parking lot, turned the key in the ignition, and hit the radio button to KNUU, the all-news station. He pulled the car out of the parking lot and headed toward I-15, which he would take toward home. As he pulled onto the interstate, KNUU was airing a discussion of the nuclear-power issue that was raging in the country that summer of 1979. In March there had been the Three Mile Island accident. In May, 65,000 demonstrators marched in Washington. And that same month a jury in another federal courthouse in Oklahoma City had awarded $10.5 million to the heirs of Karen Silkwood, who many believe died on November 2, 1972, after her car was forced off an Oklahoma highway.

It reminded Leavitt why he had been working so hard on this crazy Chicken Ranch arson case. He thought of Heidi, the young girl from the Shamrock who had died the same way on February 4, 1973, three months after Karen Silkwood's death. He pictured her flattened body lying on that miserable stretch of desert highway north of Lathrop Wells. He thought of Beverly Burton and pictured her, in her cheap little yellow slacks and spaghetti-strap top, running hysterically back and forth across that steaming blacktop highway while that punk Kolojay went after her in his Lincoln.

For the next two weeks Leavitt took before the grand jury every possible witness he and Perry could find. They

called in Ray Shamblin, who had been the officer in charge
of the Pahrump sheriff's station the morning of June 10,
1979. He denied that anyone—Glen Henderson or Jay
Howard or anyone—had ever told him not to respond to
the fire. He said he didn't respond because he didn't consider it an important fire, didn't realize how serious it was.
Blackwell told him the fire department was already there,
so he decided to go to the accident instead.

They pulled in Steve Blackwell, the big, boyish-looking
deputy who had been on the dispatcher's desk that morning
and had met Perry at the fire scene, saying he was there to
direct traffic. Blackwell came into the courthouse, as Leavitt would say, "sweating bullets." A year before, when
Larry Massoli had returned to Nye County and began to
investigate the arson, Blackwell had told him that he had
called Shamblin as soon as he had heard about the fire, but
Shamblin had mumbled something into the phone and told
him to call back at six o'clock with his regular wake-up
call. Now he was telling Leavitt that when he had called
Shamblin he had not told him the fire involved arson, so
Shamblin would have had no reason to think that he had to
respond to the fire.

After taking Blackwell before the grand jury, Leavitt sat
him down in his office and grilled him for two hours straight
until even Jim Perry felt sorry for him. But Blackwell
wouldn't break. He told Leavitt that all he had ever wanted
was to be a cop. Even if they gave him immunity and he
testified for them, he said, he knew he'd never be a cop
anywhere again. Less than a week after he left Leavitt's
office, Blackwell dropped off his sheriff's badge at the Pahrump station and, without even waiting for his final pay-
check, left Nye County.

They pulled in "the Arab." He said he was known as
George Isaac or Frank Mangone and was unemployed. His
basic line about Beverly Burton was, "She's a hooker and
she wanted to go to work for a whorehouse." He had just
helped her find a place as a favor to Jimmy Gentile in Pitts-

burgh, his "lifelong friend." He had received no money.
He did admit that she later called him and claimed that she
was afraid for her life and wanted to leave the Shamrock.
Isaac said he called Martin and told him not to hurt the girl.

Leavitt even went so far as to fly Jimmy Gentile in to Las
Vegas from Pittsburgh. Gentile admitted that he had found
Beverly Burton crying in a diner after her husband had left
her, and asked if he could help her. But his story matched
Isaac's: Beverly was a hooker looking for an entree to the
Las Vegas area; Gentile simply made an introduction.

Jack Tatum was no more help. He sat in the grand-jury
room like an old con, cool and calm, staring straight ahead
and not moving a single muscle. He appeared to know but
a single word in the English language: No.

"Mr. Tatum," Leavitt asked him, "on the night or early
morning of the fire at the Chicken Ranch, did you accom-
pany Elbert Easley to the Chicken Ranch brothel in the
Pahrump area?"

"No."

Leavitt tried ignoring the answer. "And assist in setting
the Chicken Ranch on fire?"

"No," Tatum said. "Uh-uh."

"Have you ever been to the Chicken Ranch brothel?"

"No."

"Did you ever talk to Elbert Easley about burning down
the Chicken Ranch?"

"No."

"Did you ever give Elbert Easley any money because of
the services he rendered in burning down the Chicken
Ranch?"

"No."

"Did you ever receive any money from Bill Martin in
exchange for your helping to burn down the Chicken
Ranch?"

"No."

"Have you ever had any conversations with Bill Martin about causing damage of any kind to the Chicken Ranch or any other brothel?"

"No."

"Have you ever talked to Ken Kolojay about burning down the Chicken Ranch?"

"No."

Tatum had just let Leavitt and every one of the twenty-three grand jurors know that he was not going to let yet another grand-jury interrogation phase him. Leavitt was furious. Just to push Tatum a little more, he asked him, in front of the grand jurors, if he would agree to take a polygraph test, even though Leavitt knew damned well that he could never introduce the polygraph in evidence. Tatum was an old con to the end. He agreed. They set a date for September 13.

"Goddamn this case," Perry said.

"Where have I heard that before?" Leavitt said laughing.

The two were sitting in a booth in the McDonald's on Fremont Street, a few blocks from the courthouse, watching the flotsam and jetsam of downtown Las Vegas shuffle by the window in the 110-degree noontime heat. The looks on their faces reminded Leavitt of his mood.

It was the first week in September, and Leavitt and Perry felt as though it was 1978 all over again. They were so goddamned frustrated. And the next thing Leavitt had to look forward to was taking Kenny Kolojay before the grand jury.

"Everywhere we turn in this case we keep hitting brick walls," Leavitt complained. He and Perry had no way of knowing that, thanks to an old habit of Perry's, the day Kolojay came before the grand jury one of those walls was going to give.

• • •

On September 6, Kolojay arrived at the courthouse to testify. Just as Leavitt expected, he had his whole story down pat. He had been asleep with Beverly Burton in Room Six of the Shamrock while the Chicken Ranch burned. She was his alibi. But he made one crucial mistake that day, one that Leavitt hadn't expected. He brought his alibi with him to the grand jury.

Beverly was sitting outside the grand-jury room while Kolojay testified when Jim Perry walked into the waiting room. Perry always made it a practice to sit there while Leavitt took witnesses to the grand jury.

"How're you doing, Beverly?" he said, sitting down next to her. "Anything we can do for you?"

"Find my husband, Bernie," Beverly said.

Anxious to do anything to soften her, Perry went down to his office and traced Bernie Burton through FBI computers to his driver's license in Texas. He came back up and told her that was the best he could do.

After letting her talk about her husband a little more, Perry gradually worked Beverly around to talking about Kolojay. She didn't like Kenny, she said. But he was the only person she had to turn to. Her family "had deserted" her and she didn't have any other friends. She said that when Joni Wines sent her home to Pittsburgh, she had been given "an ultimatum to be back in Nevada in twenty-four hours or else." She stopped short of admitting that it was Kenny who had given her the ultimatum.

"Where was Kenny the night of the fire?" Perry asked her.

"I know some things about that night," Beverly said. She sounded terrified. "I remember them and I know some of the places he was at." But that was all she would say. The only thing she would tell Perry was that Kenny and Nick di Candia did not work on the water pipes that night. They worked on them that afternoon, long before the fire.

Perry had had Beverly all to himself for over an hour when finally the grand-jury door opened. Perry and Beverly quickly stopped talking. Kolojay walked out, motioned with his head for her to get going. She quietly got up and followed him out of the room.

The following morning FBI agent Joe Murray got a frantic call from her. She had told Kolojay that she'd talked to the FBI again. She said she was afraid he was going to kill her. She had moved out of the Shamrock and was living with a roommate at an apartment in Las Vegas. She asked Murray to meet her at a nearby 7-Eleven.

Although the temperature was close to 110, Murray and Perry found her at the 7-Eleven, standing in the sun in her usual skin-tight jeans and tank top, shivering. They led her over to the small patch of shade the store offered and stood there talking to her while the uniformed cocktail waitresses and blackjack dealers and the occasional housewife going in to pick up some orange juice, or a pack of cigarettes, or a carton of milk, stared openly at the two gray-suited FBI agents and the sorry-looking little hooker.

Beverly admitted she had lied to the grand jury four weeks before. She said Kolojay had made her do it. She said Kolojay intended to talk to each and every grand-jury witness to make sure no one implicated him in the fire. Then she said Bill Martin had ordered her to refuse to talk to the FBI. Murray and Perry couldn't stop themselves from looking up at each other and smiling.

Then Beverly repeated the story she had told when she was first questioned by Murray. It was the story they needed to help make their case. She went to sleep by herself the evening before the fire. Ken Kolojay was not sleeping with her when the fire occurred. She awoke early the morning of June 10 because she was the early-up girl and there was a Shamrock customer waiting for "a date." It was that "date" who told her about the Chicken Ranch fire.

After agreeing to set the record straight before the grand jury, Beverly went back to her apartment. The next morning she called Perry three times. She was in a panic.

"Kenny is going to kill me, Kenny is going to kill me," she said each time she called.

She said that Kolojay had hired her roommate, Charlene Pellegrini, to spy on her. Charlene had followed Beverly to the 7-Eleven the previous night and had told Kolojay she had talked to Perry.

It seemed to old Joe Murray he had spent half this year chasing this dizzy little girl through the heat of a Las Vegas day. For the second morning in a row, he and Perry rushed out of the federal courthouse, jumped into Perry's gray Plymouth, and drove across town as the temperature soared to 110. They found Beverly's apartment. It was in one of the hundreds of stucco-and-wood-trim apartment buildings that are home to the thousands of people who came to town to work in the hotels and casinos. They all offered leases on a month-to-month basis. And they all looked as though they'd been put up in one day.

Perry and Murray knocked on the door. No one answered. They knocked and pounded until the door frame rattled, but were greeted only by silence. So they went to the apartment manager. The manager raised his eyebrows at their FBI credentials, and let them into the apartment. But Beverly and Charlene were gone.

As far as Perry and Murray were concerned, it was just business as usual on the Chicken Ranch case. They returned to their offices to take care of the rest of their work. They knew that Beverly would turn up, probably with another story, another tack on the winds of her unhappy life.

She called Perry at six that evening. He knew right away that something was wrong. She sounded as if she were calling from inside a deep well. Her voice was garbled, her words slurred. She managed to get bits and pieces of her story out: She had fought with Kolojay. A terrible fight. She had taken whatever drugs she had in her purse and medicine cabinet. Charlene had rushed her to the emergency room. Beverly had had her stomach pumped. She was going to get on an airplane that night and go to see her brother, Dean, in Florida. He was in the Navy down there.

Perry called Beverly's brother in Jacksonville. He wanted to make sure there was a brother. He also wanted to make sure the brother would be some help to her and not make matters worse. He told him what his sister had been through the past few months of her life. Dean seemed like a good sort to Perry, at least over the phone. He said that he wanted to help Beverly and that she was welcome down there. So at eleven o'clock that night Charlene took Beverly to the airport and escorted her on an Eastern flight to Jacksonville.

Beverly was still so high that she couldn't remember the next day how she had gotten to Jacksonville. She called Joe Murray two days later. She said she wanted to come back and testify, then leave Nevada forever and start a new life. Murray asked her if she was sure Kenny didn't know how to find her in Jacksonville. She swore he didn't.

On Thursday, September 13, Perry flew to Reno to meet Jack Tatum at the FBI office there, where Tatum had promised to take a lie detector test. It was a relief to leave the heat of Las Vegas and fly north to the edge of the Sierra, where it was a beautiful 75-degree day. It was also a relief to get away from Beverly. Leavitt always said that you got so caught up in your witnesses' lives that they "almost became like family." Getting caught up in Beverly's life was making Perry sad and crazy.

Tatum showed up on time for the test. The polygraph operator sat him down in a small room, attached him to the machine, and ran through a list of questions Perry had brought with him. After just a few questions, the examiner told Tatum that the chart showed he was lying. For the first time, Perry saw the old con lose his cool. He became very upset and said he wouldn't answer any more questions. So they took him off the machine.

Perry stayed with Tatum awhile after the polygraph operator left. Perry thought if he kept talking to him, kept pushing him, Tatum might break. For a few minutes Perry was sure Tatum was close to "flipping," close to giving them the break they needed in exchange for a reduced sentence. Then his expression changed back to the blank stare Perry was used to.

Tatum looked at Perry and said, "I can serve the time."

On Wednesday, September 19, Beverly Burton arrived back in Las Vegas. Perry met her at the airport, checked her into a hotel, then took her to Leavitt's office so that they could talk to her before taking her in front of the grand jury. In the middle of the interview, Perry dreamed up the idea of hooking up a tape recorder to a phone in the FBI office to try to set up Kolojay for tampering with a federal witness.

Perry had Beverly call Kolojay from the FBI office and ask his advice about her upcoming testimony. But it was as if Kolojay had psychic powers: he just knew the phone was tapped. It was a bust.

"Now listen," Kolojay said. "I ain't gonna, ah, say things on the phone and, and then, and then, oh, them get me for tampering with a federal witness. 'Cause I'm not, I'm not gonna say what you should do, what you shouldn't do. Because if I did, and then, you know what would happen, no matter what you said, then they got me anyway."

Perry, listening in on earphones, motioned for Beverly to cut off the conversation, drawing his hand across his throat like a razor. But Kolojay still had enough of a hold over Beverly that she was unable to end the conversation, unable to make the final break. Beverly kept talking until Kolojay cut her off.

"I wish they'd get some sophisticated equipment on this phone," he yelled. "Because the taps are awful bad. I have phone taps that're better than this! Why don't you fix this tap? Perry, would you fix this fucking phone! Jesus Christ. Six billion dollars you guys get a year, and you can't even fix one son-of-a-bitchin' twenty-five-dollar phone. Jesus Christ. . . ."

Leavitt took Beverly Burton before the grand jury the next morning. The atmosphere in the room was in startling contrast to the one the last time he had had her in this room. This time Leavitt sat at the opposite end of the long conference table and, like a strong, supportive father, slowly and quietly asked her about the testimony she had given in this same room six weeks before.

Beverly was still as mute and expressionless as she had been the day Leavitt first saw her. She was trying hard to cooperate with Leavitt, but every once in a while, in the middle of the questioning, she would start to choke up and Leavitt would have to wait a few minutes before he started again.

"Did I ask you before this grand jury if Kenneth Kolojay ever told you to lie about where he was June 10, 1978, the night of the Chicken Ranch fire?" Leavitt asked her.

"Yes, you did," Beverly replied.

"And did you tell me that Kenneth Kolojay never told you to lie about where he was that night?"

"Yes I did."

"And was that false?" Leavitt asked quietly.

"Yes," Beverly said. "Any question you asked about, about whether Kenny told me to say that, I denied that he did."

"And who told you to deny that?" Leavitt asked.

"Kenny," Beverly said.

"Did I ask you before this grand jury what knowledge you have of Kenneth Kolojay's whereabouts the night of the Chicken Ranch fire?" Leavitt asked.

"Yes," Beverly quietly replied. "I told you he was with me."

"And was that false?"

"Yes," Beverly said.

At the end of two long days of testimony, Leavitt escorted her to the U.S. Attorney's waiting room, where she would once again pick up her $35-a-day witness fee. He asked if there was anything he and Perry could do for her. She said no. She said she had a friend who could get her a job in the gift shop of the MGM Grand Hotel and that she was going to take that and then get an apartment.

"OK, Beverly," Leavitt said. "Now, you take care of yourself."

As he turned to go into his office, he looked back at her. Maybe there really is a chance she'll straighten out her life, he thought. But he couldn't tell whether he really felt that or whether he was only engaging in wishful thinking.

CHAPTER

Twenty-six

"It is our opinion," the petition read, "that Joni Wines is an embarrassing failure as our county sheriff."

On Wednesday, September 20, while Beverly Burton was testifying about Bill Martin and Kenny Kolojay before the federal grand jury in Las Vegas, two hundred miles north in Tonopah friends of Martin and Kolojay walked into the County Clerk's Office at the Nye County Courthouse to file a formal petition demanding the recall of Joni Wines.

The petition read a lot like the complaint that Bill Fox, Glen Henderson's former Lathrop Wells deputy, had filed with the court three months before, in the wake of the fight over Beverly Burton. "She has all but totally destroyed our Sheriff Department, both as to personnel and as to reputation," it read. "Nye County and its people are entitled to better publicity and public relations than that suffered as a result of the unsatisfactory performance of Joni Wines."

As soon as recall leaders Ellen Woods, Elmer Bailey, and Jerome Mundt had filed the petition, the county clerk picked up her telephone and dialed Joni Wines, who was sitting in the sheriff's office a few doors away. She told

Joni that the petitioners now had sixty days—until November 20—to collect 756 signatures, or 25 percent of the votes cast in the election that had put Joni Wines into office. If they got the signatures, and they were ruled valid by Judge Beko's court, then the court would set a date for a recall election.

"Thank you for calling," was all Joni Wines said. The county clerk was surprised that she sounded so composed. She didn't know that Joni Wines had been steeling herself for several weeks against the day the call came.

On September 26, while Recall Joni Wines leader Ellen Woods was driving around the Amargosa Valley collecting signatures on her brand-new petitions, Jim Perry was driving those same roads in his Plymouth Fury, looking for a way to corroborate Elbert Easley. A double murderer, waiting on Death Row at San Quentin to be killed in the California gas chamber, Easley was, as Leavitt had said the morning he saw Easley's confession, probably the least credible witness in the history of American jurisprudence.

Leavitt had Bo Hyder and John Deer, who would testify that Martin had asked them to set the fire. He had Beverly Burton, who would testify that Kenny had tried to use her as his alibi the night of the fire. And he had Easley, who would testify that he and Tatum and Kolojay had set the fire. Now Leavitt needed one more thing to make the arson case: someone to corroborate Easley's testimony of the events the night of the fire.

All their hopes were resting on that blue-and-white trailer Easley had pointed out to Perry the day Perry had driven Easley around the Amargosa Valley in shackles, the day Easley begged Perry to let him "buy some pussy" at the Chicken Ranch. So Perry drove out on the interstate once again, past the Lathrop Wells corner, and turned left on Highway 373 to Death Valley until he got to the blue-and-white trailer.

The couple who lived there were Anne and John New-house. Newhouse told Perry he'd been a radiation safety monitor at the test site for twenty-one years. Perry asked them if they remembered a morning the previous summer when three men had stopped to ask for help with an over-heated car. Yes, Mrs. Newhouse said, she remembered the morning. She remembered that it was early and she was getting dressed to go to a Weight Watchers meeting in Las Vegas and that after that meeting she went to do her weekly shopping at Safeway.

Mr. Newhouse remembered that there were three men in the car. He described them as white males, two of them in their twenties and thirties, the third in his fifties. He said they wore work clothes, and one was bigger than the rest; he was built like a bouncer. Mr. Newhouse asked them to move the car away from one of his olive trees because he was afraid that the steam spewing up from the radiator would hurt it. Mr. Newhouse remembered getting a roll of black electrician's tape to repair the radiator hose. Perry showed the Newhouses pictures of Kolojay and Tatum and Easley, but they could not identify them.

"Is there any way you could pinpoint what date it was?" Perry asked.

"Sure," Mrs. Newhouse said. "When my husband and I go together to shop at Safeway, I always write a check for extra cash so we can go out to lunch together. But I remember my husband didn't go that day. So it would be whatever Saturday I didn't write a check for extra cash."

Mrs. Newhouse brought the checkbook over to where she was sitting with Jim Perry. While Perry waited, she slowly flipped through the pages of the check journal. Fi-nally she stopped.

"Here it is," she said, "June tenth, 1978."

Perry felt like jumping up and touching the ceiling of the blue-and-white trailer.

He could hardly wait to get back to Las Vegas to tell Leavitt. He drove back out to the highway, turned right at the Shamrock, and an hour and a half later was walking through the door to Leavitt's office, a wide grin on his face. Leavitt listened to him quickly spill out his story. Then he leaned back in his chair and slowly lit a cigarette, savoring the moment.

"The descriptions fit," Leavitt said, as if running down a checklist. "And the details match Elbert's story so perfectly. I mean, steam from a car harming an olive tree. Jesus Christ! That's the kind of details even witnesses like Elbert can't make up."

He looked up at Perry, a sly smile of satisfaction on his face. "Jimmy, it's time to start talking about drawing up some indictments."

The next day they walked over to the coffee shop at the Golden Nugget—a step up from Jo Jo's and McDonald's, they went there for special occasions. They sat down to try to figure out how to get some indictments.

"We've got a solid arson case now," Leavitt said. "I think we've reached the point where we have to stop. The trouble is, that puts us back where we started with this goddamn case, with nothing to prosecute but the arson."

For two years Leavitt and Perry had hoped they could prosecute Bill Martin under RICO, the Racketeering-Influenced and Corrupt Organization Act which allowed the feds to prosecute what would otherwise be state offenses if there was a pattern of racketeering activities associated with the crimes. But that required coming up with a second offense besides the arson. And Leavitt and Perry couldn't make one stick.

"The white slavery comes down to all the men in the case versus Beverly," Leavitt said. "Kenny, Nick di Candia, the Arab, even that clown Gentile from Pittsburgh—boy, was that bastard sweating in the grand-jury room. It's all of them against Beverly. And I can't do anything with John Deer's claim that Martin keeps a ledger in his office listing political payoffs. I'd never get a judge to give me a search warrant to go into Martin's office for something somebody saw ten years ago. Let me just try to march that in to Foley and make it work!''

Perry laughed. "You know, sometimes a lot of publicity will bring people out of the woodwork. I've seen it happen. But not in this case. We're not going to get another thing out of that county. It's us against them now. The only reason we got John Deer was because of Joni Wines's lady friend. I still think the best way to break open this county is to get Martin for the arson, then flip him.''

They stopped talking about the case while the waitress came over to take their order. A club sandwich, potato salad, and coffee for Leavitt. The diet hamburger plate for Perry. The U.S. Attorney's Office didn't care how much you weighed; the FBI did.

"I'll tell you what I'll do," Perry said after the waitress had left. "I'll ask around the office and see if any other agents have heard of a case where the feds prosecuted an arson.''

Two days later Perry walked into Leavitt's office. "One of the guys remembers a case back in Tampa, Florida,'' he said. "He says they convicted several suspects on 844(i).''

Leavitt grabbed the royal-blue-bound copy of the federal criminal code that always sat on his desk. Statute 844(i) was a 1970 law Congress had passed to try to combat radical bombings. It said that anyone who destroys or damages property used in interstate commerce by means of "an explosive" shall get ten years and a $10,000 fine. If someone is injured by the "explosive," the penalty goes up to twenty years and a $20,000 fine.

"The only thing that worries me," Leavitt said, studying the statute, "is whether we can successfully argue that the gasoline and kerosene Easley says they used constitutes an explosive under this law. Before we go any further, I better send a request to the ATF lab in Washington and get them to render an opinion."

Almost two-and-a-half years of work on this case and it was all going to come down to this one Bureau of Alcohol, Tobacco and Firearms decision. He looked up at Perry and shrugged.

"We'll just have to sit back and wait."

It was almost noon several Saturdays later when Larry Leavitt stumbled out of bed. Pulling on a robe, he staggered out to the kitchen, poured himself some coffee that Barbara had left him, and sat down to read the Las Vegas *Sun*. There in the *Sun* was an interview by Scott Zamost with Nye County District Judge William Beko.

> During a candid interview at the Nye County Court-house, Beko said he would be "shocked" if either Shamrock owner William Apfel, alias Bill Martin, or former Lt. Glen Henderson were indicted by a federal grand jury in Las Vegas investigating last year's blaze of the brothel located in Pahrump. "I'd be shocked," Beko said of Henderson, whom he has known for 25 years. "Glen Henderson has a heart bigger than his head. I wouldn't believe it even if he is indicted."

Leavitt sat and stared angrily at the paper. " *'I wouldn't believe it even if he is indicted,' "* he bitterly repeated to himself.

As soon as he arrived at his office on Monday morning, he looked up the Nevada Code of Judicial Conduct. Instead of simply Xeroxing the relevant section, he wrote it out in longhand on a sheet of yellow legal paper, as if the very act of writing would assuage some of his anger: "Canon 3(a)6. A judge should abstain from public comment about a pending or impending proceeding in any court. . . ."

When Leavitt was finished, he underlined the last three words with thick strokes of his black felt-tipped pen.

• • •

"I just want to die," Beverly told Jim Perry. "I just want to die."

On October 3 Beverly Burton had finally gone over the edge, as everyone watching her thus far feared she might do. Jim Perry received a call from the Las Vegas police, saying they had her in custody. She had been in a nightclub called the Brewery, where she had gotten herself mixed up with a pimp. She'd gone back to his apartment, refused to work for him, and he'd beaten her silly. She'd been up all night with the police, requesting to talk to the FBI.

Each in his own way, Beverly Burton and Elbert Easley were slowly grinding toward oblivion on curiously parallel paths. When Perry and Murray saw her, she might have been Easley's spiritual sister in detention, shocked, dazed, bloodied and scratched, her face cut, swollen from crying, her makeup smeared, bruises all over her arms.

"I just want to die," Beverly told Perry. "I just want to die." She begged him to take her back to her apartment so that she could take another overdose of pills.

Perry refused. "I know you're going to take them," he said.

"Yes, I am. I want to die," she said.

Joe Murray was begging Perry to leave her. He wanted to take her back to her apartment so that they could go to lunch. But Perry felt responsible for Beverly now. It was as Leavitt said: these witnesses became almost like family. He had no intention of leaving her in her apartment to die. He took her to the state mental hospital and spent the remainder of the day trying to get someone to commit her. The doctors didn't want to do it. "She'll just get worse in here," they told Perry. They suggested putting her into Valley Hospital. But that required Beverly's consent.

"I'll kill myself if you send me there," Beverly told Perry.

Finally he sat her down with a psychiatrist, who convinced her to check herself into Valley Hospital for a few days. On her fourth day there she began calling Perry every five minutes. She wanted out. She begged and pleaded, threatened and cajoled, until Perry called the psychiatrist, who suggested that he sign her out. So Perry signed her out and let her go back to her apartment.

She called Perry from Sunrise Hospital three days later. Kolojay had called her and said he was going to be indicted. If he was, he had told her, he was going to leave the country rather than go to jail. She got upset, thought it was all her fault, so she took more pills. "She came as close as you can come to dying," a nurse told Perry.

When she was released from the hospital, Beverly said she had a new boyfriend, a cab driver. So Perry took her to the trailer park where the cab driver lived and had a long talk with the man about Beverly's problems, to make sure he could take care of her.

A few nights later Beverly called. She said she was going back to her brother in Florida. She asked Perry to take her to the bus station at the Stardust, where the Greyhound bus stopped to take the gamblers out of town after they'd lost so much they could no longer afford air fare home. On the way Beverly told Perry about her last conversation with Kolojay after she left the hospital. He had told her that it would have been better if she'd died from the second over-dose of pills.

CHAPTER

Twenty-seven

"RECALL PETITION AT 70 PERCENT IN FIRST 14 DAYS."

The October 5, 1979, edition of the *Pahrump Valley Times* ran that headline in bold black letters above the lead story, which reported that 528 people had already signed the recall petition. Only 228 more signatures, the paper said, were needed. Below that was another bold headline to a second story: BARNETT BLASTS SHERIFF'S PRESS ACCUSATIONS AS DISSERVICE TO NYE. In it Glen Henderson's old friend, Nye County Commissioner Don Barnett, denied Joni Wine's claim that he had asked her to stop investigating people in Nye County. "I don't know what or who is behind all of these statements," Barnett said, "but they're misleading and they skirt the truth. This constant running off at the mouth with these half-baked charges seems to me to be a damn serious disservice to the county."

As if that wasn't bad enough for Joni Wines, on page two, editor Milt Bozanic published a letter he had received from Mr. and Mrs. Arnold Mason of Pittsburgh, Pennsylvania:

Recently we read of large scale crime, corruption, and white slavery in Pahrump in the national *Star* magazine.

We had planned to move and retire in Pahrump next year, but will hold off now until more information is received. We hope things will settle down, as we thought it was a nice valley.

Joni Wines was in deep trouble and, for the first time, she was trying to do something about it. On Monday, October 15, she scheduled a meeting at the Pahrump Community Center to face the people squarely and try to convince them that they should not recall her.

But it was too late. That morning the whole nation awoke to a brand-new issue of *Us* magazine. In it was a huge photograph of Joni Wines with a sweet, silly smile on her face and a World War II Thompson submachine gun in her hands. Standing behind her, broad grins on their faces, were Larry Massoli, Frank Homstad, and Deputy Tony Falcone, who had worked under Glen Henderson at Lathrop Wells until they had a bitter falling out. Below the photograph was the headline of the story: "A MACHINE-GUN TOTING GRANDMA TAMES HER WILD WEST TOWN."

It was just what the people of the Pahrump Valley wanted to hear. In another era they would have threatened to hang her at that meeting. By eight o'clock that evening any good that Joni Wines might have done at that meeting had already been undone by the photograph. Her opponents had made sure that everyone in the town who wasn't legally blind had seen a Xerox of the photo. Stacks of copies waited for those entering the cinder-block Community Center building just in case anyone was arriving at the meeting by way of Pakistan and hadn't already seen it.

The room was packed with almost one hundred people—men, women, and children—seated in rows of folding chairs. Another fifty stood behind them. The men were dressed in leisure suits or in jeans, plaid work shirts, and cowboy boots. Some carried a .22 inside a boot. The women were dressed in polyester pantsuits and big brightly colored blouses. Except for a few of Joni Wines's original supporters, the crowd was wholly composed of people who wanted to lynch the Sheriff. Or at least ride her out of town.

They were people who had moved out to the desert where they thought life would be easy. But the life had turned out not to be so easy. They could never escape from the sun, and the heat, and the wind. The wind never stopped blowing, swirling all around them, blowing the heat at them like a blast of air from an oven, picking up the fine white sand and blowing it into their eyes, blowing it till it caught in their ears and stuck to their faces and their clothes, blowing it till they could taste the fine white dust in their mouths.

There was a thick layer of dust everywhere in that room that night, and a lot of resentment. These people facing Joni Wines had worked all their lives to buy their plots of land in the desert, worked all their lives to buy the American dream. But the dream had not turned out quite the way they had planned. And now Joni Wines and all these young reporters were reminding them about it. And so a certain bitterness had set in around their eyes, and a certain hardness around their mouths. It was a hardness as hard as the land itself.

Joni Wines sat facing these people from behind a long folding table which was set up on a low platform in the front of the room. Larry Massoli sat on one side of her and Tony Falcone on the other. The yelling began from the moment the meeting opened. When a question was fired at the Sheriff, Massoli would try to answer for her. Then the crowd would yell, "Let her talk! Let her talk!" Joni Wines would start to answer in a soft voice, and the people would start to yell, "I can't hear you! I can't hear you!" Soon people in the crowd began to stand up and make speeches instead of asking questions. They were so angry their bodies shook. Fights broke out spontaneously in the crowd as people popped up out of their chairs and hurled invectives across the room.

At one point Jay Howard stood up and laid into Joni Wines, a pleasure he had clearly been looking forward to for a long time. Tony Falcone's feisty little platinum-blond wife happened to be sitting right in front of him. She stood up and turned around.

"Jay, you'd better shut your mouth," she said, "or I'll tell these people what kind of man you really are."

Jay Howard just snorted and kept talking.

"Jay Howard," Cindy Falcone insisted, "if I were you, I'd sit right down before I start tellin' 'em about all the stuff I heard while you were sheriff, while you were talkin' and playin' innocent." Her voice rose in accusation as the crowd became interested in what she was saying. "And you talk about corruption!" she shouted. "I'll tell 'em. I'll tell 'em all!"

Jay Howard sat abruptly on his folding chair and stared away from her. June Howard, sitting next to her husband, snapped at Mrs. Falcone, "You don't know anything."

"I know enough, so just drop it," Cindy Falcone said.

Jay Howard turned to his wife. "Just stop," he said. And she did.

The dramatic high point of the evening came when Tim Hafen, a former state assemblyman and one of Pahrump's largest landowners, stood up. It was on the road that bore his name—Hafen Ranch Road—that Walter Plankinton had opened the very first Chicken Ranch.

"I am sick and tired of all these accusations flying around and all these stories that everybody is being investigated," he said. "I want to know: Am I being investigated?"

"We haven't said we're investigating everybody," Massoli replied.

"I want to know if I'm being investigated," Hafen insisted.

"No," Joni Wines said, "you're not being investigated."

Jay Howard popped up out of his chair again. "I want to

know if I'm being investigated," he yelled up at the podium. "Tell me I'm not being investigated."

Joni Wines looked directly at him. "Well, I'm sorry, Jay, I can't tell you that. Because you are being investigated."

Wave after wave of laughter washed over the crowd as June Howard tugged at her husband's jacket to get him to sit back down.

But Joni Wines was not to have the last laugh. That Thursday she held another meeting in Beatty, where her only supporter was Brian Thayer, the former highway patrolman who had been first on the scene when Heidi, the prostitute who was running away from the Shamrock, was found dead by the side of her car. The meeting ended with Joni Wines on the platform in tears.

The following day Pete Bertolino, Joni's undersheriff, resigned, saying his farewell through the pages of the Pahrump Valley *Times*. He told a reporter that the Nye County Sheriff's Department was being run more like *Playgirl* magazine than a law enforcement office.

Monday morning *New West* magazine hit the stands with a full-page cover photo of Joni Wines standing in front of Larry Massoli and Frank Homstad. Portions of the story were read over KOLO-TV in Reno, which is picked up by viewers in Tonopah. The story sparked a new wave of petition signing, pushing the number to 926, or 170 more than necessary to hold the recall election.

The magazine article described Nye County as a place "where many of the men come when they feel burned out by Las Vegas and many of the women come in the company of a pimp." For weeks afterward the people of the county went around asking each other with bitter irony, "Did *you* come 'cause you felt burned out by Las Vegas?" And: "Did *you* come in the company of a pimp?"

On November 6, in Las Vegas, Larry Leavitt was lighting his first Carlton of the day and idly sorting through the heavy pile of mail that always awaited him on Monday mornings. He was thinking less of the mail than of his Saturday golf game with Perry. One of Leavitt's and Perry's great joys in life was beating a hotshot young Drug Enforcement Administration undercover agent. And they had done that on Saturday.

While Leavitt's mind was soaring through the deep-blue autumn desert sky, following a once-in-a-lifetime 140-yard drive with a nine iron that had put his ball eight inches from the cup, his eye fell on a letter in the middle of the pile. It was from the U.S. Bureau of Alcohol, Tobacco and Firearms.

He tore open the letter. It was from a chemist named Rick Tontarsky, who told Leavitt that, in his opinion, a mixture of gasoline and kerosene—the mixture that Easley said was used to light the Chicken Ranch fire—fell under the definition of "explosive" in federal statute 844(i).

"Jimmy, my boy," Leavitt yelled into the telephone not more than twenty seconds later, "we have a case!"

On November 15 Ellen Woods, Elmer Bailey, and Jerome Mundt, the leaders of the movement to recall Joni Wines, presented to the county clerk 1,119 signatures, 363 more than necessary, to set a date for a recall election. This time the clerk didn't have the heart to call Joni Wines. Instead she dialed Massoli, and Massoli walked down the hall and told his boss.

Joni Wines just stared straight ahead for a moment without saying a word. Then she looked away and whispered, almost to herself, "Oh, well, we figured they'd do it."

Judge Beko disqualified himself from presiding over the recall proceedings. David Zenoff, a former Nevada Supreme Court justice, was named to preside. The first matter to be decided was whether the signatures were valid or not, and Joni Wines—still too naïve for her own good—hired Plankinton's attorney, Leonard Smith, to represent her.

At the initial hearing the county clerk reported that only 22 of the 1,119 signatures were invalid. That left 1,037 valid signatures to contend with. Smith requested a continuance to give him time to examine the signatures. Judge Zenoff gave Smith and Wines two weeks to disqualify 301 signatures if they were to invalidate the recall petition.

That night Joni Wines went to Frank Homstad's house for a big spaghetti dinner, along with Larry Massoli and his wife, Robin, and Leonard Smith. Joni was beaten down by then. She sat through the whole dinner fighting back tears. She kept asking what had become of the federal indictments that were supposed to vindicate her. She couldn't understand why they were taking so long. She kept asking Marty Homstad, Frank's wife, and the others for some assurance that she might survive this ordeal with her dignity and peace of mind intact. But no one could honestly give her that assurance.

The Grand Jury charges:

> That on or about June 10, 1978, in the District of Nevada, defendants Kenneth Kolojay and James Luther Tatum did willfully, unlawfully, and maliciously, by means of an explosive, damage and destroy a brothel known as The Chicken Ranch, the said act of malicious destruction having been willfully and knowingly aided, abetted, procured and induced by defendant William Apfel, also known as William Martin.
>
> The Grand Jury further charges: That from on or about April 1, 1977, and continuously thereafter up to and including on or about June 13, 1978, in the District of Nevada and elsewhere, defendants William Apfel, also known as William Martin, Kenneth Kolojay, James Luther Tatum and Glen W. Henderson willfully and knowingly did combine, conspire, confederate, and agree together and with each other to maliciously damage and destroy, by means of an explosive, a brothel known as The Chicken Ranch, and to influence certain deputy sheriffs to ignore and neglect their duty promptly

to investigate the intended arson, and thereby place the
lives of the occupants thereof in extreme jeopardy.

It was nine-thirty on Monday morning, December 3, in
Las Vegas when Larry Leavitt finished reading the entire
seven-count, thirteen-page indictment to the twenty-three
grand jurors on the fourth floor of the United States Courthouse. In addition to the arson and conspiracy charges, the
indictment included the charge that Kolojay "corruptly in-
fluenced" Beverly Burton to lie to the grand jury, and that
Bill Martin, Jack Tatum, Glen Henderson, and Ken Kolojay perjured themselves before the same grand jury.

When Leavitt had finished, he and the court reporter left
the room and waited in the small grand-jury waiting room
—the one where Leavitt had first seen Bo Hyder and Glen
Henderson the day the grand jurors first heard about this
crazy case. Fifteen minutes later the foreman opened the
door. He told Leavitt the jury had decided to indict on all
counts. Careful to keep himself from smiling, Leavitt took
the indictment and signed it himself. Then, with the twenty-
three jurors in tow, he walked down a hallway to the magistrate's courtroom.

"Mr. Foreman," the magistrate said, "do you have a
report to make?"

"Yes, Your Honor. The grand jury has met and considered the matter of the arson at the Chicken Ranch
brothel and has today returned indictments in that matter."

The magistrate turned to Larry Leavitt. "Mr. Leavitt,
what is the government's pleasure?"

"Your Honor," Leavitt said, "the government seeks the
issuance of warrants for the arrest of William Apfel, also
known as William Martin, Kenneth Kolojay, Glen W. Henderson, and James Luther Tatum."

"It is so ordered," the magistrate said.

Leavitt and the magistrate's clerk took the indictment to
the federal court clerk's office on the third floor and waited
while arrest warrants were typed. Then Leavitt took the

arrest warrants back to his office and waited for a phone call from Perry, who was already on the highway with a convoy of nine FBI agents, in three unmarked cars, heading up to Lathrop Wells.

At eleven Perry called from a gas station at Mercury, at the entrance to the nuclear test site.

"We got it, Jimmy," Leavitt said excitedly, "all seven counts. Now you can go get those bastards."

"Dynamite," Perry said. "We're on our way."

"You know," Leavitt said to him before hanging up the phone, "this is the one time in my life I wish I was an agent."

All three cars pulled into the gravel parking lot at once. One car stopped in front of the Shamrock, one in front of Martin's house, and the other in the rear to prevent anyone from running out into the open desert undetected. The FBI agents got out and knelt down, laying shotguns over the hoods of the cars. They chambered rounds and aimed at the doorways of the ramshackle buildings.

Perry wanted to have Martin in handcuffs before any trouble started with Kolojay and the girls. So Perry and Dan Kelsay, his supervisor, went up to Martin's door. Perry knocked on the door. Martin's girlfriend Beverly Nichols opened it. Perry identified himself, though of course she knew who he was.

"I have a warrant for the arrest of William Apfel, also known as William Martin," he said.

"He's just gone across the street to get the mail," she said, pointing to the post office on the other side of the highway.

"May we come in and search the house?" Perry asked.

"Yes," she said.

Perry and Kelsay drew their revolvers and walked into the front room. The sunlight was against them, making it hard to see inside, putting them at a disadvantage. They went through the house quickly, pointing their guns into each room before entering it, then moving to the next. They weren't so much searching for anything as they were clearing the area to make sure there weren't any surprises waiting for them. They didn't want anyone hurt, especially not themselves.

Perry drew back a curtain. Outside, the other agents were still poised, kneeling with their shotguns thrown over the hoods of the cars. A truck rumbled past on the main road. Perry walked out into the sun and crossed the highway to the post office. One of the agents turned around to follow his progress and cover him with a scattergun.

Perry pushed the post office door open and asked the postmaster, "Where's Bill Martin?"

"Bill hasn't been in yet this morning. A girl picked up the mail."

So Martin's girlfriend was lying.

Perry walked back across the highway and went into the Coach House Bar. He approached the British barmaid, Pam, and told her he had a warrant for Martin's arrest.

She was as tough as she could be. She hadn't seen him, she said, she'd check his office. She went to the office behind the bar. A couple of minutes later she came back, saying he wasn't there.

"There's a federal statute that makes it a crime to harbor a fugitive," Perry said to Pam. "If he's in there, we're taking you with us, too."

Pam was still swearing that Martin was not there when the walkie-talkie spoke up: Kolojay was coming out of the back door of the Shamrock. Perry and Kelsay hurried out and found Kolojay standing there talking with the FBI, innocent and friendly as a hound.

"Hi, Jim, what do you want me to do?" he asked.

"You're under arrest," Perry said, snapping on a pair of handcuffs. "You have the right to remain silent. . . ."

The other agents drew their revolvers and went into the brothel to look for Martin.

Perry put Kolojay into a car, then went back into the bar. He told Pam that he was going to search Martin's office. The five-foot-six-inch woman moved to block the door. Perry grabbed her and threw her over the bar and moved toward the office. Pam came at him with all her 145 pounds and caught him in the back with her fist.

"FBI, Martin, open up. We have an arrest warrant for you."

The demand was met with complete silence.

"FBI, Martin! Open up. If you don't, we'll have to break down the door."

Silence.

One of the agents banged on the door.

"Come on, let's break it down."

Silence.

"Come on . . ."

Suddenly the door swung silently open and out walked Bill Martin, pale and drained.

"William Apfel, you are under arrest . . ."

One of the agents snapped a pair of handcuffs as Martin said, "Can I take that envelope?" indicating a thick accordion envelope on his desk.

"What's in it?"

"Some cash for bail," he said.

When they had Martin safely put away, a few agents went down the highway and rounded up old Glen Henderson. The former Nye County sheriff's lieutenant had only two things to say. He had to call a neighbor to feed his goat, Betsy, and he had always thought the FBI was the highest caliber of law enforcement.

CHAPTER

Twenty-eight

Out on the desert small whirlwinds occur from time to time. They are called dust devils, and they come up for no apparent reason. They whirl around, catching whatever is not tacked down, lift it high into the air, and then, again for no reason and without apparent cause, they disappear, leaving whatever they have carried to fall back to the ground some distance away.

So it was with the people of Nye County. In the Christmas season of 1979 something whipped the people into a frenzy. Judge Beko blamed it on the press a few months later, when it was all over. And what the people picked up during that frenzy was Joni Wines. They picked her up, spun her around, and set her down in a heap without so much as a please and thank you.

The federal indictments only served to harden the will of Joni Wines's opponents and make them even angrier than they had been before. There was a hysterical pitch to everyone's voice; everyone became a great cross-examiner. "Is that firsthand information," they would demand, "or is that just hearsay?" One day Lola Binum, the woman who had first dared Joni Wines to run for office, got into an argument with a Pahrump man in the parking lot at Saddle West. When he grabbed her arm in the middle of the fight, she pulled away from him and cracked a bone in her elbow.

During November and December of 1979, Joni Wines's women friends spent hours in the County Clerk's Office on the first floor of the Tonopah courthouse comparing the names and addresses on the voter-registration lists against the signatures on the recall petition. They managed to find discrepancies on 308 names—seven more than they needed to invalidate the petition. The signatures they sought to disqualify were those of people who had not signed their middle initials, people who had forgotten to list their addresses, people who had neglected to place "Mr." or "Mrs." before their names.

On December 14, 1979, eleven days before Christmas, Leonard Smith presented the list of signatures to Judge Zenoff, who gave the recall supporters until January 8 to reply to the challenges. Throughout the holiday weeks, the recall leaders worked frantically to contact every one of the 308 people on Joni Wines's list to gather proof that their signatures were valid.

As the weeks went by, the frenzy increased. A Recall Trust Fund was established. The Pahrump Valley *Times* published the 308 names to encourage those people to come forward. And a "caravan of Pahrump signators" was organized to take the Tonopah courthouse by storm on January 8 and argue that their signatures should be counted.

Throughout those weeks, it was Joni Wines and the women who supported her who seemed to suffer the most. One of them was Donna Scarlett, a tall, lean woman with a sun-weathered face whose family had been one of the first to settle Pahrump in the early 1950s, when the government was conducting open-air nuclear tests nearby. There had been no electricity back then, no telephone, and no indoor plumbing. And only rutted dirt roads to take you in and out of the valley. Donna Scarlett had married and moved to Las Vegas and had been divorced. Then she had remarried and moved back into the valley. Now she sold mobile homes for a living.

"My own relatives turned against me because of my believing in the same things that Mrs. Wines believed in," she said. "Boy, you couldn't walk down the street without starting a fight. They would all tell me, 'This is none of Joni Wines's business. She's prying into business that doesn't concern her at all.' Everybody stayed home 'cause they didn't want to meet each other. The stores suffered. We were renting two acres from my aunt and uncle and it got so bad in our family that my husband and I were forced to leave because of the recall.

"Friends that were friends for many years weren't friends any longer. It got so bad in the school that this little blond girl of mine, she got so upset I took her to a doctor. She was trying to be a friend to everybody and it tore this child up. She wanted to leave Pahrump. 'I hate it, Mom,' she kept saying. 'I hate it.' It was unbearable."

Joni Wines hated it, too. Leonard Smith told her they could keep fighting in the courts and postpone the recall election for six months. But she had no intention of forcing herself, and everyone in Nye County, to live through six more months like this. She didn't even go to the January 8 court hearing to face the "caravan of Pahrump signators." Leonard Smith went in her stead.

He walked into the courtroom, approached the bench, and told the Judge, "Your Honor, the Sheriff has asked that we stop all arguments and call for a recall election as soon as possible."

The courtroom was as still as the desert after a sandstorm. Then people began to whisper, "What did he say? What did he say?" and a general rumbling of startled voices overtook the courtroom.

Judge Zenoff split the sound with his gavel and announced that there would be a ten-minute recess. When he came back, he set the date for the recall election: Tuesday, February 5, 1980.

Joni Wines was defeated by almost two votes to one. In the end she never fully understood the complex issues she had become caught up in, issues of public leadership and public pride, issues of personal power and political protection. She was sad and bewildered that night. She kept saying she didn't know why people did not want her to investigate the fire, or to help out that pitiful little Beverly Burton.

As soon as Joni Wines realized that the election was over, she drove her white Nye County Sheriff's car over to the Pahrump sheriff's station, while Blaine followed in the family's Honda. When they walked through the front door, everyone from the department was standing around in silence. Without saying a word to anyone, they went straight to her desk and started putting her personal belongings in brown supermarket bags they had brought from home. While they were doing that, Pat Edenfield, her former campaign manager and best friend, walked into the station.

"It's a bust," she said quietly to the dispatcher.

"I know," he said.

Then Pat Edenfield walked over to Joni, who was standing behind her desk, crying.

"Get away from me," was all Joni said.

By midnight, Joni and Blaine had packed their car and were headed north on the interstate out of Nye County. While Joni slept, curled up on the Honda's small back seat, Blaine drove right through Lathrop Wells, where Bill Martin and Kenny Kolojay were celebrating at the Coach House Bar. Two hours later, he drove, unnoticed, through Tonopah, where Peter Knight sat at the Mizpah bar, celebrating with John Adams, Bill Beko's other protégé.

The next morning in Nye County, Frank Homstad received a message from one of Glen Henderson's friends. The message said: "Once you drop your badge, you're fair game." That same morning, Larry Massoli picked up the telephone at his Pahrump trailer and a disembodied voice left the same warning: "Drop your badge and you're fair game."

Massoli immediately called Jim Perry in Las Vegas and asked Perry to have some men available in case they needed help before they were able to get their wives and children out of town. Then the two men packed everything they owned into their cars, pulled their kids out of school, and as quickly as they could, left Nye County.

The good old boys on the Nye County Board of Commissioners—the men Walter Plankinton had opposed when he first came to Nye County to set up his business in 1976—appointed Harold "Stick" Davis as the new sheriff. He was a quiet, unassuming eighteen-year veteran of the department who could be counted on not to make waves. Judge Beko presided over the swearing in of the new Sheriff before a packed courtroom. After the ceremony Beko lashed out at the press for trying people in the media instead of in the courts. "The last fourteen months," he said, "have been a period of greater political and personal turmoil than I can remember during the fifty-seven years of my residence in this county."

What he didn't know was that it was about to get worse.

Back in December, even as Bill Martin was paying his bail with the $40,000 cash he had stuffed into that brown envelope before the FBI banged on his door, newspaper reporters were interviewing Peter Knight and Bill Beko. Knight told the *Sun* that Bill Martin and Glen Henderson were "sound, law-abiding citizens." Beko said, "The indictment hasn't changed my mind one iota. I still don't think they would be involved in any criminal activity."

Since Beko and Knight had already declared Martin and Henderson innocent, it should have come as no surprise when Knight decided to make sure a federal-court jury would do the same. Three weeks after Henderson's arrest, Knight, who had done virtually nothing to investigate the arson when it occurred, assigned John Adams to the case. Adams was the man Bill Beko had persuaded Joni Wines to hire as her lieutenant, the same man who had told her the Sheriff's Department did not have the resources to investigate the Chicken Ranch arson. He had quit the Sheriff's Department after Massoli had gotten the Easley confession, and had gone to work as an investigator for Knight.

One of the first calls Adams made was to Jack Ruggles, who had just been hired as an investigator for the U.S. Public Defender's Office in Las Vegas and assigned to work on Glen Henderson's defense. Ruggles was no stranger to the people in the Chicken Ranch arson case. In one of those bizarre coincidences that could happen only in a small, Byzantine state like Nevada, Ruggles had been a Las Vegas city policeman in the early 1950s and had walked a beat with a former New York City cop named Bill Apfel. Ruggles was also a longstanding acquaintance of Bill Beko.

Ruggles and Adams met at Henderson's trailer in the Amargosa Valley and then spent the next few days in Lathrop Wells and Pahrump, interviewing people about the case. Then, on January 16, the two drove to Modesto to see what they could find out about Elbert Easley. When Modesto Police Detective Steve McDonough saw the two walk into his office, he looked at his buddy Ron Ridenour and said, "*What* are these two guys doing together?"

McDonough and Ridenour decided this was too strange for them. They told Ruggles and Adams they weren't going to talk. Then they called Mike Land, the assistant district attorney who had prosecuted Easley. "Look," Land said, "I don't know what the hell's going on in that county, but we might as well just tell them the truth and let the chips fall where they may."

So McDonough and Ridenour took Adams and Ruggles to a bar near the station. "They told us what a good old boy Glen was," McDonough would later tell a Nye County grand jury. "And what a 'dingbat' Joni Wines was. They

really put her away. Then they went into a spiel about how
Bill Martin would never mess with any of this. By the end
of the conversation, there was no question that Adams was
looking to get these guys off.''

While McDonough was suspicious of what Ruggles and
Adams were doing together—a highly questionable state of
affairs in and of itself—Frank Homstad, the quiet country
boy, could not have been more trusting. As soon as they
returned from Modesto, Adams and Ruggles took Homstad
to a bare office in the Tonopah courthouse, turned on a
tape recorder, and started to talk to him about what a great
joker Glen Henderson was. Yes, Homstad told them as the
tape reels turned, Glen was a great joker. In fact, he was
such a great joker that you really could not tell when he
was kidding and when he was being serious.
  The next morning a rather sheepish-sounding Frank
Homstad called Larry Leavitt. When Leavitt heard what
Homstad had done, he was enraged. Those bastards, he
said to himself, quickly lighting a cigarette, they're trying
to break my case. He called Perry and told him to get up to
his office right away.
  "I want you to call Peter Knight," he said. "I want that
bastard to know that we know what he's up to. Tell him we
heard he was out investigating the Chicken Ranch arson
case. Then tell him, if he comes up with anything good,
we'd like him to let us know." Leavitt grinned broadly. He
leaned back in his old leather-backed chair, and, with a
broad smile wreathing his face, sat and listened as Perry
placed the call.
  "It was amazing," Perry said as soon as he put down the
receiver. "Knight didn't even know what to say. I've never
seen a lawyer who didn't know how to handle himself in
that kind of conversation. He was so flabbergasted he
couldn't even talk. He really didn't say anything. He
couldn't get a complete sentence together."

"I love it!" Leavitt said.

With that telephone call completed, Leavitt turned to his next order of business. He grabbed a copy of the *Nevada Revised Statutes* and looked up the laws governing the conduct of district attorneys, to wit: "No District Attorney or partner thereof shall appear within his county as attorney in any criminal action, or directly or indirectly aid, counsel or assist in the defense in any criminal action, begun or prosecuted during his term."

Then Leavitt placed one more telephone call. He dialed the Nye County Sheriff's Office in Tonopah and asked to speak to Larry Massoli.

"I just feel obliged as a good citizen," Leavitt coyly said to Perry while he was waiting, "to bring the statute to his attention."

Larry Massoli, in turn, picked up the telephone and read the statute to Ed Ostrander, an irascible former Detroit cop who was chairman of the Nye County grand jury and one of the few people left in Nye County in those weeks before the recall election who still believed in Joni Wines.

At 1:45 P.M. on March 11, 1980, at the Tonopah Convention Center, Peter Knight stood, flushed and nervous, before the Nye County grand jury, to try to explain why he had not investigated the Chicken Ranch arson in June 1978, and why he had only decided to investigate it in December of 1979 after Martin, Henderson, and Kolojay were finally indicted.

As a special prosecutor, who had been appointed to conduct the unusual investigation, hammered away at Knight, juror Pat Thayer, who had rented a house from Knight when she and her husband first moved to Beatty, watched him sink lower and lower in his seat. It was her husband, Highway Patrolman Brian Thayer, who had found the crushed and bleeding body of Heidi, the young prostitute from the Shamrock.

When the special prosecutor was finished wringing Peter Knight out, the Nye County District Attorney walked over to Pat Thayer as if he was looking for a friend. He said he had a terrible headache, and asked her if she had any aspirin.

Pat Thayer just stared at Knight. Buddy, she said to herself, are you ever asking the wrong person.

Twenty-nine

The desert winter burned into spring, and the grim business grew even grimmer. Kolojay's attorney, Paul Schofield, filed a motion asking Federal Judge Roger Foley to dismiss all charges on the grounds that the Chicken Ranch fire was not set by an "explosive." Schofield submitted statements from the Las Vegas Fire Department Bomb Squad saying that the mixture of gasoline and kerosene that Easley said they had used was not an explosive at all, only an accelerant. Judge Foley took the motion under consideration, and the possibility that the entire prosecution would fall apart on that technicality hung over the case on into the summer.

In the meantime, the same desert wind that had picked up Joni Wines and shaken her picked up Larry Leavitt and began to make him wonder why he had ever started this case. Jack Tatum, who had been arrested at his sister's house in Roseville, California, and had been transferred to the North Las Vegas jail, gave a message to a guard that he wanted to see Perry. When the guard called Perry, she told him that a man named Kenny Kolojay had visited Tatum several times since Tatum arrived there. She said that the day before, when Tatum had said he wanted to see Perry, he had just gotten a message from Kolojay. The message was that Kolojay wouldn't be coming to visit Tatum today, but he would try to get money for Tatum's bail as soon as possible.

Without checking with Leavitt, Perry went straight over to see Tatum. Tatum told Perry he wanted to cut a deal. He had a bad heart, he said, and he didn't want to die in prison. He had firsthand information he could give them. Perry went back to the courthouse and up to Leavitt's office.

"I think we should do it," he said excitedly. "We really need him. We can't just rely on Beverly and Easley. They're such flaky witnesses."

Leavitt was much cooler to the idea. "Before we even contemplate talking to him," he said, "I think you should go back and ask him a few questions to get a hint of whether he can really tell us anything."

So Perry drove back across town to the North Las Vegas jail, and Tatum told him yes, he could give them firsthand information about the fire. Then he said he could also give them information about possible criminal involvement on the part of the district judge up there, Judge Beko, and the district attorney, Peter Knight.

Perry was as excited about this case as he'd been since the day Walter Plankinton first walked into his office over three years before. He drove back to the courthouse and told Leavitt, who picked up the phone and called Ted Manos, a criminal attorney the court had appointed to represent Tatum.

"Go see your client," Leavitt said.

So Manos went to see his client and called Leavitt the next day. "He's willing to talk," Manos said. "But he wants a pass. He doesn't want to do any time."

Perry wanted to cut the deal. But Leavitt wanted none of it. For the first time since they had started work on the case, Perry and Leavitt began to argue. The more they argued about it, the more adamant Leavitt got.

"It is absolutely unacceptable," he told Perry. "Here I have a star witness who's a condemned murderer on Death

Row in San Quentin who's not going to be prosecuted for this arson. Can you imagine me then rolling in Tatum, a guy who's looking at eleven unexpired years on a parole term, and cutting him loose, too? I mean, I would never live that down."

On April 16, things got even worse. Ken Cory, the federal public defender representing Glen Henderson, walked into Leavitt's office that day carrying a tape recorder. He told Leavitt he wanted to talk about dismissing the indictment against Henderson. Cory said that Henderson would deny some of the conversation that took place that hot spring day in 1977 in the Nye County patrol car with Larry Massoli and Frank Homstad. Then Glen would explain the rest by saying he was just joking. To seal his case, Cory placed the tape recorder in front of Leavitt and played a portion of the interview Peter Knight's investigator, John Adams, and Cory's investigator, Jack Ruggles, had conducted with Homstad.

Leavitt knew when he was beaten. He had worried about Henderson from the day he first saw him in the grand-jury room. He was the kind of defendant who could charm a jury and dilute the case Leavitt had against three far less charming men: Martin, Kolojay, and Tatum. As soon as Cory clicked off the tape recorder, Leavitt looked up at him. Without a trace of any emotion in his face, he said, "What can Glen do for us?"

"I'll bring him in this afternoon and we can talk," Cory replied.

At noon that day, as Leavitt was leaving the courthouse for lunch, he was stopped by one of the security guards.

"Hey, you know that young hooker who's your star witness in the whorehouse case?" he said. "She was here today with Ruggles. She was up in the Public Defender's Office."

"Oh, my God," Leavitt said.

Beverly Burton had switched sides again.

• • •

Glen Henderson lumbered into Larry Leavitt's office in the hands of Ken Cory and Jack Ruggles. He was dressed in his rumpled old khaki pants and a bright-red shirt. He crammed his enormous body into one of the old leather chairs that sat in front of Leavitt's desk, and stared at Leavitt. Boy, Leavitt thought to himself, you can feel the heat in this room.

Leavitt was as cool and correct as he could be. He told Henderson that he would agree to dismiss all charges against him in exchange for some kind of statement. But even as he said it, Leavitt realized that this indignant old man sitting before him was not going to give him one bit of useful information.

"Sure Bill Martin complained about Plankinton," Henderson said. "He said: 'This son of a bitch is causing a lot of trouble, he ought to get his head busted.' But that's just ordinary talk. You don't take that talk seriously. About Blackwell, I wouldn't be surprised if there was some kind of a deal between Blackwell and Jay Howard about not responding to the fire. But I don't know anything about it." Then Henderson decided to volunteer a little information about Blackwell that he knew would be no use to anyone. "He's hooker crazy," Henderson barked. "He likes to go to whorehouses like dogs go to garbage."

As soon as the three men left his office, Leavitt got himself a cup of coffee, then sat down, lit a cigarette and dialed Jim Perry. The whirlwind had caught Leavitt and would not let him go. He was tired and he was angry. He was supposed to be running the show, directing his prosecution, but the show was directing him.

"I really felt silly," he told Perry. "I've never given that much away without getting anything from a defendant. I'm almost ashamed of myself."

• • •

In Tonopah on April 6, while the secret negotiations between Glen Henderson and Larry Leavitt were still taking place, the Nye County grand jury voted to indict Peter Knight for using his office to assist Henderson in his legal defense. After Ed Ostrander, the foreman, had signed the indictment, he and the deputy forewoman, and the grand-jury secretary, walked into Judge Beko's office to present the indictment to him.

Beko was distraught. He pleaded with the three grand-jury officers not to indict his young protégé. "I know Peter wouldn't do anything illegal," he said. He sounded like a father talking about his son. "If he was doing anything illegal I would know about it, and I wouldn't tolerate it."

Then Beko got tough. He said he knew that the Assistant U.S. Attorney in Las Vegas, Larry Leavitt, was going to drop his charges against Henderson.

"Obviously you'll look silly charging Peter Knight with a gross misdemeanor for assisting in his defense," Beko said, "when the charges are going to be dropped."

Ed Ostrander was startled to hear that Beko knew about what most surely were secret negotiations between Henderson and Leavitt. But he didn't say anything. Beko handed back the indictment to Ostrander and asked the grand jury to reconsider.

In the four years since Walter Plankinton had arrived in Pahrump to open his brothel and begin the bitter struggle that had torn Nye County apart, Bill Beko had managed to stay out of the fray. He had managed to preserve his image of the county judge who no longer let himself be drawn into petty political squabbles—a man above and apart, always disqualifying himself instead of presiding over matters in which he could be said to be personally involved. But this time he had stepped right into the middle of it.

Ten days later the Associated Press ran the story on news wires all over the state:

Fifth District Judge William P. Beko of Tonopah, Nevada, has asked the Nye County Grand Jury to reconsider the indictment issued against his close friend and former legal partner, Nye County District Attorney Peter L. Knight, charging the District Attorney with assisting former Nye County Sheriff's Lieutenant Glen Henderson in his defense in the Chicken Ranch arson case.

The story said that Beko had asked the grand jury to reconsider the indictment because he knew that the federal prosecutor in Las Vegas was going to drop the charges against Henderson. The entire sticky web of intrigue and collusion, now exposed to the light of statewide publicity, looked even worse than anyone had suspected it would.

Beko was quick to respond. "I do not intend to dignify rumors reportedly made by 'unnamed reliable sources' or other crackpots who don't know what the hell they are talking about," he said. He told reporters that his conduct with the grand jury had been "totally and completely consistent with the law."

That same afternoon in Las Vegas, Larry Leavitt signed the order dismissing the case against Henderson. As soon as the order was filed in the clerk's office, the courthouse reporters called Ken Cory. Cory told them that if Henderson was called as a witness in the Chicken Ranch arson trial he would testify about what he knew. "It's our position," Cory said, "that he doesn't know much about what occurred."

The following night Bill Martin threw a party in the gravel parking lot of the Coach House Bar for everyone who wanted to celebrate Henderson's good fortune. The drinks were on the house. A rock band played in the parking lot, and even the new Sheriff, Stick Davis, showed up to hoist a couple in Henderson's honor. Bill Martin spent the night telling everyone that it was only a matter of time before all the indictments were thrown out, just like Henderson's. This case, everyone in Lathrop Wells agreed that night, was never going to go to trial.

• • •

Eleven days later the Nye County grand jury voted again to indict Peter Knight. This time Beko didn't try to block it. It was too late for him to do anything to help his protégé. As soon as the indictment was returned, Knight told reporters he had no intention of stepping down as district attorney.

Judge Beko, as he had been forced to do so many times in the last four years, disqualified himself from hearing the case. Judge Joseph O. McDaniel of Elko, a former district attorney, was appointed to preside in his place. Knight's attorney filed a fifty-six-page petition asking McDaniel to dismiss the case because "there is no evidence that Knight did anything illegal." McDaniel agreed. He responded with his own lengthy ruling that included a ringing defense of Peter Knight and Nye County. "The facts of this case did not occur during normal times in Nye County," he wrote. "They were troubled and uncertain times." Then he blamed most of that trouble on Joni Wines and dismissed the case against Knight. The day the decision was handed down a triumphant Peter Knight told the Tonopah *Times-Bonanza* that the decision represented "a vindication of me, my office, and Nye County."

That summer of 1980 was a terrible time for the men and women who had tried to solve the Chicken Ranch arson case. They had been waiting for so many years to see some action taken, had waited so many years to see someone go to jail, that in that hot Nevada summer even they were beginning to believe what Bill Martin was saying: that this case was never going to go to trial.

Larry Leavitt had broken up with his girlfriend, Barbara, and had moved out of the house they had shared. He was living alone again, in a summer rental, and looking for a town house to buy. He and Perry had come down from their high of the year before when they had, back to back, successfully prosecuted two political-corruption cases.

This summer they were working the routine cases that come in and out of the federal courthouse.

Joni Wines was living in Las Vegas and filling out applications for secretarial jobs at the Las Vegas City Licensing Department and Southern Nevada Memorial Hospital. Frank Homstad, unable to find a job on a police force, was working the night shift as a security guard at a Pomona, California, Miller Beer plant.

Larry Massoli and his wife, Robin, and their two young children were living in Las Vegas with his mother-in-law while he tried to find work. He applied for a job with the North Las Vegas Police Department and was told he didn't get it because he was a "troublemaker." "You're righteous, and what does righteous get you?" Robin Massoli asked that summer. "Righteous doesn't pay the rent. Righteous doesn't put food on the table. Sorry, they say, we don't want someone with integrity. We want someone who keeps his mouth shut." They were discouraged, fed up, resentful. They thought they were never going to get any good news.

On a 115-degree day at the end of July, they finally got some. That afternoon Judge Foley filed the ruling everyone had waited all summer for, the ruling on whether the indictments should be dismissed because the fire at the Chicken Ranch had not been started by an "explosive."

> This Court is unprepared to conclude that the United States could not, by appropriate testimony or other evidence, show that the means used to start the fire at the Chicken Ranch does indeed fall within the definition of the statute. In view of the foregoing, the Motion to Dismiss filed on behalf of Defendant Kolojay is hereby denied.

Then Judge Foley added one last sentence to the ruling: "The Clerk of the Court is directed to set this case for trial."

CHAPTER
Thirty

It was one of those events that had gone beyond being merely an event. It had developed its own subculture, the way the rodeo, or a rock concert tour, or the big-top circus does. And now, on November 18, 1980, the first day of the trial, everyone who was anyone in the Chicken Ranch arson case was showing up for the denouement.

Joni Wines was there with Pat Edenfield, and Pat's daughter, Michelle. Lola Binum was there. Glen Henderson was there, roaming the hallways in his rumpled khaki pants and a bright-yellow sports shirt. John Adams was there, as was Jack Ruggles. Walter Plankinton was there, sitting nervously in a corner, waiting to be the first to be called to testify.

The only one missing was Jim Perry, the man who might be called the father of the Chicken Ranch prosecution. In September, two months before, he had been promoted to supervisor of white-collar crime in Nevada and could no longer assist Leavitt in the day-to-day presentation of the case. He had to stay at his desk, two floors below, and anxiously wait for reports from Leavitt.

On the right side of the courtroom, Leavitt sat at a long

glass-topped walnut conference table next to FBI agent
John Bailey, who would assist Leavitt during the trial. Although he had lost only four out of the sixty-five cases he
had tried since becoming a lawyer, Leavitt still had the
butterflies in his stomach that he always had on the first
day of a trial.

At the front and center of the room, at the high wooden
bench behind which hung the bronze seal of the United
States, sat Judge Roger Foley. A slight man with a balding
head who looked much older than his sixty-three years,
Foley peered out over the courtroom through oversized
horn-rimmed glasses. On the left side of the room sat the
three defendants and their attorneys, all uncomfortably
crowded together at another conference table.

Jack Tatum sat at one end of the table, staring, as he
would for the entire length of the trial, at no particular spot
in the room. Martin and Kolojay sat on opposite sides of
the table, facing each other. They chatted across the table,
smirking and laughing as though they had not a care in the
world. They had about them the cocky manner of two men
who knew they shouldn't be in the courtroom, two men
who knew the government didn't have a case against them,
but who were willing to just sit there and wait it out until
the trial was over and the jury had returned a verdict in
their favor.

At nine-thirty on Wednesday morning, November 19, after
the jury had been selected and the opening arguments had
been made, Judge Foley turned to Larry Leavitt and ordered that the testimony begin.

"Mr. Leavitt, you may call your first witness."

"Walter Plankinton," Leavitt said.

At the back of the courtroom the double doors opened,
and Plankinton walked in and took his seat in the high-
backed leather witness chair that sat on a platform between
Judge Foley's bench and the jury. Plankinton's voice was

shaking slightly as Leavitt slowly and carefully took him through the events that had led up to the fire. There was none of the bravado that usually characterized his speech, none of the swaggering talk. Today he was determined to sound low-key and earnest.

By the time Leavitt brought him up to June 10, 1978, Plankinton had settled down on the witness stand and was ready to bring his own special touch of drama to the night he heard that the Chicken Ranch had burned.

"I was in Las Vegas," he said. He turned to face the jurors, and his voice began to quaver. "Around five o'clock in the morning, my son called me and informed me that the Ranch had just been attacked by some individuals, that gasoline or something of that nature had been spewed around and set afire . . ." Plankington paused. His voice cracked. ". . . and that the Ranch was gone."

Leavitt let a few seconds of silence go by.

"Did the Nye County Sheriff's Department," he asked Plankinton, "undertake an investigation to determine who was responsible for the fire?"

"No," Plankinton answered emphatically. "The morning of the fire, there was no response on behalf of the Nye County Sheriff's Office."

At the defense table, Kenny Kolojay's lawyer, Paul Schofield, jumped to his feet.

"Your Honor!" he said. "I object to that last answer and ask that it be stricken. He stated that he was in Las Vegas. I wouldn't think that he had any personal knowledge . . ."

Judge Foley nodded in agreement. "Yes," he said, "based on hearsay, Mr. Leavitt. It will be stricken. The jury will disregard."

Leavitt wasn't going to let that stop him.

"Were you ever interviewed during that period of time, June of 1978, by Nye County sheriff's deputies concerning the fire?" he asked Plankinton.

Plankinton realized exactly what Leavitt wanted. He turned to face the jurors and delivered his answer slowly and emphatically.

"I don't ever recall being interviewed to this day by the Nye County Sheriff's Department about the fire."

By eleven-thirty the same morning, after Leavitt had gotten the $15,000 payment for Easley's appeal on the record to be completely up front about it and get it out of the way, he turned Plankinton over to the defense. They started, as they would with every witness, with Kolojay's lawyer, Paul Schofield, a tall man with a lanky, aw-shucks walk. Schofield seemed the least prepared of the lawyers in the courtroom, occasionally confusing dates and locations of events so badly that members of the jury shook their heads in embarrassment. Schofield would be followed by Tatum's court-appointed attorney, Ted Manos, who would start to tighten the screws on Leavitt's witnesses. A small, excitable overweight man, Manos paced the courtroom, trying to unnerve prosecution witnesses by rushing up to the podium and, without letting a second slip by, firing away with a series of short, rapid questions.

Manos was followed by Bill Martin's attorney, Charlie Waterman, who would turn the screws on Leavitt's witnesses all the way. Waterman was like a viper. Tall, white-haired, he wore his clothes in various shades of pink and red, blue and black. He strutted around the courtroom, his voice dripping with sarcasm, sweeping his arm across the room, waving his glasses, staring with cold blue eyes, and taunting the witnesses with street talk: "Ya lied, didn't ya? Didn't ya, ya lied, didn't ya, didn't ya, didn't ya!"

Waterman had come into this courtroom not only to defend Bill Martin, but also to defend Bill Beko, Peter Knight, and all of Nye County against the lies and accusations of this "pimp" named Walter Plankinton. Waterman said his style was simply part of his strategy: that if he made it clear how angry he was, the jury would feel angry, too. But it seemed more than that. Joni Wines had publicly accused him of offering her $3,500 from "two men in Lathrop

Wells,'' an offer Joni Wines had said she considered a bribe, and he had had to live with that every day, waiting for the chance to get even.

It had come now. And as he expressed his personal rage, he also expressed the frustration and rage of the people of Nye County, not only a rage at what had been said of that place, but a rage born of the place itself, a rage born out of a century of enduring the sun and the wind and the sand and the heat every day.

The only thing Leavitt knew about Waterman was that he had won a recent victory in federal court in a labor racketeering case. The jurors in that case had said that if they needed an attorney, they would want someone like Charlie Waterman. That scared Leavitt. It was clear from the first day of cross-examination that the outcome would depend upon whether the jury responded to the cool, controlled, cautious manner of Larry Leavitt or the outrage of Charlie Waterman.

Waterman lit into Plankinton with all the pent-up furies of Nye County.

"So far now, Mr. Plankinton, who have ya included in the Tonopah Mafia? Certainly ya included Pete Knight, who ya say solicited a bribe of seventy-five thousand dollars?"

"That's right," Plankinton said. "Correct."

Waterman waved his glasses at Plankinton. "And certainly ya included Bill Beko, because ya said repeatedly, publicly, that Bill Beko was a part of the Tonopah Mafia! Isn't that right?"

Plankinton nodded. "Bill Beko is the smart man there," he said.

After letting Plankinton dig himself a hole, explaining that Bill Beko was the head of the Tonopah Mafia, Waterman shouted, "What evidence do ya have of that, Mr. Plankinton?"

"It is just a general trend of things," he said. "Mr. Beko gives the orders . . ."

"Evidence, Mr. Plankinton!" Waterman yelled, waving his outstretched arm. "What evidence do ya have of that?"

Plankinton slumped slightly in the big leather witness chair. "I don't have any evidence, sir," he said.

Waterman waltzed up and down the courtroom, getting Plankinton's anger up, stopping him short, leading him by the nose, then tripping him up. Plankinton, completely unprepared for a broadside artist such as Waterman, walked right into the traps. At the defense table, Martin and Kolojay nodded and smiled as if to say to everyone, "We told you so."

With a minute to go before the midday recess, Waterman screamed at Plankinton, "The reason ya have gone around the length and breadth of Nye County saying these things is because ya have a paranoid idea, is it not, Mr. Plankinton, that ya must get your way. And when they wouldn't let ya open a brothel, ya decided to get them. Didn't ya?"

"That's not correct!" Plankinton yelled helplessly.

Waterman turned and walked toward the defense table. " 'That's not correct,' " he muttered sarcastically under his breath, just loud enough for the jury to hear.

During the break Leavitt tried to make up for the coaching he clearly should have given Plankinton before, but it was little use. Waterman forced Plankinton to accuse Beko of outright corruption. And when Plankinton couldn't come up with solid evidence to back the accusation, Waterman made mincemeat out of him. Plankinton ended the day shaking and sweating, his voice quavering, defending his statements by saying, "Fourteen of my friends and my oldest son pretty nearly perished in that fire."

Charlie Waterman and Walter Plankinton continued to skirmish for the rest of the long afternoon. At the end it was hard to tell who had been hurt the most by the cross-examination, Waterman or Plankinton. Near the very end

of the day, an angry Charlie Waterman asked Judge Foley
to admonish Plankinton to answer a question. Judge Foley
stared slowly out over the courtroom, then leveled his gaze
at Waterman. "If I start handing out admonitions," he
said, "I don't think you'd be too pleased."

At that moment the jury exploded into bursts of loud
laughter. As they continued laughing, their bodies visibly
relaxed, as though they were relieved that the afternoon of
unrelenting cross-examination was finally over.

Leavitt spent the third afternoon questioning Larry Massoli, who would have been a key witness if Leavitt hadn't
dismissed the indictment against Glen Henderson. When
Massoli tried to tell the jury that Henderson had warned
him Bill Martin was going to have the Chicken Ranch
burned down, he was cut off by Judge Foley. The federal
rules of evidence prevented Massoli from testifying about
the conversation, since Henderson was no longer a defendant. As a result, the jury spent the afternoon looking
bored and restless, as if they wondered why Massoli had
been called at all.

At 3:17 P.M. all that changed. The double doors at the
back of the courtroom opened and in walked John Deer.
His shoulders and arms were so big that he looked as if he
could crush a man bare-handed, but his face had been
creased and molded by a deep and abiding fear. He had told
his friends that before this investigation of Bill Martin was
over "someone's going to end up dead." That day he
looked as if he might be that someone.

Asked where he lived, John Deer could scarcely speak.
Asked to identify Bill Martin, John Deer could look up only
for a second. His gaze was riveted on his hands, which
were clasped together in his lap.

"Did you work for Bill Martin in Lathrop Wells?"
"Yes, I did."
"What kind of work did you do for him?"
"Mechanic."

"Working in a gas station?" Leavitt asked. He realized he was going to have to drag the answers out of Deer.

"Yes."

"How many hours a week, generally, did you work for him?"

"I don't really know. It varied. Seventy or eighty hours a week."

"How much did you get paid a week?"

"That varied—a hundred and a half, a hundred and a quarter."

"For seventy to eighty hours a week?" Leavitt asked incredulously.

For the first time John Deer looked up for more than a second. "Yeah," he said, sounding glad to respond.

"Did there come a time, Mr. Deer, in February of 1978, when Mr. Martin called you to his office to have a conversation?"

John Deer sighed. His gaze returned to his lap. "Yes," he whispered.

"Tell us," Leavitt said, "to the best of your recollection, what happened when he called you in there."

John Deer stared at his lap. His thick muscles tensed across his shoulders. He seemed to contract into himself. If he had had a shell, it would have been sealed shut. For a long time it seemed as if he simply wasn't going to answer. Then he said, "Well, it was possibly over station business."

"What else?" Leavitt shot back. What if John Deer rolled over and played dead now? What if he was so afraid of Bill Martin that he wouldn't testify?

"And . . ." John Deer stopped again. Then he sighed, as if he had just given in to the certitude of his own doom, as if he had finally signed his own death warrant. "He was complaining about the Chicken Ranch," Deer said.

"What was he saying about it?" Leavitt asked, plunging ahead to keep from losing the momentum, lest Deer withdraw back into himself.

"He just said he'd have to do something about it."

"Did he direct you to do anything?" Leavitt asked.

"Well, myself and Bo Hyder."

"What did he direct you to do?"

"He was talking about sending us over to burn it down."

"Do you recall how he put it to you? To the best of your recollection."

"Well, to the best of my recollection, he said that he was thinking about sending us over to burn it down. Mr. Martin told me, Bo and I, that Mr. Plankinton was rockin' the boat in the county too much and he'd have to send Bo and I over to burn it down."

"What did you do?"

"Nothing. I just—later on I told him I didn't want any part of it."

"In June of 1978, did you hear about the Chicken Ranch having been burned down?"

"Yes."

"And a few days after that happened, did you have the occasion to be in Lathrop Wells at Mr. Martin's property?"

"Yes."

"Did you see Mr. Martin on that day?"

"Yes."

"Tell us to the best of your recollection what was said."

A curtain seemed to come down between Deer and Leavitt, and for the longest time Deer simply stared at his big angular knuckles in his lap. Finally he looked up.

"I just asked him about it, and he said, 'Well, I had to do something.' "

Leavitt turned on his heel to face the defense table. "Your witness," he said, with the slightest hint of glee on his face.

Not even Charlie Waterman went after John Deer too hard. The defense didn't even try to attack his story of what Bill Martin had said. They knew this was one witness you didn't want to push.

●   ●   ●

Bo Hyder had spent two days sitting in the hallway just outside the courtroom, his huge body squeezed uncomfortably into a courthouse chair. Every time the lawyers and the defendants left the courtroom for a break, Hyder would take Leavitt aside and say he hoped, this time, Kenny Kolojay would take a swing at him, so that Bo would have an excuse "to get him."

This was Edwin "Bo" Hyder. This was not John Deer. He walked into the courtroom with his head held high. The last time he had testified in this building, his head had been completely shaven. This time he wore his thick dark wavy hair down to his shoulders and had grown a long, droopy mustache to match. With nine felony convictions and two of his own trials behind him, Hyder knew all about testifying. He took his seat in the witness chair, cool, cocky, sure of himself. Instead of appearing vulnerable, as Deer had, he came across as frightening and tough.

Leavitt began by getting Hyder's nine felony convictions on the record to leave as little room as possible for the defense to take advantage of them. Then Hyder repeated his story about the day Martin called him into his office. "He told me the son of a bitch in Pahrump had been going too far and has to be taught a lesson," Hyder said. "Then he told me he wanted to burn the whorehouse down and break the guy's arm and leg." There was a sudden stir in the courtroom. In the spectators' section an old man gasped out loud. Bill Martin and Kenny Kolojay exchanged disgusted glances.

The defense left Hyder largely to Charlie Waterman. Waterman came on the same way he had come on to Plankinton, shouting and strutting and flinging his arms around the courtroom to show the jury how outrageous—outrageous!—it was that this nine-times-convicted felon was up here on the witness stand testifying against a good citizen, an upstanding businessman, like Bill Martin.

This time it was an even match.

Waterman tried to get Hyder to admit that the only reason he was here testifying was that he hated Bill Martin and was just trying to put him into jail. But Hyder was too clever for that.

"Ya have a very deep hatred for him, don't ya?"

"Dislike, not hatred," Hyder snapped back.

"Have ya ever told any person that ya were going to see to it that Bill Martin went to prison?"

Hyder glared at Waterman. He had seen him out at the Coach House Bar enough times when Waterman had come to call on his client Bill Martin. He was not afraid of him.

"No," Hyder said.

Thirty-one

Elbert Easley walked into the courtroom with a macho swagger and a sneer on his lips. He was dressed in a baroque costume: brown slacks that flared dramatically at the cuff and a sleeveless black undershirt with narrow straps that showed through a sheer polyester shirt. His long black hair had been combed the way he liked it, like Elvis's, and he had grown a pencil-thin mustache and a small goatee.

Easley had been brought from San Quentin to Las Vegas' Clark County Jail a week before. Since that time he had been tormenting Jim Perry and Larry Leavitt with demands that had to be met before he would testify. He was a condemned murderer. He didn't have to do anything for anybody unless he felt like it. What were they going to do? Put him into jail?

He wanted Roger Hanson to come to Las Vegas to discuss his death-penalty appeal. He wanted a conjugal visit with Lorrie Ross, who was in town to testify about the night Elbert showed her several hundred dollars wrapped in aluminum foil and claimed he'd been given it for burning down a whorehouse. He wanted slacks with legs that flared exactly twenty-one inches at the cuff. He wanted a barber

who could cut and layer and blow-dry his hair. And he
wanted a hair gel called Blue Magic. "If I look good and I
feel pretty inside," he told Leavitt, "I'll testify right for
you." So Leavitt spent one evening, when he should have
been home preparing for the next day's testimony, driving
all over Las Vegas on a shopping spree, looking for the
obscure ointment.

When Leavitt finally got the prisoner onto the witness
stand, the situation went from bad to worse. Easley swiveled aimlessly in the big leather-backed chair, his eyes half
closed as if he was in a trance. Each time Leavitt asked him
something, Easley stopped, shook his head, and squeezed
his eyes, as if the whole world was just too much for him.
Then he would open his eyes again as if he was trying to
get the courtroom in focus.

"After you were in Lathrop Wells for a few days," Leavitt asked, "did you hear Mr. Tatum or Mr. Kolojay or Mr.
Martin talking about the Chicken Ranch?"

"Mr. Who?" Easley asked in his slow Oklahoma drawl.

It was a frustrating beginning. It took Easley quite a
while to warm up to the idea that he was here to tell the
story of the burning of the Chicken Ranch. But when it
happened, it happened suddenly. When Leavitt brought
him up to the day before the fire, Easley finally got the
courtroom into clear focus.

"That afternoon Jack came out and woke me up out at
the bunkhouse, and we went over to the brothel and met
Ken. Ken was talkin' about burnin' the brothel. He said he
had been watchin' it periodically. And prior he had a girl
out there, one of his girls, to kind of spy on the place. And
he knew that the best time to burn it would be around three
o'clock because that was the slowest part of the night.

"Then Kenny walked over to Martin's house and asked
Beverly, 'Is Bill up? Ask him to come out when he's up.'
And shortly thereafter he came out with his housecoat on.
And Kolojay walked over to him.

"I couldn't hear what Kenny Kolojay was sayin'. But I

heard Bill Martin. Kolojay was talkin' to Bill Martin, and Bill Martin just went off and started screamin' and yellin', you know, because he found out that a trick was forty dollars at Plankinton's place. It cost Jack forty dollars just for a straight lay.''

At the defense table, Martin and Kolojay looked across at each other and shook their heads, half out of embarrassment and half out of anger.

''Kolojay asked Martin if he wanted to postpone the plans,'' Easley continued in his Okie drawl, ''because he found out where Walter Plankinton lived. He had been talkin' prior to that about killin' Walter Plankinton, gettin' some girl to poison him because he had a bad heart. And Bill Martin just went off and started screamin', 'No, just burn the motherfucker up!' ''

Leavitt stood a few feet from Easley, refusing to let his face register how delighted he was feeling. If only Perry could be here to see this, Leavitt thought to himself.

''Then Kenny said, Well, he would see if he could get a car. So he left and went to Las Vegas and he didn't come back until way late, after midnight, with a blue '69 Chrysler New Yorker. And Jack Tatum came over and asked me if I wanted to just drive the car out there for a thousand dollars.''

The courtroom was hushed now. There was not a sound in the room except that of Easley's slow, spacy Oklahoma drawl.

''We pulled the Chrysler around the back behind the bunkhouse out there and started findin' cans and buckets and stuff around. We took some kind of chemical, I don't know if it was coal oil or some other kind of chemical. Then Kenny went with a big can over to the gas station and he got some gas in it.

''Then we went out there. On the way we stopped. We parked on the side of the road and got out and started mixin' the chemicals. Jack just mixed the chemicals into a pan and just kept addin' gas to it and poured a little bit onto the ground and lit a match to it and see if it would burn. And there was just a little blaze come up off the ground about this high.''

Easley stopped and indicated with his hands how high the blue flame had been. The jury stared at the space between his hands as if there were actual flames dancing there.

"So Jack would add a little bit more gasoline until the fire was the right color. Then we started drivin'. Straight up to the Chicken Ranch. We just pulled straight in to the door and off to the side maybe just a little bit.''

Leavitt, realizing how dramatic this was and how it was getting to the jury, stopped Easley. He wanted to heighten the drama. He let a moment go by.

"Tell us what happened," Leavitt asked in a soft voice, "when you stopped the car.''

"I left the motor runnin' and the lights out. Kenny got out on the left side and walked to the end of the porch. Jack walked straight up to the door. Kenny was already waitin' at the door, his shoulder against the wall, squatted down, you know, waitin' right outside the sliding glass door so the woman wouldn't see him. And Jack rang the bell. She opened the door, you know, where she didn't see his face, just all in one motion. And then he pulled a nylon sock down over his head as she was openin' it and put the hat back on.

"Then as the door opened—well, as she started openin' it, he just pushed her out of the way so she wouldn't get burnt or nothin'. As he was pushin' her to the right out of the way through to the curtain, Kenny reached in the door and splashed the stuff and Jack put a book of matches on the couch as he was backin' out.''

Again Leavitt let some time pass. The room was so silent that it seemed as if the silence had a sound all its own.

"What happened then?''

"It just went up. Fire," Easley breathed, as if he too had been caught by the eeriness of it all, remembering the night the Chicken Ranch burned, the screaming women, the flames crawling up a tower of greasy smoke toward the sky. "Just shot up," he said. "It almost exploded, you know."

Easley had been so spooked by it at the time that he had started backing the car out of there before Kolojay even had a chance to get in. "Jack was tryin' to shut the door and Kenny Kolojay was tryin' to get in and he just jumped over Jack with the rifle. And somehow or other the rifle got stuck into the steerin' wheel. I just sped out of there."

"Then what?" Leavitt said softly.

"We looked back to the right, and we could just see . . . the whole sky was red."

With only two days left before Thanksgiving, Leavitt had two more scenes he wanted to have Easley set for the jury. He had Easley describe the stop he and Kolojay and Tatum made at the blue-and-white trailer on the way back to Lathrop Wells to repair the old Chrysler's radiator hose. Then he had Easley describe the moment Bill Martin made the payoff for the Chicken Ranch arson.

"I seen Bill Martin hand Jack Tatum the money, an envelope. A business envelope." Easley was enjoying this now. He started acting out the scene for the jury. He hit it on the back of Jack's hand like this. Then Jack and me just kind of walked together up to the apartment. And Jack paid me a thousand dollars. He said, 'Well, that wasn't bad for just drivin' a car, was it?' "

"Now," Leavitt said, "two or three days or so after the fire, you saw Mr. Martin in the bar?"

"I remember seein' him, yes, in the bar, when it first came out in the paper. He read somethin' that Plankinton said. And he was laughin' about it. He said it was a good job. He bought a drink. He was laughin' about Walter Plankinton's heart, somethin' about his heart. I said, 'Well, are you sure that he'll suspect you?' And he said: 'Yeah, I know damn well that he knows I did it. But there's nothin' they can do about it, because it is still a crime on the state level.' "

Martin was saying that he felt Peter Knight wouldn't prosecute him, that he was probably immune from the law in Nye County, Nevada.

If there was one witness the defense had to break it was Easley. If they were to have any hope of keeping Martin, Kolojay, and Tatum out of prison, they had to discredit him. When the busloads of tourists began arriving at the downtown hotels for their complimentary chips and complimentary turkey dinners—Cross-examination of Easley went right up to Thanksgiving—and continued one more day after it.

Schofield tried to portray Easley as a confused, spaced-out drunk who could not be trusted to remember anything, let alone the details of an elaborate conspiracy. He hammered away at the most trivial details—whether or not there were rain barrels behind the Shamrock and whether the gasoline and kerosene were mixed in a pan that was twelve or eighteen inches wide—trying to get Easley to make a mistake.

Manos tried to get Easley to admit that he had raped Tatum's young daughter-in-law, that Tatum had run Easley out of Lathrop Wells, and that the only reason Easley was testifying here today was that he was out to seek revenge. But Manos couldn't get Easley to break. Easley cracked his knuckles and rubbed his eyes, and now and then he stared into space before answering. But despite the haze through which he seemed to view everyone in the courtroom, he made few mistakes.

The problem was that he had to make only one big mistake. And he made it with Charlie Waterman.

"So, ya lied, didn't ya, Mr. Easley!" Waterman bellowed. "So ya lied!"

It was at the bitter end of Waterman's cross-examination that Easley made his first big mistake. Waterman came at him like a bull, his head down, charging again and again, the same accusations, the same gutter talk, relentlessly. "So ya lied, didn't ya, Mr. Easley! So ya lied!"

And finally, as sure as stone is worn invisibly away by water, Easley was worn down by Waterman. He began "filling in the pieces," as criminal lawyers call it, trying to place every one of the defendants at the scene of the crime. For the first time he insisted not only that he and Tatum were present the day Martin made the payoff, but that Kolojay was there as well.

"Now, in any of your grand-jury testimony," Waterman demanded, strutting across the courtroom, waving his glasses in the air, "did ya mention Mr. Kolojay bein' present?"

Easley nervously ran his long bony fingers through his greasy black hair. "I wasn't asked," he said weakly.

"Did . . . ya . . . mention . . . him . . . bein' . . . present, Mr. Easley?"

"I didn't, no," Easley conceded angrily.

"Now, in your deposition, Mr. Easley, did ya mention the name of Ken Kolojay as bein' present during that transaction?"

Easley swiveled in the leather chair, cracked the knuckles of one hand, which now had Blue Magic hair grease on it. "It wasn't asked in that particular part," he said.

"But ya didn't, did ya?" Waterman was still shouting.

"No."

"Now, you had an opportunity to tell this story to your own lawyer, Roger Hanson, in the Modesto jail. Do you remember that?"

Easley clearly knew what was coming, but it was as if he'd been tied down and could only wait for it to stampede toward him. "I don't remember all that well," he said. "Just parts of it will come to my mind. We were talkin' about my murder case too."

"And ya didn't mention that Mr. Kolojay was present in that statement, either, did ya?" Waterman yelled.

For the first time in four days, Easley began to whine defensively. At the prosecution table Leavitt glanced over at John Bailey. Although it was impossible to read any emotion into Leavitt's face, Bailey knew what the glance meant. Leavitt was worried. He had begun to have a sense, over the last four long days, that the jury was believing Easley. Now he wasn't sure what they would make of this.

"I was tellin' him what I remember, how I remembered it. And he was writin' and I was talkin', I kept drifting off into my . . . you know."

"Did ya sign that, Mr. Easley?" Waterman shouted, waving Easley's original confession in the air.

"Yes, I did," Easley shouted back.

"Was it true?" Waterman shouted louder.

"Yes," Easley shouted louder still.

"Well, if it was true, why didn't ya tell him that Ken Kolojay was present?"

Easley swiveled uncomfortably in his chair. "If I didn't tell," he said testily, "then I didn't remember it."

Waterman walked over to Easley. Standing between him and the jury, he made a sweeping gesture with his arm in the direction of the jury and began slowly shouting each word: "What you are asking this jury to believe now is that ya didn't remember it."

Easley spun in his chair until he was staring straight at the jury. He smiled his cold, taunting smile, a smile that might have been on his face when he stuffed small black rubber balls into the mouths of the young German man, Reiner Junghans, and his pretty blond wife, Ingrid, and stabbed them a hundred times.

"I'm not askin' them to believe anything," he said angrily. "I don't care what they believe."

Waterman was jubilant. "Well, all riight, Mr. Easley! All riight."

CHAPTER

Thirty-two

The Wednesday morning after the Thanksgiving recess, FBI agent John Bailey walked a few blocks to the Rainbow Vegas Motel to get Easley's girlfriend Lorrie Ross, who was staying there while she waited to testify. As soon as Bailey walked into the motel office, the manager started screaming at him. Since the day she arrived, it seemed, Lorrie Ross had been taking in tricks, twenty-four hours a day.

Bailey started to laugh to himself. The government had paid her air fare, put her up in the motel, and was paying her the standard $75-a-day witness fee for every day she was there. On top of that money, Lorrie had decided to earn a little more.

Trying to keep a straight face, Bailey calmed the motel manager down. "Please," he said, "let her stay. She's an important government witness."

Lorrie Ross was the first of a series of witnesses Leavitt began bringing to the witness stand as soon as Easley left it. They were all there to do one thing: corroborate Easley's testimony, and convince the jury they could believe the man whom Charlie Waterman liked to call "this bought-and-paid-for, lying murderer."

Lorrie Ross told the jury how Easley had folded back the foil wrapping of his payoff money in a Fresno motel room and told her he had burned a whorehouse down. Easley's father told how he had listened in while Easley was talking on the phone with Jack Tatum and heard Tatum tell Elbert "that he had him a deal with Bill Martin."

Easley's sister, Charlene, testified that Elbert had told her "that he was involved in something to do with the burning of a brothel." John and Anne Newhouse told how three men in a large, light-colored car had stopped at their house trailer on June 10, 1978, to fix a busted radiator hose.

When they were finished, Leavitt then brought on a new set of witnesses to show the jurors how horrible it had been inside the burning aluminum trailers of the Chicken Ranch brothel at 4:30 in the morning of June 10, 1978. He called the grandmotherly night maid, Barbara Perri, who set the scene by describing how a masked man grabbed her by the throat, threw her on her back, and then splashed gasoline into the room so that his accomplice could ignite it.

Then he called Maria Mechanic, the six-foot-tall prostitute who had seen the car pull up to the Chicken Ranch door. Wearing a slinky green dress, she sauntered into the room on stiletto heels, tossing her soft henna-red curls about her shoulders, obviously enjoying her walk across the courtroom as much as everyone was enjoying watching it. She took a seat in the black leather witness chair and, swiveling flirtatiously, proceeded to tell the story of the fire in a deep, husky, sexy voice.

Suddenly it seemed that all the advantage Leavitt had gained with Barbara Perri had been lost. Maria was so busy vamping for her audience that it looked as if she was causing the jury to forget that she and thirteen others had almost lost their lives that night. Even Leavitt's latest girlfriend sat in the spectators' seats laughing.

Meanwhile, directly above the courtroom in the U.S. Attorney's Office, even more of a circus was going on. Suzi, the one woman who had been injured, and very nearly killed, in the Chicken Ranch fire, had appeared at the courthouse wearing skin-tight slacks and a low-cut clinging blouse that stretched so tightly over her breasts she looked as if she was ready to start work for the evening. FBI agent John Bailey knew one thing: she certainly wasn't ready to start testifying in court. He quickly escorted her to the office and asked one of the secretaries for a safety pin. "I'm not going to touch her!" he laughingly told the secretary.

Suzi tried to get her blouse to stay together, but it wouldn't work. Bailey had two secretaries go with her into a closed office to work on the knotty engineering problem, but they were unable to sort it out. At that point, Suzi began to cry. "Boss say no show titties in court," she said. "Boss say no show titties. Boss say look like respectable lady."

Bailey found the best-endowed woman in the U.S. Attorney's Office and asked her to give Suzi her blouse; Bailey gave her the top of the U.S. Attorney's jogging suit to wear until Suzi had finished testifying. But that didn't work. That blouse was still too tight. Finally Bailey had Suzi call her teenage daughter and get her to find the most conservative skirt and blouse her mother had at her apartment. The girl hurried over to the courthouse in a cab.

After all that, Suzi was not called to the witness stand until the next day, by which time she had found a tasteful black wool skirt and a smart red-and-black blouse. Still, it didn't make any difference. Suzi looked so startling, her voluptuous breasts looked so amazing sitting atop her tiny body, her thick black waist-length hair looked so breathtaking, that two of the men in the jury nearly fell out of their chairs leaning forward to pay attention. The jury sat and giggled as she told them, in broken English, of the fire that nearly took that beautiful hair and body and turned them into ashes.

The jury stopped laughing only when Leavitt, after reminding them that Easley and Tatum had visited the Chicken Ranch before the fire, asked Suzi if she recalled ever having seen any of the men in some photographs Jim

Perry had once shown her. For the first time in the trial, everyone at the defense table looked genuinely concerned. Ted Manos stood up at his seat and leaned over the table, as if getting a few inches closer to the witness would somehow make a difference.

Leavitt took his time now; the courtroom was his. He picked two small brown envelopes from the prosecution table, walked over to the clerk's desk, and handed them to Judge Foley's clerk. The clerk marked the envelopes Plaintiff's Exhibits 30 and 31. Leavitt picked up the first one, took out a set of photographs, and placed it on the wide wooden railing in front of the witness stand. He was clearly enjoying the moment.

"Now, Miss Damkoehler," he said to Suzi, "for the record, Government's Proposed Exhibit Number Thirty consists of an envelope attached to which are a series of six photographs. I want to show you the photographs and ask you which of these people, if any, you picked out when Mr. Perry showed you that."

The courtroom was silent. The men in the jury who had been leering at Suzi now sat up straight in their chairs. Suzi pointed to one of the photographs.

"For the record, Your Honor, that is a photograph of Elbert Easley," Leavitt said.

He opened the second envelope and set the contents before Suzi. "Now I'd like to show you Government's Proposed Thirty-one, which likewise is an envelope and a series of eight photographs. Miss Damkoehler, do you recall which photograph you picked out when Mr. Perry showed you these photographs last year?"

Again Suzi pointed to one of the pictures.

"This photograph, Your Honor, is a photograph of James Luther Tatum."

There was a slight gasp from the jurors. At the defense table Kenny Kolojay and Bill Martin anxiously looked at Charlie Waterman as if they were waiting for him to rescue them. Waterman did not return their glances.

Thirty-three

"Beverly Burton."

It was two-thirty on Tuesday, December 9, when Larry Leavitt stood up at the prosecution table to call Beverly Burton as his last witness in the Chicken Ranch arson trial. As he stood there waiting for her to enter the courtroom, he had no idea how that sad little redheaded girl whose picture he kept in his office drawer was going to testify.

Since the week before the trial, Leavitt had been conducting his own private cold war with Beverly. He had discovered that she had come back to Las Vegas from her new home in New Jersey. She was with a man she called her fiancé, and they were talking to Jack Ruggles and Kenny Kolojay. So he made no effort to contact her. He decided he wouldn't try to talk to her at all before she testified. He would simply put her on the witness stand, cold.

Then, the first week of the trial, he got a call from her. She was clipped, curt, the old Beverly. "Mr. Leavitt," she said, "I want to know when I'm going to testify."

Leavitt decided he could be just as cold. He didn't know if his reaction would mean anything to her at all. But on the theory that she was a girl who badly needed approval, he decided to withhold his. He wanted her to know he was mad at her.

"I don't know when you will testify," was all he said to her.

A few days later, she showed up in the U.S. Attorney's waiting room. Leavitt was pleased to see how much she had changed since she lived at the Shamrock, although he was not about to let her know it. Her hair had reverted to its natural carrot color. She wore no makeup, and her peaches-and-cream freckled complexion showed a kind of schoolgirl wholesomeness Leavitt had never believed she could possess. She wore a plaid wool skirt and a beige turtleneck sweater.

"I want to see my grand-jury transcripts," she said.

"Why?" Leavitt shot back.

"I just want to see one portion."

"You're not going to see them."

"I have a right to see them," she said. "I have a right."

"Well, Beverly," Leavitt replied icily, "not only do you not have a right to see them, but you're not going to see them. And I don't have anything more to say to you." He spun on his heel and walked back to his office.

A week later she called again. She said she had to see him about her testimony. Leavitt said he would see her, but only if she had her own lawyer present.

"What do you want?" Leavitt asked her when she arrived with a lawyer.

"I want to take the Fifth Amendment."

"Then I will grant you immunity and order you to testify," Leavitt snapped back.

Then Leavitt turned to her attorney. "In no way must my remarks be construed as any kind of threat," he said, "but if Beverly comes back into court now and changes her story again, I think she's opening herself up to a problem."

Of course, Leavitt and everyone else in the room knew it was a threat.

• • •

She walked up to the witness stand, through the narrow space between the prosecution and defense tables, trying to stare straight ahead. But you could see her body tense as Kenny Kolojay, the man who once had so controlled her life, swiveled in his chair to stare at her. As she took the witness stand, the double doors at the back of the courtroom quietly opened and Jim Perry slipped into a seat in the spectator's section. This was one part of the trial he was not going to miss.

Leavitt took her quickly through the history of how she had been flown out to Las Vegas from Pittsburgh and brought to Lathrop Wells, Nevada, and forced to become a prostitute. He wanted to waste as little time as possible before he got to the single question—whether she had slept with Kolojay the night of the Chicken Ranch fire—that would tell him, and everyone, which way she was going to testify.

"After work each day at the Shamrock, did you sleep with anybody?" Leavitt asked her.

"Yes," Beverly said. Her tone was clipped, tough.

"And who was that?"

"Ken Kolojay."

"Now, on or about June 10, 1978, in the early-morning hours, the Chicken Ranch brothel was burned down. On the day before, did you see Ken Kolojay?"

"Yes. Earlier in the day."

"Where was that?"

"At the Shamrock."

Leavitt took a deep breath.

"When is the next time you saw Ken Kolojay?"

At the defense table Martin and Kolojay stared tensely at Beverly. Martin, Kolojay, Leavitt, and Perry had been waging a brutal tug-of-war over Beverly for over two years now, taking turns pulling her in opposite directions. Now all four men were waiting to see into whose arms she would finally fall.

"I'm not sure," Beverly replied.

By the looks on their faces it was evident that Martin and

Kolojay were sure that she had chosen them. Leavitt took another deep breath.

"To the best of your recollection."

"Twelve o'clock noon," she said. "The next day."

"That would be Saturday, June tenth, at twelve o'clock noon?" he asked.

"Yes," she said.

Martin, Kolojay, and Waterman exchanged angry glances. The long battle for Beverly Burton was over, and Leavitt and Perry had won.

With Beverly on his side, Leavitt now felt secure in taking her through the nightmare that had begun for her one evening some months after her husband had left her. Beverly Burton had sat crying in the Colonial House in New Kensington, Pennsylvania that night, contemplating how harsh life had been to her and how hopeless it all seemed. She had been eighteen years old at the time, when two men named Ernie and Jimmy offered to help her find her husband.

It was the first glimpse the jury had of what prostitution was like in Nevada, where, because it was legal and because it was regulated, the world's oldest profession had supposedly been cleaned up. But the only thing about it that had been cleaned up was that the customer knew that the girl he bought had probably been to a doctor within the last week.

Beverly described how she arrived at the Shamrock with no money and no way to get home.

"I got very upset," she said. She still sounded scared and tough. "I was told I had to stay to pay back the two hundred dollars Bill Martin had paid for me. I was very upset. I tried to get hold of the two guys that sent me out here. And I couldn't get through to them."

She stopped for a second. Her body relaxed, and suddenly her voice was softer, more vulnerable. "I don't know," she sighed. "I was pretty hysterical the whole day."

"At that point, had you ever heard of Ken Kolojay?" Leavitt asked.

"No."

"What happened when you met him?"

"Well, he talked me into staying there to make some money so I could leave."

"And were you supposed to make money by prostitution?"

"Yes."

"Had you ever done that before?"

"No."

"How old were you at that time?"

"Eighteen."

Leavitt let the jury absorb that. That was the age of a high-school senior, a homecoming queen.

"What sort of relationship did you develop with Ken Kolojay?" Leavitt asked.

"I guess I fell for his stories, and his charm and everything else."

At the defense table Kolojay began to laugh.

"Now, when you saw Kenny at noon the morning after the Chicken Ranch fire, where did you see him?"

"In the kitchen of the Shamrock."

"And what was he doing there?"

"He was just sitting there when I first seen him. I told him about the burning of the Chicken Ranch. About six o'clock in the morning, I had a customer who had told me he had gone to the Chicken Ranch before he came to the Shamrock and that it was burned down."

"What did Ken Kolojay do when you told him?"

"He was just laughing about it. And I was joking around at the time, you know, about how I thought he had done it."

"Shortly thereafter, did you and Ken Kolojay have any conversation about where he was on the night of the fire?"

Charlie Waterman and Ted Manos knew what was coming. They were half out of their seats.

"I think the first time anything was brought up was when we were driving in his car here in town. I seen Elbert Easley's picture in the paper. I had told Ken I recognized him. I had seen him out in Lathrop Wells. And Ken just told me he doubted if I would ever be asked, but if I ever was, to say that I didn't see Elbert Easley."

"Did he say anything to you at that time about himself?"

"Yes, he did."

Waterman and Manos were still sitting on the edge of their chairs, ready to spring.

"What did he say?"

Manos jumped up. "Objection, Your Honor! Foundation!"

The jurors' eyes darted quickly from Manos to Leavitt to Judge Foley.

"Go ahead," Judge Foley said to Leavitt.

"Thank you, Your Honor." Leavitt turned back to Beverly Burton. "What did Ken say to you?"

"He said that if I was asked, I was supposed to say I was with him at four o'clock in the morning that night of the fire."

Leavitt's voice rose dramatically. "Was it true that you were with him at four o'clock in the morning?"

"No, it wasn't," she said.

Leavitt spun on his heel and turned back to the prosecution table, catching Jim Perry's eye for a split second. Perry looked absolutely elated. He couldn't get over how well Beverly had held up. She didn't even look like the same girl. If anyone had told him a year ago that she would be sitting there testifying like that, with that strong voice, answering the questions, never wavering, he would have said it was impossible.

With Kolojay's alibi destroyed, Leavitt went on to let Beverly describe to the jury in excruciating detail what her life—the life of a white slave—had been like in her tiny bedroom at Bill Martin's Shamrock Brothel in Lathrop Wells, Nevada.

She had been at the Shamrock only two weeks when she tried to run away the first time. She told the jury she had taken her $1800 share of the $3600 she earned in two weeks, which gave the jury some idea of what the stakes were in this brothel war. She and another girl had run away to Las Vegas, but Kolojay had found her, and "he put me in the Corvette and he took me back out to the Shamrock." He took away her money, and that was the last she ever saw of anything she earned for Bill Martin's Shamrock Brothel.

A few months later she and another girl ran away again. They "asked a guy in a truck to wait for us after we closed, and we went out the front door and met him out on the highway." He took them to Reno, where they caught a plane for Portland. They were in Portland three days when Beverly realized the other girl had phoned Kenny. She grabbed a taxi to the airport, but Kolojay caught her there. "I started to buy a plane ticket," she testified, "and before the ticket was made out, Kenny came into the airport, and there was another man with him, and Kenny just handed the plane ticket back to the lady and said I wouldn't be needing it, and he grabbed me by the arm and walked me outside and put me in his Lincoln and we headed back to Lathrop Wells."

She tried to leave "quite a few times" after that, but each time Kolojay brought her back. Then in April 1979 she had a bad argument with Kolojay. "I was leaving and I ran out to the highway. And he came out with his Lincoln Continental after me, and he tried three or four times to run me over. And I screamed and it didn't help. I finally stopped a car in the middle of the highway."

She told the jury the driver took her to Beatty, where she talked to the Nye County sheriff's deputies, who took her to Las Vegas to talk to the FBI. Then she told the jury how she had returned to Kolojay the day before she was supposed to testify.

"I was scared," she said quietly. "I had just gotten in so deep so fast. And I went back. I was just very insecure. I hated what I was doing. But I didn't know how to leave him."

The only sign of Beverly Burton's life in Lathrop Wells was a certain hard set to her mouth, a certain caution in her eyes, a toughness, a wariness in what would otherwise have been a soft, young girl's face. It was a toughness that, on this late-December afternoon just two weeks before Christmas, was about to serve her well. For Beverly Burton was about to begin nine hours of brutal cross-examination.

She had told conflicting versions of the same series of events so many times that she was the kind of witness defense attorneys dream of. For the first day Paul Schofield hammered away at her, taking her over and over the many times she had told two completely different versions of the same story. Beverly never wavered. For the first time in her life, she was standing up to the men who had used her, and she was standing up well. "I was lying then," she kept telling the jury. "I am not lying now."

On the second day, Charlie Waterman and Ted Manos tried to show everyone in the courtroom that she was nothing but a dizzy hooker who loved being a prostitute and was here testifying today only to get back at Kenny Kolojay for kicking her out of Lathrop Wells.

"And as a matter of fact," Waterman shouted, his voice rising as he strode across the courtroom waving his glasses in the air, "the time that ya ran out of the Coach House ya had an argument with him about other girls, didn't ya!"

"No, I did not!" Beverly shouted back.

"Isn't it also a fact that ya were insanely jealous of other girls?"

"No, I was not!" Beverly shouted back again.

"And it was that emotion," Waterman shouted, stopping

and waving his arm to encompass the entire courtroom, "that predicated what is happening here in this courtroom today! Isn't that true?"

Beverly was tough. Her voice was steady. "That is untrue," she said.

"Now," Waterman said. There was a new note of sarcasm in his voice. "There did come a time, did there not, in your tenure at the brothel, when ya got to kind of like being a prostitute?"

Beverly glared at him.

"Never," she said.

"Ya never did?" he asked, raising his eyebrows and smirking.

"Never did," Beverly said.

"Well!" Waterman said. There was a note of triumph in his voice. "Ya kind of did things to further your appearance during that period of time, didn't ya?"

Beverly looked puzzled.

"Further my appearance?" she said.

Then her shoulders fell. Beverly realized exactly where Charlie Waterman was going.

"Yes," she sighed, "you mean have an operation."

"To make yourself more attractive!" Waterman shouted at her.

Beverly nodded bitterly across the room to where Kenny Kolojay was sitting.

"That was his doings," she said.

"Ya had a breast operation, didn't ya, during that period of time!" he shouted across the room.

"Yes, I did," Beverly said quietly.

"Ya left the brothel!" Waterman shouted. "And ya went to town! And ya had an enlargement! Isn't that true?"

"That's true," she said.

"And the purpose of having that enlargement was because you wanted to be more attractive to your customers!" Waterman shouted. "Isn't that also true?"

"That's not true," she said, motioning toward Kenny

again. "The reason was he wanted me to make more money."

Waterman's voice was at a fever pitch. "The point is, ya did want it, didn't ya! No one held ya on the table!"

Beverly was quiet now, resigned.

"No, they didn't," she said.

Ted Manos was even rougher.

He rushed up to the witness stand. "Did your mother know you were a prostitute?"

Beverly looked as if Manos had literally slapped her.

"She knows some of it," Beverly said quietly. "But she doesn't know all that happened."

"So you haven't told her the whole truth?" Manos shouted.

"No," Beverly said. "There is no reason to."

"Did your brother know that you were a prostitute here in Las Vegas?" he shouted again.

"Some of it," she said.

"You haven't told him the whole truth!"

"I haven't lied to him. If I would have told him everything, it could have been painful."

"Nobody in your family before you ever has been a prostitute, have they?"

"No," Beverly said.

Larry Leavitt jumped out of his chair. He had had enough.

"Objection!" he yelled.

"Sustained," Judge Foley said, without even waiting to hear from Manos. The objection meant nothing to Manos. He had no intention of stopping.

"The point is!" he shouted back at Beverly. "That you were the only prostitute in your family!"

Leavitt jumped up again.

"Objection!" he shouted. "What is the relevance of this?"

"Sustained," Foley said again.

This time Manos turned to Foley.

"Your Honor," he said, "if I might proceed. This gets to impeachment. The whole purpose is to establish her motive for lying."

Foley looked down at Manos.

"You can cross-examine," he said, "but I don't think you should lecture."

Manos turned back to Beverly. He began to shout at her again.

"Now, you felt bad about being a prostitute! Didn't you?" he shouted.

"Yes, I did," she said. Leavitt could not believe she was standing up to this.

"You are angry that Ken Kolojay played a part in your being a prostitute!" Manos shouted again.

"No," Beverly shouted back. She was angry now. "I didn't even want to come to court. All I wanted to do was just forget."

Manos was still shouting. "Isn't it true," he said, "that, had you been able to forget it, had you not had to go to court, you never would have had to tell your mother, or your brother, or anybody even half-truths?"

"That's not true," Beverly shot back.

"Isn't it true," Manos said, screaming at her now, "that in order to explain your past to your family it is necessary for you to establish that you were forced into all of this? And that is all part of the lie that you are telling today!"

"That is totally untrue," Beverly said. Her voice was clear and strong. "I am not lying today."

CHAPTER

Thirty-four

From the day he was arrested at the Coach House Bar "for conspiring to destroy the Chicken Ranch brothel by means of an explosive," Bill Martin had been telling everyone in Nye County that the federal government would never be able to make that explosives charge stick. Now the time had finally come to see whether Bill Martin was right.

On Friday morning, December 12, as soon as Leavitt had rested his case, Judge Foley dismissed the jurors, and Paul Schofield rose to make the motion that everyone had been waiting for since the day the trial began. He asked for "a judgment of acquittal" on the grounds that the government had produced insufficient evidence to let the case go to the jury.

The three defense attorneys told Judge Foley that Kolojay's obstruction charge must be dismissed because the only evidence to support it was from Beverly Burton, "an admitted perjurer." The judge, they said, should also dismiss the charge of conspiracy to destroy the Chicken Ranch by means of an explosive, on the grounds that the fire had been caused by simple combustion. They based

most of their argument on a Nashville case involving
René's New & Used Furniture Store, which was destroyed
by fire. In that case Junior Lee Birchfield was accused of
opening the store's skylight, pouring gasoline in, then lighting some paper and dropping it onto the gasoline. Federal
prosecutors in Nashville had used the same federal statute
that Leavitt was trying to use now. The federal judge in
Tennessee had rejected their argument.

Armed with extensive testimony from Bureau of Alcohol, Tobacco and Firearms chemists, Leavitt asked Judge
Foley to reject Birchfield as precedent because "the Tennessee court was without benefit of the expert testimony"
that Leavitt now had. "We are breaking new legal ground
here," he pleaded with the judge in what he would later
characterize as his attempt to "ask Foley to have some
balls."

The four attorneys argued to the end of that Friday afternoon, and when court resumed the next Tuesday, they continued to argue well into the middle of that afternoon as
well. At nearly 3 P.M., when Charlie Waterman stood up to
make yet one more argument, Foley looked up from the
notes he had been making all day.

"I don't think that's necessary," he said.

Suddenly the eyes of everyone in the courtroom were
focused on him. He looked back at his notes. The minutes
ticked quietly by. Then, after what seemed an almost unbearable length of time, Judge Foley straightened his oversized spectacles and began reading slowly from his notes.

"This court believes that counts one and two must fall,"
he said. "The court believes that gasoline does not consti-
tute an explosive unless as part of a device such as a Mo-
lotov cocktail, and that Birchfield was correctly denied."

At the defense table, Martin and Waterman, smug I-
knew-it-all-along looks on their faces, nodded their heads
in agreement. At the prosecution table, Leavitt did not
even allow himself to blink.

"Now, turning to the testimony itself. The court feels

that to have the naked testimony of Elbert Easley as the sole support of a criminal conviction is unconscionable. The same could be said of the testimony of Beverly Burton. Neither witness has the slightest regard for the truth. And they are totally unreliable in this court's opinion. Although the testimony of Elbert Easley is to some extent corroborated by other evidence in the case, there is little if any corroboration of Burton's trial testimony. Therefore the court feels that the jury would have to have a reasonable doubt as to the obstruction-of-justice charge against Kolojay as set forth in count three. Count three must fall.''

Foley had eviscerated Leavitt's case, leaving only the perjury counts to go to the jury. Leavitt and Bailey sat perfectly still. Martin stood up quickly, turned to Waterman, and solemnly shook his hand. Then he rushed out of the courtroom and down the hall to the pay phone to tell the good news to everyone in Tonopah and Lathrop Wells.

Waterman, Schofield, Kolojay, and Tatum gathered up the papers spread over the table before them and followed Martin out of the courtroom. They were halfway down the hallway, heading for the pay phones, when Ted Manos finally left the room. As he walked through the courtroom's double doors and out into the hallway, he called to the other men in a buoyant, booming voice.

"It is an honor to be associated with you gentlemen!" he yelled. The word "honor" bounced off the marble walls and echoed down the hallway.

Larry Leavitt and FBI agent John Bailey walked up the back stairs of the courthouse to Leavitt's office, where they were soon joined by Jim Perry, a couple of courthouse reporters, and almost every other attorney in the U.S. Attorney's Office.

Leavitt took a seat behind his desk and lit a cigarette while the others milled around the small office. There was something of the atmosphere of a wake that attended these events. There was very little conversation about the case. For what was there to say? Everyone had simply shown up to view the body, which in this case was Leavitt's.

Leavitt pulled out a brown manila envelope from under his desk and handed it to Jane Morrison, the Las Vegas *Review-Journal* reporter who covered the courthouse. Today was her birthday and Leavitt had bought her a package of shot glasses as a joke. But it had not turned out to be much of a joking occasion. After she had opened the present, Leavitt took it back from her and pulled out three glasses. Then he slammed them down on his desk, one at a time.

"This one's for Leavitt," he said. "This one's for Bailey. And this one's for Perry."

Larry Leavitt drove home alone that night, turned on the lights in the new Las Vegas town house he'd moved into in September, walked into the kitchen, and started a pot of water boiling. He walked into the living room, clicked on the television set, and listened to a local anchorman say, "A jubilant Waterman told reporters that 'no one in Nye County except Walter Plankinton believes Bill Martin was behind any of this. In Nye County,' Waterman said, 'Bill Martin's name has never been sullied.' "

Leavitt clicked off the set, walked back into the kitchen, and dropped a plastic bag containing Stouffer's frozen beef stroganoff dinner into the boiling water. He watched it bob on the surface for a moment as the water rolled to a boil once more.

The phone rang. It was a friend in the U.S. Attorney's Office in Reno, calling to offer condolences.

"Hey," Leavitt said. "This isn't over yet. We're still in this case. We still have three perjury counts to try."

He was tired. He was angry. He wasn't used to losing cases. And he wasn't used to losing cases that had attracted as much publicity as this one. But he knew he couldn't let himself be blown away by this. He still had the rest of this case to try. He sat down with his briefcase and his frozen beef stroganoff dinner, and began pulling out documents.

Thirty-five

Leavitt expected the defense to call a lot of witnesses, including Glen Henderson and Judge Beko, neither of whom was going to be easy to handle. Leavitt had a source in Las Vegas who kept telling him that Beko was coming to testify. "He doesn't want to," Leavitt's source said, "but he'll come if it's absolutely necessary."

The morning after Judge Foley's ruling, the defense decided it wasn't absolutely necessary. Sensing victory, they decided to cut their case short. They would spend Wednesday and Thursday presenting a series of supporting witnesses, including Nye County District Attorney Peter Knight. Then they would bring on Bill Martin and Kenny Kolojay to testify in their own defense.

They began with Jack Luther Tatum's son, Levi, a scrawny twenty-one-year-old with that distant look of someone who had taken a lot of drugs. He and his girlfriend, Candy Harder, said that Jack Tatum was at Candy's house in Rio Linda, California, on June 9, 1978, and that they drove to Lathrop Wells on June 10, arriving hours after the Chicken Ranch had already burned.

Leavitt went after the young couple in that same calm,

controlled manner he had used with his own witnesses. Rather than trying to wear them down with the shrill, unnerving voice Charlie Waterman used, he tried to wear them down with the voice of a stern, disapproving father. He had Levi Tatum's testimony to the FBI from ten months before. The boy had said he was "probably working the graveyard shift at the gas station in Lathrop Wells" the night of the fire and had no idea where his father was that night. Leavitt quietly and mercilessly hammered away at the boy and the girl until Candy was reduced to tears and Levi was slumped back in the big leather chair, saying in exasperation, "Man, I don't know."

There followed a procession of people who could support Tatum, Martin, and Kolojay or impeach one of the prosecution witnesses. John Grisez, Elbert Easley's public defender, told the jury that Walter Plankinton had said he would pay Roger Hanson to represent Easley if Easley would testify specifically "against Bill Martin." Sherri Lyn Maine, a pale, obese young woman who was a barmaid at Bill Martin's Coach House, said Bo Hyder had tried to see Bill Martin the night before Hyder testified before the federal grand jury, and when Martin refused to see him "Bo told me he would make that motherfucker sorry he did not talk to him."

John Coulsen, a Las Vegas parking-lot attendant and friend of Ken Kolojay, told the jury that on the morning of June 10, 1978, he had gone out to the Shamrock to see Ken about selling Shamrock T-shirts. When he arrived at the Shamrock at eighty-thirty, he said, Kenny was at the whorehouse.

Coulsen was the one defense witness who got to Larry Leavitt and FBI agent John Bailey. John Newhouse had testified that the drivers he had helped had arrived at his trailer at seven, which would have given Kolojay plenty of time to be back at the Shamrock by eight-thirty. But Easley had placed the time closer to nine.

"Jesus Christ," Bailey said in the hallway after Coulsen

left the witness stand. "You can find anybody in this town to lie for you!"

When Peter Knight was a young boy living in the Emery Hotel, an old two-story frame building his parents owned in Thermopolis, Wyoming, his mother decided to send him away to the military academy in Faribault, Minnesota. His father laughed and told his friends it was because "Faye doesn't want him to grow up to be a dumb cowboy like me." By the end of the day on December 18, Peter Knight probably wished he had become one. As he took the stand, his face pink and flushed, his sandy hair carefully wetted down and combed back from his forehead, he looked like the son of an old Wyoming bronc buster who had never quite learned what this courtroom business was all about.

"Mr. Knight, how are you employed?" Charlie Waterman began.

"I'm the District Attorney of Nye County."

"Since you were the District Attorney of Nye County, have you had occasion to read in the newspaper an account where Walter Plankinton described you as having taken or solicited a bribe?"

"Yes, I have."

"After you read that in the newspaper, did you then initiate a letter to Mr. Plankinton?"

"Yes, I did."

"You called Mr. Walter Plankinton an unmitigated liar in that letter," Waterman said, his voice rising. "Was that with reference to your having solicited a bribe from him?"

"That is directly what it referred to, because he did make that statement. That I had solicited a bribe. Which isn't true."

"Did you ever ask Walter Plankinton for a piece of the action at his brothel?"

"No, sir."

Waterman turned to Leavitt, a thin smile on his face. He

had wanted the jury to hear Knight call Plankinton a liar and leave it at that. He knew that if he didn't question Knight about the four years Knight had spent trying to keep Plankinton out of Nye County, Leavitt would not be able to cross-examine Knight about those four years.

"No further questions," Waterman said.

Leavitt stood up and crossed the room to face Peter Knight. This was the man Leavitt had been fighting for two and a half years. Boy, Leavitt thought to himself, just as he had when he sat across his desk from old Glen Henderson, you can feel the heat in this room.

"Mr. Knight," he said in the same stern disapproving voice he had used on young Levi Tatum, "when Walter Plankinton accused you of soliciting a bribe from him, was he referring to a meeting that you had with him?"

"Yes, I did meet with Mr. Plankinton," Knight said nervously. He kept looking at Waterman for help, but no one could help him now.

"Was that in your office?"

"Yes, sir."

"What was his purpose in coming to you, as he stated it?"

"He indicated to me that he had the desire to open a brothel in Nye County."

"And you, of course, had no problem with that, right?" Leavitt said, toying with Knight.

Knight looked thoroughly befuddled. "I beg your pardon?"

"You didn't have any objection to that, did you?" Leavitt was clearly enjoying this.

Knight looked at Waterman and shifted nervously in the big leather chair. "Well, what he actually said, Mr. Leavitt, was that he intended to open a brothel in Pahrump. And I did have a problem with that. And I voiced the problem to Mr. Plankinton by noting for him the fact that there was Pahrump Town Ordinance Number Three which made the operation of a brothel in the town of Pahrump illegal."

"Did you show him a copy of it?"

"I don't recall."

"Now, Mr. Knight," Leavitt said. He was beginning to set his trap. "Is it your testimony that the only problem that you had with Mr. Walter Plankinton opening a brothel in the county of Nye was that, in your judgment, the location that he selected would have been in violation of the town ordinance?"

Knight fell right into it. "That's the only problem that I foresaw. With the proviso that it was my belief that the Board of County Commissioners was not in favor of authorizing any more brothels to open up."

Leavitt sounded absolutely gleeful. He had Knight right where he wanted him. "Was it necessary, Mr. Knight, to get permission from the Nye County Commission to open a brothel in Nye County at that time?" Leavitt asked.

"No."

"Was it necessary, Mr. Knight, to get the permission of the District Attorney to open a brothel in Nye County at that time?"

"No."

"Was it necessary to get anybody's permission to open a brothel in Nye County at that time?"

"No," Knight said.

"Then what possible bearing would the County Commissioners' feelings have on a businessman who wants to open a business that's not illegal and that does not require a license?"

"At that time the law of the State of Nevada was still represented by the Cunningham decision, which had held that brothels were a nuisance per se, and upon actual knowledge by a county commissioner or a district attorney there was an incumbent duty on that person to move to abate such nuisance."

Incredibly, Knight seemed not to realize what he'd just done. Leavitt was having a difficult time concealing his glee at the trap he had set and how easy it had been to get the District Attorney to fall into it.

"So," Leavitt said, "all it would take would be actual

knowledge on the part of the District Attorney that a
brothel was in existence, and that would be grounds for
getting rid of it. Is that what you're saying?"

"Yes."

"All right. Did you have personal knowledge that there
was a brothel operating in Beatty by the name of Bobby's
Buckeye?"

Waterman was on his feet. "Your Honor!" he yelled.
"This is far outside the scope of direct examination. The
only question I asked this witness was relative to the solic-
itation. It had nothing whatever to do with this."

"It goes to impeachment, Your Honor," Leavitt shot
back.

Judge Foley nodded. "Go ahead," he told Leavitt.

"Did you have personal knowledge, Mr. Knight, that in
Beatty there was open and operating a brothel by the name
of Fran's Star Ranch?"

Knight started to whine defensively. "Not actual, personal knowledge."

Leavitt's voice was thick with contempt. "You mean
you hadn't been there?"

"That's right."

"But plenty of people had told you about it, right?"

"Sure," Knight said testily.

"Did you know that Bobby's Buckeye was open and
operating in Tonopah just a few blocks from your courthouse?"

Knight sighed. "On the same basis, yes."

"Now, did you have personal knowledge that the Shamrock Brothel was open and operating in Lathrop Wells?"

"I knew that Bill Martin had a place called the Shamrock
down there. I never did know for sure what it was all about.
I didn't go in to inspect it, quite frankly."

"You've been to Lathrop Wells many times, haven't
you?"

"I've gone through it lots of times."

"Been at the Coach House Bar many times?"

"Yes, sir."

Leavitt waited a few seconds to let everyone see how ridiculous Knight's answers were sounding. "Mr. Knight," Leavitt began again, "do you take your duties as district attorney very seriously?"

"Yes," Knight said petulantly.

"And is it your duty to administer and carry out the laws of the State of Nevada and Nye County uniformly and evenhandedly?"

"I believe so."

"In 1977 did you know anybody who had actual knowledge that the Shamrock Brothel was open and operating?"

"I don't know."

"I see." Leavitt's voice finally began to rise in anger. "Did you know Bill Martin?"

"Yes," Knight said. His eyes darted nervously toward the jury.

"And you don't know whether the Shamrock Brothel was open?" Leavitt asked incredulously.

Knight sighed and once again glanced nervously at the jury. "I don't know what Bill Martin knows," he said.

"I have no more questions."

It was exactly two o'clock on December 19 when Bill Martin took the witness stand. For the first few minutes, there was none of the sour smugness, none of the cockiness that usually characterized his speech. His voice was quiet and quavered nervously. But after only several minutes he became smug, sour, cocky, completely at ease. He took time to instruct the jury in pop psychology, brag about his "financial astuteness," and offer his analysis of Bo Hyder's conduct based on his experience as a policeman.

Charlie Waterman had him begin by telling the jury how he had first come to Nevada in 1945 as a pilot in the United States Army Air Force and, carefully skipping his years as a New York City policeman, how he had come back to

Nevada in 1954 "to make it my home." He had worked as
a Las Vegas patrolman, he said, then as a Nevada highway
patrolman. Then he "went into business in Lathrop Wells
and opened up a brothel."

Then Waterman asked Martin if he had ever offered
money to John Deer or Bo Hyder to burn down the
Chicken Ranch. There was a new tone of respect in Waterman's voice that the jury had never heard before.

"No," Martin said, shaking his head emphatically. "I
did not. I never have."

"Now," Waterman said, "did there come a time shortly
after you testified before the federal grand jury in Las
Vegas when Mr. Hyder attempted to have discussions with
you?"

Martin nodded smugly. "I believe that would be
Wednesday evening, the twenty-first of June, at about eight
o'clock in the evening."

"Are you aware of what Mr. Hyder wanted to discuss?"

"Oh, sure I am. His grand-jury testimony the next day.
He told me I could buy the testimony one way or the
other."

"What did you do when he said that?"

"I told him to get the hell out of my bar."

Waterman turned on his heel to face Larry Leavitt.
"Your witness, Counsel."

Leavitt stood up and slowly approached Martin. He had
awakened that morning with a 102-degree fever. He felt just
miserable. He didn't have the energy to haul off at Martin.
But he hoped if he could go in quickly and score a couple
of good, strong points, that would be sufficient.

"Mr. Martin," Leavitt began, "you came down and testified before the federal grand jury on June twenty-second,
nineteen seventy-eight. Is that right?"

Martin was as smug and in control as he had been with
Waterman. "Yes," he said, nodding.

"Bo Hyder testified before the grand jury on the same
day, didn't he?"

"Yes."

"Now, it was the night before when he came to Lathrop Wells and tried to shake you down?"

"That was the inference I drew."

"What did he say to you that night?"

"He told me I could buy his testimony."

"All right," Leavitt said. "The next morning you appeared before the federal grand jury."

"Correct," Martin said.

"And I asked you a lot of questions that day, didn't I?"

"Yes, sir."

"And I asked you the following question: 'Did you ever have a conversation with Bo Hyder relative to burning down the Chicken Ranch?' And your answer was, 'No.' And then you said, 'I was going to volunteer some information for your information, but perhaps I had better not.' And I said, 'Go ahead.' And you said, 'This man is not a very reputable character. He is a narcotics addict, a drunk —the man is weak, completely weak. He is an ex-convict. He is an informer. This man is so unreliable that it is unthinkable to me that anybody would even consult him about a thing like that. He is always under the influence of drugs or alcohol, one or the other.'"

Leavitt looked up at Martin. His voice was uncharacteristically loud, insistent. "Did you tell the grand jury on that day, less than twenty-four hours after it happened, that Bo Hyder had tried to shake you down about his testimony?"

"No, I didn't."

"Did you tell the grand jury at all that day, in any part of this transcript, about the shakedown attempt the very night before he came up here to testify?"

"No, I didn't."

Leavitt stared silently at Martin.

"That is all I have."

Thirty-six

It was Tuesday afternoon, December 23, in Las Vegas, Nevada. In the empty stretches of land where the houses stop at the edge of the desert, the green Oregon Christmas trees were set up in the sagebrush, their pine needles drying out in the hot sun and heavy wind. At the Wee Kirk o' the Heather Wedding Chapel the staff was preparing Christmas corsages for the annual rush of Christmas Eve weddings. And across the street from the wedding chapel, at the United States Courthouse, the defense attorneys in the Chicken Ranch arson case were preparing for what they were sure would be their final victory: the motion to dismiss the remaining three perjury counts for lack of evidence.

As the afternoon session began, you could feel the tension in the air. Jim Perry had come up from his office to hear the argument. Joni Wines had taken a week off from her job as secretary in the emergency room of Southern Nevada Memorial Hospital and brought her son Shannon to watch. Jack Ruggles was roaming the hallway.

Ken Cory, who had worked with Ruggles and Knight's investigator, John Adams, to get Glen Henderson off, stood up to make the motion as part of the defense team.

"Your Honor," he said, "I make a motion on behalf of all the defendants for a judgment of acquittal. The issue here is one of jurisdiction. It is a well-established general rule that perjury cannot be charged by a grand jury that has no jurisdiction over a person or subject matter."

His voice rose like a new preacher in a new church. He turned to look at Leavitt. "It was the government, it was Mr. Leavitt, it was the United States Attorney, who brought this matter before the grand jury. While certainly we can empathize with their motivations, the bottom-line question is, Did they bring a matter before the grand jury that Congress authorized to be investigated by the federal grand jury? It was a case where the government thought that they were authorized to investigate a burning of a brothel before a federal grand jury. And the legislative history shows that the government was simply incorrect. And no amount of empathizing with their motivations can change that fact."

Cory argued until the end of the day, when Judge Foley announced that the court would hear Mr. Leavitt's rebuttal the next morning. And everyone in the courtroom went home that night certain they were coming back tomorrow for a Christmas Eve acquittal.

Everyone, that is, except Jim Perry and Larry Leavitt. They knew that the question of whether anyone would ever be punished for deliberately setting fire to six aluminum house trailers with fourteen people inside—would be decided by the four letters Perry wrote on the top of his FBI memos in that summer of 1978. The four letters were RICO, which stood for the Racketeering-Influenced and Corrupt Organization Act in Title 18 of the U.S. Code, which allowed the federal government to prosecute what would otherwise be state matters if there was a pattern of racketeering activities associated with the crimes.

As Leavitt approached the bench the next morning, he could just barely keep from rubbing his hands together with glee at the thought that not one of the four attorneys arrayed against him had thought of the acronym: RICO. "The

answer, Your Honor, is so simple and so obvious that I
believe it has escaped notice by counsel. In order to provide the answer, I think I should give the court a little bit
of the history of the grand jury's investigation into this
matter.

"In the summer of 1978, Your Honor, the grand-jury
investigation concerned itself with whether or not there
were violations under the RICO statute. The grand jury,
Your Honor, was trying to determine whether or not Mr.
Martin's brothel was being operated through a pattern of
racketeering. Through white slavery, Your Honor.
Through arson, Your Honor. Through obstruction of justice. If Your Honor would inspect the FBI file on this matter, you'll see that all sheets in the FBI file carry this case
as a RICO investigation."

The defense table had gone into a collective state of
shock. In the gallery, Perry was watching to see who would
fall over first.

"It was my judgment that there was reason to believe
that the Shamrock Brothel was an enterprise doing business through a pattern of racketeering. It was not until the
investigation came down toward the winter of 1979 that it
was my judgment that the RICO charge ought not to be
brought. And so I turned my attention to the explosives
statute."

Foley looked up from his notes. "Was that after Kolojay
and Tatum testified?" he asked.

"I believe it was," Leavitt said.

"In other words, it was after all three defendants' testimony?"

"I believe it was."

Leavitt sounded buoyant. He was pretty sure he had won
that round. Now he had one more to go. Still smarting from
the fact that Foley had called it "unconscionable to have
the naked testimony of Elbert Easley and Beverly Burton
as the sole support of a criminal conviction," Leavitt still
had to convince Foley that he had presented enough solid

evidence corroborating Easley and Burton to justify letting the case go to the jury.

Leavitt had argued the issue less than a minute when Foley startled everyone in the courtroom by cutting him off. "I agree with you," the judge said. "Motion will be denied."

"As to all three counts?" Leavitt asked incredulously.

"All three," Foley said.

Leavitt spun on his heel and walked back to the prosecution table. For the first time since the trial began, there was a smile on his face.

The final arguments began on the Tuesday morning after the long Christmas weekend and lasted for eight hours until the middle of Wednesday, December 30. Paul Schofield played off from Judge Foley's remarks about Elbert Easley and Beverly Burton and attempted to tear them down in the jury's eyes. It wasn't difficult. "One is a man who was escorted in and out of this courtroom under guard," he said. The other was "a liar. . . . She is a person who lies with reckless abandon."

Ted Manos went wild in his closing arguments. "Now, in seven weeks," he said, "there have been a lot of words thrown around this courtroom that reflect great prejudice. We all know words like 'kike' and we all know words like 'nigger.' And they're terrible words. But something has come up in this trial which really and truly I never was attuned to before. Words like 'pimp' and 'whore.' And what it basically boils down to is, the defendants in this case, Bill Martin and Ken Kolojay, are called pimps because they are involved in the management and ownership of a house of prostitution."

Manos' voice rose as his hand swept toward the defendants. Then he launched into a bad paraphrase of Shakespeare's *The Merchant of Venice*.

"Well, when you sit at a table for seven weeks, you come

to know that they're people just like you and me. They're
people—they have hurts, they have fears, they have cares,
they have families. They were all born with a mother and
father. Most of them have children. They grow up and they
get married. They cry. They laugh. They love. Just like you
and I. They're people. And that's what we're here about.''

Then Charlie Waterman got up and ranted and raved,
waving his arms in the air and yelling stridently about what
an outrage it was that they were even in this courtroom.
He attacked the government's witnesses again. He attacked Walter Plankinton for starting it all. He accused
Plankinton of buying Joni Wines, who sat in the back of the
courtroom fighting back tears. "This case, ladies and
gentlemen,'' he shouted, "will go down in the annals of
legal history in Clark County, Nevada, as being the only
case ever tried in this county by innuendo! By slander! By
character assassination! And by a government that has allowed itself to be duped—to be duped!—by an unmitigated
lying brothel owner!''

At the end of it all, Leavitt had his chance to respond.

He stood up and answered Manos first. "Mr. Manos
made what I thought was a rather remarkable observation
concerning the fear that he had that a certain kind of prejudice might creep into this case. I find it rather astounding
to compare racial prejudice or prejudice regarding national
origins with prejudice against a group of individuals who by
their own volition choose to follow certain vocations. Are
pimps an oppressed minority? Are robbers an oppressed
minority? Should we not be prejudiced against murderers
and rapists?'' He stopped and shook his head. "That's
really absurd!''

Then Leavitt defended his use of witnesses like Elbert
Easley. "How does the government find a witness who will
tell about the inside of a conspiracy like this?'' he asked.
"You have to have one of the co-conspirators. You need

an accomplice. A guy like Elbert Easley. This is a tough business. If we couldn't use witnesses like that, we wouldn't be able to solve these crimes."

Finally, at the end of the eighth hour of arguments, Leavitt recreated the entire crime for the jury, from the time Bill Martin sent three thugs to burn down the Chicken Ranch to the moment a masked man slid open the glass door of the house trailer, pushed Barbara Perri onto her back, and lit the match that started the fire.

"It was an inferno in that front room," Leavitt said solemnly. "There were fourteen human beings in that brothel at that time." He turned and pointed at the defendants. "The evidence in this case has established beyond a reasonable doubt that these men, Bill Martin, Ken Kolojay, and James Luther Tatum, these men sitting right here, conspired, engaged in a hideous crime."

He turned to face the jury. "I ask you to come back to this courtroom with a verdict that plainly tells them they must be brought to justice."

The cars and buses full of couples coming to Las Vegas for New Year's Eve were already starting to back up on Interstate 15 between Los Angeles and Las Vegas when the jurors left the courtroom to begin deliberations on December 30.

They had deliberated for only one hour and twenty-five minutes when Forewoman Joanne Todd, a smart-looking blond real-estate saleswoman, told the bailiff that the jury wanted to have John Deer's testimony read to them. Then she surprised him by handing him two sealed envelopes, each containing a verdict. The bailiff called everyone and told them to be in court at nine the next morning for a rereading of John Deer's testimony. He didn't tell them that the jury had already reached two verdicts.

Leavitt and Perry, who were waiting in Leavitt's office one floor up from the jury room, were angry, upset. They went to Antonio's, a courthouse hangout, to have a scotch. They were afraid this meant that the jury had decided to believe John Deer and not Bo Hyder. Hyder had testified that Martin offered him money to burn down the Chicken Ranch; Deer had testified that Martin simply asked him to burn it down. The question that Leavitt had asked Martin before the grand jury, the question on which the perjury conviction would turn, was whether Martin had ever "offered anybody any money" to burn down the Chicken Ranch. Perry and Leavitt feared they had lost Martin.

Leavitt sat sipping his scotch and saying almost nothing, while Perry worriedly worked over the subject. Perry was so upset that he even began working over old wounds.

"We should have cut a deal with Tatum," he said. "I knew it at the time. We should have cut the deal with Tatum."

Leavitt just stared at him. He didn't say a thing.

"All rise."

Judge Foley opened the door at the side of the courtroom at nine the next morning, crossed to the bench, and took his seat. He peered at Joanne Todd through horn-rimmed glasses. "We received a note from the jury at four-forty yesterday afternoon," he said, "stating that the jury would like to see the direct testimony of John Deer. We're prepared to have the court reporter read back all of John Deer's testimony." Then, without missing a beat, Foley said, "Do I understand that you reached a partial verdict?"

A slight gasp could be heard everywhere in the room. The attorneys and the defendants turned to stare at the forewoman.

"Yes, Your Honor," she said.

"All right. I just opened the partial verdict, so we'll take that first."

It seemed as if everyone in the room stopped breathing. Judge Foley scanned the two sheets of paper. He handed them to his bailiff. The bailiff walked back to his desk and, standing beside it, began to read.

" 'United States of America, plaintiff, versus Kenneth Kolojay, defendant. We the jury in the above-entitled case, upon our oath, do say that we find the defendant, Kenneth Kolojay, guilty of the offense charged in count five of the indictment. United States of America, plaintiff, versus James Luther Tatum, defendant. We the jury in the above-entitled case, upon our oath, do say that we find the defendant, James Luther Tatum, guilty of the offense charged in count six of the indictment.' "

It was 9:06 by the courtroom clock. Jack Tatum, who had spent most of his adult life in federal prisons, shook his head angrily. Kenneth Kolojay sat quietly in his chair, chewing gum and staring straight ahead. Bill Martin, who was sitting perfectly still, his hands folded on the glass-topped table, ran his tongue around the inside of his mouth and swallowed.

Forty-five minutes after the jury went out to consider Martin's fate, the telephone rang in Leavitt's office. The jury was ready. Leavitt, Perry, and FBI agent John Bailey walked down to the third floor, along with half a dozen staff members from the U.S. Attorney's Office, and Leavitt's secretary, Becki Simmons, who had used the forty-five minutes to run out and buy champagne. Half an hour later Waterman and Martin walked down the courthouse corridor. Then everyone filed into the courtroom, where Joni Wines was already seated, to wait for the final decision.

As soon as everyone was seated, the clerk opened the door at one side of the judge's bench. The jurors walked in laughing and chatting happily among themselves. When Bill Martin saw them, a sour look crossed his face. He shot a look at Waterman, as if to say, "What's that supposed to mean?"

"All rise."

Judge Foley crossed to his bench. As he called the court to order, the double doors at the back of the room opened and Walter Plankinton walked in and quietly took a seat in the rear behind Joni Wines and the U.S. Attorney's staff.

"The record will show the presence of Mr. Martin and his counsel," Judge Foley announced. Then he turned to the jury forewoman. "The court's been advised that the jury's reached a verdict. Is that correct?" he asked.

"We have."

She handed the sealed envelope to the bailiff, who crossed the room, reached up, and handed it to Judge Foley. Foley opened the envelope, quickly read the verdict to himself, then handed it back to the waiting bailiff.

Waterman and Martin were alone at the defense table now. The glass table top sat between them like a cool expanse of water. All was calm in the courtroom; the fighting was over. They both turned to stare at the jury as the bailiff began reading.

" 'United States of America, plaintiff, versus William Apfel, also known as William Martin, defendant. We the jury in the above-entitled case, upon our oath, do say that we find the defendant, William Apfel, also known as William Martin, guilty of the offense charged in count four of the indictment.' "

There were only twelve hours and thirty-seven minutes left in 1980. Bill Martin placed one finger over his mouth and continued to stare silently at the jury. He had been using that sour stare for twenty-five years to intimidate men and women in the sad little world he ran in Lathrop Wells, on the edge of the nation's Nuclear Testing Site, where he was sure the law would never touch him. Now it didn't work any longer. As he moved his eyes from one juror to another, the color slowly drained from his face.

Epilogue

It was not Larry Leavitt's style to engage in public celebrations. As soon as Judge Foley declared the Chicken Ranch arson trial officially over, Leavitt quickly made his way out of the courtroom and up the back stairs of the courthouse to his fourth-floor office, where Becki, his secretary, had the bottle of Moët & Chandon waiting.

Just as they had done sixteen days before when Foley threw out the arson and conspiracy charges, half the staff of the U.S. Attorney's Office crowded into Leavitt's office. But this time the mood in the room did not remotely resemble that of a wake. While people wandered in and out, wending their way between the white Styrofoam cups stacked by the coffee machine a couple of doors away and the bottle of champagne on Leavitt's desk, Perry walked into the room. In the middle of the laughter and the sounds of high-pitched voices, Perry quietly walked over to Leavitt. Without exchanging a word, the two men looked at each other, smiled widely, and reached out across the desk to shake hands. For the first time in almost three years Jim Perry did not say, "This goddamned case."

Seventeen minutes after the verdict, John Bailey picked up the phone on Leavitt's desk and dialed the number of the Pastime Bar in Tonopah and asked to speak to Bo Hyder. He wanted to give Hyder the satisfaction of being the first man in Tonopah to get the news. Then Bailey called the Chicken Ranch. A few minutes later, a call came in for Jim Perry. It was Walter Plankinton, who called to thank Perry "from the bottom of my heart."

It didn't take long for the bottle of Moët to be emptied. So John Bailey and Becki Simmons quickly took up a collection and went out to buy three bottles of André's, the cheapest champagne they could find, and three pizzas with everything but anchovies and olives. After everyone had sat down with the new supply of champagne and pizza, Perry decided to call Beverly Burton, who had gone home to New Jersey with her fiancé as soon as her testimony was over. When Perry told her about the verdict, Beverly had only one thing to say:

"How much time will Kenny get?"

It would be two o'clock in the afternoon of March 30, 1981, before that would be decided. The scene in the courthouse hallway that day looked as it had the day the trial began. Once again everyone who was anyone in the Chicken Ranch arson case was showing up for the sentencing. Joni Wines was there. Jim Perry was there. Ellen Woods, the leader of the Recall Joni Wines movement, was there, telling Bill Martin and Charlie Waterman she had come to lend "moral support." Larry Massoli, who had had only two hours' sleep since getting off his shift at his new job at the Boulder City Police Department, was there, chatting excitedly with Plankinton's private detective, Gene Alesevich. Kenny Kolojay was there, pointing out Massoli and Alesevich to Martin and saying, "Did you ever see anything like those two maggots?"

Walter Plankinton was there, looking the way he had

looked in the winter of 1976 when he first came roaring into Nevada. He was all duded up in a western cowboy shirt and his hand-tooled boots and had a little twenty-year-old girl in skin-tight jeans and a see-through white cotton blouse hanging on his wrist like a Rolex. He was telling everybody, "I came here for the hanging." The one man who was not there was Jack Tatum, who had decided that the best approach to his current predicament was to skip bail, and had not been seen by anyone, including Ted Manos, since New Year's Eve.

It took barely five minutes for Judge Foley to sentence Bill Martin to five years in prison and a $10,000 fine (the maximum he could give Martin under the perjury conviction), and to sentence Kenny Kolojay to three years in prison (instead of the five he could have given him) and the same $10,000 fine. When the sentences were announced, everyone in the courtroom remained impassive, except Ellen Woods, the Recall Joni Wines leader, whose mouth dropped open, and Walter Plankinton, who dramatically wiped his hand across his forehead and smiled his broad, toothy smile.

As soon as it was over, Plankinton walked out into the hallway to hold court for the waiting reporters. "The thing I feel bad about," he declared, "is that the men who are really behind all this are sitting loose up in Nye County. The men who set it up are in Tonopah. And these men here are doing those men's time."

While Plankinton continued to entertain the reporters, Jim Perry was inside the courtroom trying to make sure that the "guys who set it all up," as Plankinton called them, would indeed do time. Perry walked over to Bill Martin to shake his hand. He figured that the closer Martin got to actually going to prison, the better chance he had of getting Martin to flip.

"Well, Bill," Perry said. "I'm sorry it went the way it did. But if you want to talk to us someday, we're always willing to listen."

Bill Martin, who, despite the verdict, was about to leave for Lathrop Wells to host his annual New Year's Eve party at the Coach House Bar, simply smiled at Perry. It was a smile that seemed to say, I'm almost ready.

BILL MARTIN never did get the chance to talk to Jim Perry. On the evening of April 28, 1982, two days after the U.S. Ninth Circuit Court of Appeals upheld his conviction—thereby almost certainly guaranteeing that Martin would go to prison—a twenty-nine-year-old Pahrump man named Gerald Aesoph walked up to the door of Martin's little white frame house behind the Shamrock. When Martin opened the door, Aesoph fired two .25-caliber bullets into Bill Martin's head, hitting him under his right eye, shattering his eyeglasses. Martin fell to the floor with a loud thud that brought his girlfriend, Beverly Nichols, running out from the kitchen. Aesoph grabbed her, pushed her into the house, then turned and shot Martin a third time, hitting him near the left temple. Aesoph then took Beverly Nichols with him and drove her fifty miles across the desert to Shoshone, the California town near Death Valley where Jim Perry had once fruitlessly searched for Jack Tatum. Aesoph surrendered to police there, six hours after the shooting. Bill Martin was placed on a Flight-to-Life helicopter in Lathrop Wells and flown across the desert to Valley Hospital in Las Vegas. He died there two hours later, never having regained consciousness.

The morning after the murder, Las Vegas reporters were already asking whether Martin had been murdered because he was ready to talk. But Nye County District Attorney Peter Knight, whose office would be responsible for investigating the murder, declared that there was no evidence of that. "I have absolutely no reason to think it was a contract killing," Knight said.

This time the facts seemed to support him. Martin had been fighting with Aesoph—as he fought with almost everyone in Lathrop Wells—over the Coach House Bar, which Aesoph and a partner were trying to buy from Martin. At his trial in the Tonopah courthouse, Aesoph testified that the first two shots he fired at Martin were fired in self-defense and the third was fired accidentally. The jury decided differently. They found Aesoph guilty of murdering Bill Martin. Shortly after the murder, Martin's widow, Sallie, sold the Shamrock Brothel to a Las Vegas businesswoman named Sandy Prince. The brothel, which friends said Sallie Apfel "had always hated," brought her $900,000.

KENNY KOLOJAY welcomed in the new year after the verdict along with Bill Martin at Martin's New Year's Eve party at the Coach House Bar, where he cockily assured everyone that the Ninth Circuit Court of Appeals was certain to overturn the jury's verdict. When that court upheld Kolojay's conviction, Paul Schofield filed an appeal with the U.S. Supreme Court, which refused to hear the case.

That left Kolojay with only one way to stay out of prison: ask for a new appeal on the basis of newly discovered evidence in the Chicken Ranch arson. To help him get it, Nye County District Attorney Peter Knight sent his loyal investigator, John Adams, to San Quentin to interview Elbert Easley in March 1982, over a year after the Chicken Ranch trial ended.

After the interview, Adams signed an affidavit swearing that Easley told him he had lied when he implicated Bill Martin, Kenny Kolojay, and Jack Tatum in the Chicken Ranch arson. Schofield immediately filed a motion for a new trial with Judge Foley, citing Adams' interview with Easley. As soon as Leavitt saw the motion, he ordered FBI agent John Bailey to catch the next flight to San Francisco to talk to Easley.

When Bailey confronted Easley in his small, airless cell on Death Row at San Quentin, where Easley had nothing to do all day long but sit and wait for someone to kill him, be it the government, with a ceremonial death in the California gas chamber, or another inmate, with the sudden flash of a sharpened metal bed spring, Easley told Bailey he had given Adams the statement because of his fear of the other Death Row inmates, who regularly threw "piss and shit" into his cell to punish him for being a snitch. "I've got to get rid of this snitch jacket," Easley said in that slow, spacey Oklahoma drawl that Bailey remembered so well.

Judge Foley didn't buy Knight's last attempt to keep Kolojay from doing time. When the sworn affidavits of Adams' and Bailey's interviews with Easley landed on Foley's desk, he denied the motion for a new trial without comment and ordered Kolojay to prison.

Since perjury is considered a white-collar crime, the U.S. Bureau of Prisons assigned Kolojay to serve his time at the minimum-security "country club" prison at Lompoc, California, where former White House Chief of Staff Bob Haldeman spent 18 months paying for his Watergate crimes. "That bastard," Larry Leavitt said to Jim Perry when he heard the news. "I envisioned him spending his three years at someplace like Leavenworth."

Six months after Kolojay surrendered at the gates of Lompoc, the U.S. Parole Commission agreed to release him in three months' time, on the grounds that he had been convicted only of a white-collar crime. When Leavitt got the notice from the Parole Commission, he was furious. After all their work on this case, they had Martin dead and Kolojay doing only nine months for the crime. This was exactly what Leavitt had feared would happen when he heard that Kolojay was being treated more like a tax cheat than a man who had set fire to a bunch of house trailers with fourteen people in them.

Leavitt fired off a letter to the U.S. Parole Commission, explaining that the jury in the Chicken Ranch arson trial had had to believe Kolojay guilty of the arson in order to have found him guilty of perjury. He wanted the commission to know that this was no white-collar crime. After receiving his letter, they reversed their decision and ordered Kolojay to serve two full years before he would be eligible for parole. Kolojay immediately challenged that decision, claiming that Leavitt had misstated the facts of the Chicken Ranch arson trial. When the commission asked Leavitt for his reply, he sent them the relevant part of the trial transcript. The commission then ordered Kolojay to serve the full two years of his three-year term—one year and three months more than he would have served had Leavitt not intervened.

Kolojay was released from Lompoc on December 10, 1984, and sent to Clark Center, a federal halfway house only two blocks from Larry Leavitt's office. He was released from there on February 8, 1985. Kolojay is living in Las Vegas with Charlene Pellegrini—the girl he had once ordered to spy on Beverly Burton—and working as a laborer.

JACK TATUM managed to hide from the FBI in the Sierra Nevada for a full year after fleeing Las Vegas on New Year's Eve. In February 1982, when it got too cold in the mountains to pan for gold, Tatum came down to his sister's house just outside Sacramento. He walked right into the hands of two young FBI agents who had been assigned to his fugitive case only two days before. They asked the tall, gaunt old con if he was James Luther Tatum. "No," he said, "I'm Paul Muncie." He reached into his pocket and pulled out a birth certificate and a driver's license in that name. The agents looked at the documents, then looked back at Tatum and asked him to roll up his sleeve so that they could check for his rose tattoo.

"Uh-oh," Tatum said.

Tatum was returned to Las Vegas, where Leavitt had him indicted for bail jumping. Tatum pleaded guilty, and

Judge Foley sentenced him to three years on the bail-jumping charge and five years on the perjury conviction in the Chicken Ranch arson case, but allowed him to serve the sentences concurrently. Because he had been convicted of a felony while on parole from federal prison on his 1965 counterfeiting case, Tatum also has to serve the remaining years of that sentence.

He is currently serving his time in the federal prison at El Reno, Oklahoma, just outside Oklahoma City. An old con to the end, he spends most of his time filing appeal after appeal of his Chicken Ranch arson conviction, all of which have been denied. In his latest attempt, in January 1985, he filed a civil suit against Larry Leavitt, Judge Roger Foley, and Judge Philip Pro, the federal magistrate who presided over his arraignment in the Chicken Ranch arson case, charging all three men with violating his civil rights. He is scheduled to be released from the federal penitentiary on January 18, 1999.

GLEN HENDERSON continued to live in his small white house trailer only a few feet away from Fort Henderson, the wooden shack that served as a testament to the good old days when he was known all over Nye County as "the last of the old-time town tamers." In July 1982 Henderson discovered that he had terminal cancer. He left the Amargosa Valley and went to live out the few remaining months of his life in the Veterans' Hospital in Long Beach, California, where he died on September 8, 1982.

Before he died, however, Glen Henderson wrote out an elaborate plan for his departure from this world. He wanted to be buried near Fort Henderson, he said, in an old pine box. He wanted to be dressed in the Nye County sheriff's lieutenant's uniform that, in life, he seldom wore. And he wanted his body wrapped in a Hudson's Bay Company blanket, as a tribute to his place of birth, a fishing boat off the coast of Maine. He wanted the funeral ceremony held at the Amargosa Community Center, just down the highway from Lathrop Wells, and he wanted an honor guard from the Nye County Sheriff's Department in attendance. Then, he said, he wanted to go on "a last patrol."

So on September 12, 1982, in a scene that only Glen Henderson could have created, his old friend former Nye County Commissioner Don Barnett—the man whom Larry Massoli had once threatened to arrest for swearing at Massoli in a meeting of the Board of Commissioners—got into the old Nye County ambulance, which now served as the county hearse, and drove to the county line at Death Valley, where he picked up the pine box that held Henderson's body. He lifted the pine coffin—now strangely light with the wasted body of what had once been a bear of a man—into the back of the ambulance. Then, with the fine white dust forming great billowing clouds around the ambulance, he proudly drove former Nye County Sheriff's Lieutenant Glen Henderson all around the back roads of the Amargosa Desert, on his last patrol.

In November 1983, two years after ELBERT EASLEY testified at the Chicken Ranch arson trial in exchange for Walter Plankinton's agreement to pay $15,000 for his death sentence appeal, Easley finally got some results from Plankinton's $15,000. The California Supreme Court upheld Easley's first-degree-murder conviction for the brutal killing of Ingrid and Reiner Junghans, but it overturned his death penalty conviction in the case. The court ruled that the trial judge in Monterey had improperly instructed the jury not to be swayed by "mere sympathy" for Easley, and it ordered a new penalty trial to determine whether he should be sentenced to life in prison or to death.

In April 1984, Elbert Easley, Walter Plankinton, and the Chicken Ranch's former night maid, Barbara Perri, were all in Monterey for the new penalty hearing, just as they had been at Easley's first penalty trial five years before. This time Roger Hanson served as Easley's attorney.

Easley hadn't changed at all. The trial was delayed twice:

once while Easley convinced the judge to give him $150 to buy the right-style clothes to wear in court, and once while he convinced the judge to bring in a hairdresser so that he would not have to appear in court in his Death Row haircut. After the trial finally got under way, and the prosecutor presented evidence that Easley had been paid $1,000 to set the Chicken Ranch fire that almost took fourteen lives, only four months before he was paid $4,000 to take the Jungh-hans' lives, the jury sentenced Easley to die in the gas chamber at San Quentin.

Elbert Easley remains on Death Row today. Under California law, he is entitled to one more appeal of that death sentence before he goes to the gas chamber.

When BEVERLY BURTON left Las Vegas after four brutal days on the witness stand, Larry Leavitt took her up to his office to thank her for the help she had given him and to try to encourage her, once again, to straighten out her life. When Leavitt was finished talking to Beverly, he escorted her out to the U.S. Attorney's waiting room, where her fiancé, Paul Hedrich, was waiting for her. He was a young man with long dark hair, who was wearing dark sunglasses in the windowless waiting room. Leavitt was startled at how much his manner reminded him of Kenny Kolojay's.

When Leavitt and Beverly walked into the waiting room, Hedrich made no attempt to say hello. He simply lifted himself out of the green leather government chair and, as Kolojay used to do, motioned with his head for Beverly to leave with him. Is it possible, Leavitt asked himself as he walked back into his office, that this is history repeating itself? But even Larry Leavitt could never have imagined exactly how history would repeat itself with Beverly Burton.

On December 21, 1980, only ten days after she and Paul Hedrich left Leavitt's office, Hedrich was charged with arson in Point Pleasant Beach, New Jersey, where he ran

two restaurants. Beverly was charged with aiding and abet-
ting the arson. Police claimed that Hedrich, after a fight
with the man who owned the building where Hedrich ran
one of his restaurants, had poured some kind of flammable
liquid onto wooden pallets that sat in an alleyway between
two of the landlord's buildings, then set the liquid on fire,
causing damage to the exterior walls of the structures. They
charged that Beverly had telephoned the landlord to make
sure he was at home, and not in one of the stores, before
her fiancé set the fire.

In January 1981, after a fight with Hedrich, Beverly
walked into the local District Attorney's Office to tell investigators that she had driven with Paul to the buildings
and watched him leave the car with a pan of some kind of
liquid. When he returned, she said, she looked out the car
window and saw some flames coming from the direction of
the stores. She said she was willing to testify against her
fiancé.

But she never did. She married Paul Hedrich instead, and
the District Attorney, unable to compel Beverly to testify
against her husband, had to drop the arson charges.

WALTER PLANKINTON celebrated his victory over the men
who ran Nye County with a party at the Chicken Ranch on
New Year's Eve. But he was not finished paying for the
fight he had started with those men five years before. In
June 1981, after a four-year battle in the appellate courts,
Plankinton finally was forced to serve the sixty days in
prison to which Pahrump Justice of the Peace Dow Chenoweth had sentenced him for opening the original Chicken
Ranch inside the Pahrump town boundaries. Plankinton petitioned the federal court to allow him to serve the sixty
days in a federal prison instead of in the Tonopah jail,
where he said the high altitude would aggravate his heart
condition. Judge Roger Foley agreed, and allowed Plankinton to serve his time in a small North Las Vegas motel that

had been converted into a minimum-security federal detention center.

In March 1982, having caused about as much commotion as any one man had ever caused in the history of Nye County, Nevada, he decided it was time to leave. He startled everyone in the county by selling the Chicken Ranch for $1 million to a wealthy financier from suburban San Francisco named Kenneth Greene, who sent a friend named Russ Reede, a Sebastopol, California, high-school biology teacher, to Nye County to manage the Chicken Ranch. The day Plankinton announced the $1 million sale of the business he had started with $60,000, he declared Nye County, Nevada, to be "the golden land of opportunity."

Like the wandering, untamed cowboy he had always been, Walter Plankinton could not rest. He moved to Phoenix, Arizona, where he set about fulfilling another dream, this one even more outrageous than his first. He decided to open a floating whorehouse-casino on a ship that he would anchor in international waters off Galveston, Texas, just southeast of Houston. Just as the Chicken Ranch had been only an hour's ride from Las Vegas, so his new enterprise would be only an hour's ride from the big oil and banking center of Houston. An unlimited supply of Texas high-rollers would be his.

He raised $700,000 from thirty-five investors to start his whorehouse-casino and put a down payment on the *Shackleton,* a former World War II British mine sweeper, which he planned to rename the *Fantasy.* But before he could get his whorehouse afloat, the Phoenix District Attorney's Office filed civil racketeering charges against Plankinton in connection with the scheme.

Plankinton never went to trial on those racketeering charges. After pleading innocent at a preliminary hearing, he left Phoenix for Santa Rosa, Texas, where his bad heart finally gave out on him. He suffered a heart attack and died in his sleep in Santa Rosa on August 8, 1984.

• • •

JONI WINES never got politics out of her system. She was like a performer who had heard the roar of the crowd and could not turn away. She and her husband, Blaine, stayed in Las Vegas, where she worked at several secretarial jobs and tried her hand at opening the "Joni Wines Finishing School" for children five to thirteen. But that was not enough. In 1982 she entered the Republican primary race for Congress, and was defeated. In 1984 she ran for a Nevada State Senate seat, walking door to door to every home in the district, as she had first done in Nye County six years before. She was again defeated, but by only 103 votes. She is now working part time as a prison librarian in Las Vegas and starting to walk door to door to all 300,000 homes in the state, asking voters to elect her governor of Nevada in 1986.

PETER KNIGHT announced in 1982 that he would not seek reelection as Nye County district attorney. In October of that year he moved to Douglas County in northern Nevada, where he opened a private law practice. When he left office, he sent the Pahrump Valley *Times* an open letter "To All My Friends in Nye County," thanking them for allowing him to serve them. "My absence from the DA's office will certainly insure that I will no longer be stickin' the chicken," he wrote. Then he added something of an apology for his actions over the preceding six years. "I assure you I never perceived nor intended my actions to be other than in the best interest of Nye County, which I love."

AS LARRY LEAVITT and JIM PERRY celebrated their victory in Leavitt's office on New Year's Eve, somebody in the room said to Leavitt, "Some of the good old boys finally got it." To which Leavitt drily replied, "A lot more of the good old boys are going to get it."

Larry Leavitt and Jim Perry were the only people in the room who knew exactly what Leavitt meant: that in September 1980, two months before the Chicken Ranch trial began, Leavitt and Perry had started the kind of operation they had dreamed of when they first began working together: they had launched their own version of the federal Abscam investigation.

They set up FBI agent Steve Ryber in an office in Las Vegas and a Lake Tahoe condominium near Carson City, the state capital, where he posed as Steve Reilly, an executive of Doctors Fiduciary Trust, a corporation that he said had millions of dollars to invest in Nevada real-estate projects. What Ryber, at Leavitt's and Perry's direction, was really looking for were politicians with influence to sell. Ryber offered them campaign contributions, consulting fees, and outright bribes, in exchange for favors, zoning changes, licenses, and permits.

When the FBI undercover operation was over, Leavitt indicted five politicians and created a firestorm of protest all over the state about the methods used in what Nevada newspapers quickly dubbed "Vegascam." The operation resulted in the extortion convictions of State Senator Floyd Lamb, a man whose family is one of the most famous and influential in the state, and four other Nevada politicians.

After the Vegascam operation was over, Leavitt and Perry went their separate ways. Leavitt became a prosecutor in the Las Vegas office of the Justice Department's Organized Crime Strike Force and in March 1985 was named chief of the Las Vegas Strike Force. Perry continued to run the FBI's White Collar Crime Section in Nevada, in 1984 supervising the celebrated case in which U.S. District Judge Harry Claiborne of Las Vegas was convicted of income-tax evasion.

Since the day in 1976 that Jim Perry had first arrived in Las Vegas and had begun "prowling the halls of the federal courthouse" looking for someone with whom he could launch the kind of political-corruption investigations nobody had ever tried in the state of Nevada, Perry and Leavitt had won convictions against two of Nevada's most powerful state senators, a Reno city councilman, the director of the Clark County business license bureau, two Clark County Commissioners, and the first federal judge in the history of the country ever convicted of a felony committed while sitting on the bench.

But they were never able to get the man who ran Nye County. In Nye County life went on the way it had for the last hundred years. It was still a wide-open desert where there was enough space to allow every man to do what he damned well pleased, where people minded their own business, the way they were supposed to, and let their neighbors clean their dirty laundry in private.

Even the combined forces of the United States Department of Justice and the Federal Bureau of Investigation had not been able to change that. It remained what Larry Leavitt had called it the day he and Jim Perry first met to talk about the Chicken Ranch arson case: "A place untouched by civilization, where the men who run it are lords unto themselves."

Bill Beko, damaged a bit, but by and large undaunted, continued to preside over the courthouse in Tonopah, up on his hill. After all the years of fighting and all the investigations, no one had successfully proven that Beko, as he himself liked to say, "had done anything inconsistent with the law." In 1982, Beko tried to be appointed by Governor Robert List to a vacancy on the Nevada Supreme Court. Investigators for the Nevada Judicial Selection Committee raised questions about Beko's role in the Nye County brothel wars. List passed Beko over for the appointment.

In November 1984, the people of Nye County reelected Bill Beko, by an overwhelming margin, to serve a new six-year term as judge of Nevada's Fifth District Court. Today, if you commit a crime anywhere in the eighteen thousand square miles of "Great American Desert" that is Nye County, Nevada, you will appear to answer for that crime before Judge William P. Beko.

ABOUT THE AUTHOR

JEANIE KASINDORF is an investigative reporter and former staff writer for *New West* magazine, where the idea for this book originated. She is a frequent contributor to *New York* magazine, and has also written for a variety of publications including The *New York Times, McCall's, Ms.,* and *Los Angeles* magazine. In 1981 she received the Investigative Reporters and Editors Award for Distinguished Magazine Reporting.

She has recently moved from Los Angeles to the New York City area, where she lives with her husband, Martin Kasindorf, the New York Bureau Chief of *Newsweek* and their cats, Alexander and Susanna.